Argonaut

Memories of an East Neuk Skipper

ARGONAUT

Memories of an East Neuk Skipper

BY

David Smith

MBE

Edited by Andrew Lindsay

AuthorHouse™
1663 Liberty Drive
Bloomington, IN 47403
www.authorhouse.com
Phone: 1-800-839-8640

© 2012 by David Smith, MBE. All rights reserved.

No part of this book may be reproduced, stored in a retrieval system, or transmitted by any means without the written permission of the author.

Published by AuthorHouse   12/05/2012

ISBN: 978-1-4772-4986-4 (sc)
ISBN: 978-1-4772-4985-7 (e)

Any people depicted in stock imagery provided by Thinkstock are models, and such images are being used for illustrative purposes only.
Certain stock imagery © Thinkstock.

Because of the dynamic nature of the Internet, any web addresses or links contained in this book may have changed since publication and may no longer be valid. The views expressed in this work are solely those of the author and do not necessarily reflect the views of the publisher, and the publisher hereby disclaims any responsibility for them.

Acknowledgements

These few pages were certainly never ever intended be a great work of literary art, but were written mainly at the request of my son Robert, who wanted to know something about his father's life and work. I came to realise some time later that there might be other people who could well be interested in some of my experiences during my long career as a fisherman and as a Skipper. I am grateful to the many friends and colleagues who have shared their experiences with me over the years. I must also thank the Scottish Fisheries Museum in Anstruther for permission to reproduce some of the photographs in this book, and Sean Bell for permission to use the photograph on the front cover. While compiling my outline of the history of fishing in the East Neuk I learned a great deal from the writings of local historians, notably Aitken Fyall's *St Monans: History, Customs and Superstitions* (Edinburgh: The Pentland Press, 1999); George Gourlay's classic *Fisher Life, or, the Memorials of Cellardyke and the Fife Coast* (Publishers unknown: 1879 and 2009), and his companion volume *Anstruther, or, Illustrations of Scottish Burgh Life* (New York: General Books LLC, 2009); Peter Smith's *The Lammas Drave and the Winter Herring* (Edinburgh: John Donald Publishers Ltd., 1985); William Smith's *The Lights and Shadows of a Fisher Life* (Aberdeen: J. Daniel and Son, 1885), and Harry D. Watson's excellent *Kilrenny and Cellardyke: 800 Years of History* (Edinburgh: John Donald Publishers Ltd., 1986). I must also mention Jim Tarvit's book *Steam Drifters: a Brief History* (Anstruther: St Ayles Press, 2004). Finally I wish to express my thanks to Dr Robert Prescott for his foreword, and Andrew Lindsay who edited my text and prepared it for publication.

D. S.

Foreword

THE FISHING INDUSTRY has long been an important part of the social and economic fabric of Scotland. Readers with an interest in its history have available long runs of official statistics recording numbers of boats and fishermen, the size of annual catches and port landings, published annually by the Fishery Board for Scotland and its successors. What is less readily available are the personal stories of the fishermen who go to sea to catch the fish. David Smith's account of his own highly successful fishing career is therefore important and provides us with valuable insight into this nationally significant story.

Born in St Monans in 1930 he went to sea aged 15, retiring after almost 50 years, mostly as Skipper and boat-owner, having witnessed great changes in the fishing industry. His experience has embraced great-line fishing, drift-net fishing and, more recently, the seine-net and pair-trawl methods. He built and skippered a succession of boats culminating in the *Argonaut IV*, KY157, a fine model of which is on display in the Scottish Fisheries Museum.

His memoir presented here will appeal to readers at a number of levels. Some will delight in his account of growing up in St Monans in the 1930s and 40s, a time when the East Neuk of Fife maintained a considerable presence in the fishing industry, despite an increasingly fragile infrastructure. Others will be intrigued by his treatment of the day-to-day business of fishing, along with the details of the technical developments, for a number of which he was directly responsible, and which contributed to his long-running success at the top of his profession. One cannot fail to be impressed by the picture of ingenuity, commitment and courage that emerges vividly from this account of his working life at sea.

Since retiring from the sea David has served a number of years as a Trustee and Board Member of the Scottish Fisheries Museum. He has been a good friend of the Museum and a valuable link between the Museum and the fishing industry whose history it records.

Dr R. G. W. Prescott
Vice-President, Scottish Fisheries Museum

29th October, 2012

My Beginnings

I WAS BORN in the fishing village of St Monans in the East Neuk of Fife on the first of November 1930, some nine years before the start of the second great World War. I am the eldest of a family of five, four boys and a girl. I was born the son of a fisherman, the grandson of a fisherman, the great-grandson of a fisherman, and a few generations beyond that on both sides of my family. I am also the nephew of a fisherman, and in time I was to become a fisherman myself, along with my three brothers. Later I became the brother-in-law of a fisherman, the uncle of a fisherman, and also the cousin of a fisherman, and finally I was to become the father of a fisherman, and also the father-in-law of a fisherman.

I am sure that in the fishing industry of my childhood, such a claim would not have been all that unusual, and there would have been many fishermen throughout the whole of Scotland who would have been able to say much the same thing. I'm afraid that now, especially here in the East Neuk of Fife, the situation has changed so dramatically that I must surely be amongst the very last of a rapidly disappearing breed who will be able to make such a statement ever again!

In the style of the times, as the first-born son in the family, I was named David Smith after my paternal grandfather. The second-born son was my brother John, who was named after my mother's father. The third-born son, Robert, was named after my father himself. That was the way it always was at that time. If there were any other boys in the family, then they would generally be named after a close relative. My youngest brother Albert, for instance, was named after Albert Scales of Leith, the trawler owner who was my father's employer for many years. His middle names were from Peter Tait, a banker friend from Oban where my father was fishing during the war, and also from Alec Stewart, another friend, who was a dock policemen there.

In the case of girls, the first-born girl would always be named after the mother's mother. The second daughter born would then be named after the father's mother and the third born would be named after the mother herself. "Getting their names" was always extremely important to people in those days, but now the custom is fast disappearing and it seems that for the moment, almost anything goes. I think it's a great pity, because people were proud to be able to trace their lineage back over a great number of years. At that time, the first question that would always be asked of the parents of a new arrival would be to find out who the new bairn was to be named after.

I don't think the rules were ever quite so strict in the case of a baby girl though, because my father, who was very much a stickler for all that traditional stuff, was to name my only sister Evelyn! This name had no connection with any family relative that I can ever remember, so obviously it must have just been a name that they both liked. Maybe it was the start of a break in that long tradition that I spoke about.

My own christening and that of my brothers didn't take place until I was old enough to remember it for myself. My mother had been a Sunday School teacher in Cellardyke Kirk as a young woman, and when she and my father were married she moved to St Monans to set up home. She naturally joined the "Auld Kirk" and became a regular attendee there. When we came along later, apparently the minister of the day refused to baptise us unless my father also became a member of the Kirk. This caused him quite a problem, because out of respect for his own father, who had been one of the co-founders of the Close Brethren movement in St Monans, he couldn't agree to this. Mind you, along with some of his own brothers when he grew up, I don't think that he attended all that many Brethren meetings either. We were eventually christened at the dining table in our living room!

There have been several very well-researched books written about the history of fishing along the north shores of the Firth of Forth, particularly in the East Neuk of Fife area. They tell the story of what was once a very important industry and of a way of life that had gone on for a very long time, and as I have grown older I have come to realise that I have lived through quite an important part of the latter period of this history. During my lifetime I have witnessed the total decline of the once thriving fishing industry in St Monans, to the point where there is not one single fishing vessel left in the harbour. On the other side of the coin though, during that very same period I have also witnessed the huge build-up of some sections of the Scottish fishing fleet taking place elsewhere.

I have also seen many new developments in fishing techniques and equipment, and I have witnessed during my lifetime many changes in fishing boat building materials and construction methods. I have seen the introduction of all kinds of hydraulic-powered machinery which have made fishing equipment easier to handle, and I have also seen the introduction of many items of sophisticated electronic equipment both for navigation and for fish-finding. Indeed, I would claim to have been myself responsible for several of the changes that took place in the fishing industry during my long career, which were very important at the time in the evolution of the modern Scottish fishing boat. After spending almost fifty years as a working fisherman, and for the most part of that time as a Skipper and fishing vessel owner, I intend to try and tell my tale mostly in an anecdotal manner from some of my own recollections.

Like everyone else in the village I moved on to Waid Academy in Anstruther for my secondary School education after finishing primary school in St Monans. The catchment area for Waid at that time was more or less the same as it is now, from Lundin Links in the west to Kingsbarns in the east, and all the East Neuk fishing villages and the countryside in between. Generations of local people had discovered that many of the friends and acquaintances that were made at Waid Academy were to remain friends for life.

Those were the days of course some twenty years before Thomas Beeching

My Beginnings

and his decimation of the country's rural railway systems. At that time during my youth, the railway was still running throughout the length of the East of Fife, from Thornton junction in the west, to Crail and St Andrews in the east. I remember one very curious situation that always existed in my schooldays concerning the St Monans pupils who travelled to Anstruther and Waid Academy for their secondary school education. If you were in certain classes, you travelled to school by train in the morning and returned home again by train at night, and everyone else went by bus. The funny thing though was that everyone travelled home for lunch and back again on the same bus!

Who decided what these lines of demarcation should be I shall never know, but you accepted the situation as it was, and I was one of the pupils who travelled by train. The custom most probably went back to a much earlier time when Waid Academy first opened in 1886, and only a very few people went on to a secondary school education. The railway would probably have been the most convenient way to travel. Incidentally, the railway station at St Monans, along with the whole East Neuk branch line itself, was to close in 1965, just one hundred years after its first opening.

I remember from those days in attending Waid Academy just how tidy and well cared-for the local railway station at St Monans used to be, with well-stocked flower beds running practically the whole length of the platforms during the summer. The railway company very cleverly used to award an annual prize for the best kept station and there was always great competition between them. The staff at St Monans station took great pride in their work, and were all very keen to win, and, as I recall, they very often did. Admittedly those were maybe more leisurely times, and they would have perhaps had some time to spare, but I think first and foremost it was always a labour of love. I also remember the big coal fire in the waiting room on a cold winter's morning whilst awaiting the train to take us to school. Incidentally, no trains ever ran on a Sunday!

The second great World War ended in April 1945, and it coincided with a time when more and more young people from this area, and indeed perhaps throughout the whole of the country, were being urged by their parents for the very first time to go on to further education. It was especially true of many local fishermen's families, who at that time could only remember all the lean times and all the hard work for very little reward from the pre-war era. Many of them were determined that their families would not have to experience what they had to endure. Now, for the first time since the start of the war, it was possible for a whole generation of young men to have a choice in their careers. It was no longer inevitable that they would become fishermen like their fathers before them. I took a different route though: I had decided long before my time came to leave school that I was determined that I was going to become a fisherman.

In 1945 most of the traditional fishing infrastructure was still firmly in place in most of the smaller harbours around Scotland, and with so many of my immediate family still actively involved in the fishing industry, it was almost inevitable that I would also become a fisherman. The fishing industry had been very good indeed to my own father, and he had managed to carve out a very successful career for himself as a trawler Skipper and latterly as a part owner. I imagine that he did not have all that many bad memories from his working life, so naturally he gave me every encouragement from a very young age to join him at sea. After three-and-a-half years at Waid Academy, I left school and joined the local fishing fleet in the traditional manner. At fifteen years of age, I became a boy cook on a herring drifter.

A Brief History

BEFORE I START to write about my own career, I would just like to attempt to give a very brief potted version of some of the early history of the fishing industry in this area. This is from valuable information that I have managed to glean from various published works and other recorded sources.

The earliest mention of fishing for herring in the North Sea that I can find is in 1177, and I find it quite remarkable that even by that early date the Dutch and the North Germans were fishing all the way from the Shetlands down to Great Yarmouth. They had even drawn up rules which stated that the fishing should not start each year until 24th June. They had also formalised regulations in which a standardised method for the salting of herring was included. This is quite amazing when you consider that all this happened more than 800 years ago.

As far as the fishing industry here in the East Neuk of Fife is concerned, there is an early record of a pier at Cellardyke in 1452, and there are also some reports of fishing for herring in 1550. There are also reports of fishermen from this area in boats known as "Creers", which were boats with a mainsail and a jib, fishing as far away as the Outer Hebrides in 1580. There are also records from Crail as early as 1580, mentioning indentured apprenticeships for young people in the fishing industry, and their being supplied with gear after completion of their contracts.

By 1642 it was already being reported that there was a scarcity of fish along the east coast to "the hurt and hunger of the poor and the beggaring of the fishermen." Again in 1657 and 1658 there are reports that there were very few herring to be "gotten" on the Fife side and also on the Dunbar side. In 1662 and 1663 it was said that again there were no herring to be caught. I wonder what factor apart from natural cycles would be blamed at that time? It certainly couldn't have been the fault of over-fishing, because I don't believe for one minute that the boats and the crews at that particular time were capable of influencing the stocks in any way whatsoever. Thirty years later, in 1693, a welcome change seemed to take place. It was reported that the fishing was now very good, and that strangers were flocking to this area from "other shores".

In 1703 there are again reports of a prosperous fishery, and by 1707 it is noted that the branding of herring barrels with the local village brands seemed to be well-established. There were also arrangements for the contents of the barrels to be inspected and a fee charged for doing so. Could this perhaps have been the very start of quality control in this area?

It's not easy trying to gather exact information from the past, especially from as long ago as three or four hundred years. One local fisheries historian was the late Peter Smith of Cellardyke, who was himself the son of a fisherman. After graduating from St Andrews University, he went on to follow a career as a mathematics teacher at Waid Academy, and he was to record that along with his father, he had spent twenty-two summers working as a lobster fisherman during the early part of his teaching career. He wrote in one of his books, *The Lammas Drave and the Winter Herring* (1985), that available records of fishing here in the East Neuk of Fife in Scotland were usually written by the local parish ministers, and that they might not have been all that comprehensive. He believed that it wasn't until around the year 1710 that the first detailed account of the fishery in this area can be found.

It reports that St Monans had twelve boats at the summer herring "drave", and also ten boats fishing for white fish. It has Pittenweem with fifteen boats at the herring, and six boats fishing for white fish, and Anstruther Easter was said to have had 24 boats at the summer "drave". Cellardyke is recorded as having 20 boats at the summer herring and ten boats at the white fish, all with seven-man crews. In 1755 it is reported that yet again there was a fish famine. There is also a report of a boat and crew being lost at Pittenweem in 1765, and in 1766 it is reported that yet another boat was lost at Elie with a crew of six men.

Life went on for the next ten or twelve years or so, and it wasn't until 1778 that there were more encouraging reports from a Fisheries inspector that good fishing was being carried on in Cellardyke, and that there were fifteen boats employed in the herring trade there. There were also thirteen boats employed at St Monans, eleven boats fishing from Crail, and four at Pittenweem. All the local fishers employed in the herring trade were said to be in very high spirits because of their success. There were also a few smaller boats employed in the white fish trade in each port.

From 1783 onwards, fishing in the East Neuk was once again reported as sometimes being very poor, and from the spring of 1790, what has been recorded as the seven-year haddock famine took place. Haddock totally disappeared from the area for a period of seven years almost to the day. In 1791, Crail was said to have had thirteen herring boats, six great-line boats, and six small lobster boats, giving a total of 42 fishermen. They were naturally finding very poor fishing for haddock, coupled with the herring also in decline. Like the present day there were always plenty of theories about why fish were either scarce or plentiful. One particular recorder's idea on the situation was that "the industry of man was ruining the shoals." Cellardyke in 1793 was to see the tragic loss of yet another seven men at sea.

In 1795, St Monans had sixteen "drave" or herring boats, but is said to have had only 80 men who followed the fishing from "year's end to year's end." I suppose that they would mainly be great-line fishermen who fished in smaller boats. The year 1795 is also singled out for a special mention as being the "black year", mainly because of the high price of oatmeal. Such was the distress in St Monans mainly amongst the fishing community, that the local kirk session had to make a special plea to Sir Robert Anstruther of Balcaskie and a small reduction in the price was arranged.

In 1800 another seven-man crew were to lose their lives, and on 24th June

1805, yet another crew of six men were lost. I notice from all these old reports of boats and whole crews being lost that they happened in many cases when boats were attempting to enter the harbours in bad weather. Some of these harbour entrances were very poor at that time, especially with easterly winds, and these small, open-decked and sometimes very heavily-laden sailing boats would have been very easily swamped. I'm sure that there would be very few second chances to rectify matters if they got their approaches to the harbours wrong.

The biggest boat that had been built up until 1802, was still only about 29 feet in length, and was still regarded by some as being the leviathan of the fleet. One local expert was pessimistically quoted as saying, that "she was too big to sail, and too big to row!" From a statement like that you can get the feeling that there was great opposition locally to building bigger boats.

Around 1793 it seems that a new herring fishery had just been discovered in the Firth of Forth. This fishing took place in the late autumn further to the west in the waters in the vicinity of Burntisland. It was to prove a godsend each year in extending the "Lammas drave" for a few more weeks. It eventually became so popular that boats were reported to have come through the newly-opened Forth and Clyde canal from Greenock and even as far away as Ireland to take part. Incidentally, this canal first opened in 1790 after being about 22 years in the building and was all dug out by hand.

It was during this period between 1793 and 1815, that the press gangs were very active in the Firth of Forth area. To add to all their other miseries and their very hard lives, there are some horrendous stories of how some of the best young fishermen of the day were being taken into the Navy against their wishes, to serve in the twenty-year Napoleonic wars against the French.

Towards the end of 1814, another tragic fatality occurred in the area. It seems that on this particular weekend the fleet had received some news brought to them by the Elie packet, that there were fish to be caught at the Burntisland herring fishery. By this time it had become known locally as the "up the water drave". On the Monday morning, encouraged by the news, as many boats as could manage were making their way west up the Firth of Forth in a stiff breeze. About a mile from the Island of Inchkeith, a sudden squall suddenly hit and upset one of the boats, and although a ferry was quickly on the scene and one man was saved, three men lost their lives. The boat, which was almost new, was recovered, but sadly in later years, it was again lost with yet another crew, this time whilst fishing from Pittenweem harbour.

I have seen several reports over the years of boats being lost and then later being back at sea again. I can only surmise that in many cases these small open-decked boats were simply swamped and filled with water by a sudden inrush of sea coming in over their toprails. Because they were heavily laden with fish and fishing gear, they simply sank or capsized. Often the boat itself would be undamaged, and in the shallower waters of the Forth in better weather they must have been relatively easy to locate and salvage.

George Gourlay notes in his book *Fisher Life, or, the Memorials of Cellardyke and the Fife Coast* (1879) that David Rodger was the Skipper of this lost boat in the first instance, and that his widow before her own death, had the satisfaction of seeing all of her five sons established as Captains of foreign-going sailing vessels. One son in particular, Captain Alexander Rodger, had a successful career at sea and later formed his own company in Glasgow which owned ships taking part in the tea trade with China.

In 1866, one of his ships, the sailing clipper *Aerial*, under Captain John Keay from Anstruther, was to take part in the famous and well-documented race from Foochow in China to London docks against her great rival the *Taeping*. The fierce competition between those great sailing ships took place annually, and on this particular year sixteen of these graceful ships were to take part. Their goal was always to see who would reach London with the very first cargo of tea of the new season.

That year the result of the race was very close with *Ariel* taking on board her pilot on 5th September, just eight minutes ahead of *Taeping* after 99 days at sea. *Taeping* was actually the first to dock, but the race was so close that the owners agreed to split the prize money. *Serica* arrived later on the same tide, and two other ships arrived within the next two days. It must have been quite a race!

It wasn't until 1816 that the herring shoals returned to the Firth of Forth once again, and the local fishing was said to be very successful for season after season until about 1822. Maybe it was just coincidence, but this period was also a time when the war against the French had finally ended, and the British Empire was rapidly expanding all over the globe. Sadly but inevitably, many more local fishermen were to lose their lives at sea between 1819 and 1822, and also in that year the herring fishing was once again reported as being a failure. It is also recorded that again in 1826 there were to be no summer herring.

In 1828 another fatal accident at sea was reported. After the summer herring "drave" had finished, several Cellardyke boats had followed their normal pattern and sailed to the mussel grounds of the River Eden near Guardbridge to load up with mussels. They would then bring them back to be stored locally in a communal "scaup" amongst the rocks, where the mussels would be covered with fresh seawater during each tide. This would provide them with their winter bait for their long lines, and their "sma lines". Some of the more daring of the men who were present on that day were apparently anxious to make the journey back to their home port as soon as possible, and didn't show enough regard to the signs of impending bad weather. Very soon after crossing St Andrews Bay and before rounding Fife Ness, the weather deteriorated and one of the heavily-laden boats foundered with more men losing their lives. Two St Monans boats also foundered in a heavy gale in February 1833 with the loss of nearly all hands.

Because of the size of boats in the local fleets at the time, if the fish didn't appear locally, and by that I mean literally along the Fife shores, then it would more or less have meant that the fishing would have been a failure. This must have been all very much a boom-and-bust scenario over all that long number of years, and you can hardly begin to imagine the great hardship and severe poverty that must have existed amongst the local fishermen and their families in all that period. Certainly there must have been some limited income to be had from long-lining for white fish, but fishing for herring would have always been regarded as the mainstay of their incomes.

In Cellardyke in the wintertime many of the boats that weren't being used would have to be hauled up the slipway from the crowded harbour and on to the shore. They would be dragged to berths far above the high water mark, and well out of reach of the winter gales. It was essential for their safety, because at that time many of them were not insured: they simply couldn't afford the premiums. Because there wasn't room enough for them all to be laid up near to the harbour, some would have to be dragged further east to the nearby "Town's Green".

Getting all of these boats drawn out of the water would have been no easy task, and it resulted in an elaborate ballot system being worked out to determine the order in which the boats would be hauled out. Sets of iron wheels would be attached to the boats by chains, so that they could be more easily hauled along the streets. Nearly everyone in the village would be involved in the exercise, and it usually took several weeks to complete. It was said that an award of whisky was always some part of the payment!

Something that has to be borne in mind when considering all the information from that very early period, was that up until then probably the biggest of the boats that the fishermen would have had might only have been about 30 feet in length, or even less. They were not really suitable for going away to other ports and fishing areas in winter to try and improve their earnings. The summer was different though, and we are told that as far back as 1832 it wasn't unknown for some of these small, completely undecked boats of only 28 feet in length to venture as far north as Wick to attend the herring fishing there. Apparently the men lived in accommodation onshore, and sometimes a local girl or a female relative would go with them to take care of the cooking. Some of the boats would also venture around to the west coast.

The springtime of 1836 presented quite a quandary for many of the local Skippers and crews who were trying to make up their minds whether they would sail to the north and join in the summer herring fishing there. It seems that this was a period when the fishing in the Firth of Forth was becoming more and more unpredictable each year, and except for four boats that remained at home, most of the crews took the decision to sail north to the Buchan ports. Later on in that same year in August, the word quickly went round the local piers that the gannets, each with a herring in its bill, were like "clouds in the sky". A sudden storm apparently brought that season to an end.

The next year, 1837, herring were once again seen in the Firth of Forth in great numbers, and it was said that some 40 boats were attending the fishing. Some of the great-line boats were reportedly going as far as 50 miles out to sea in search of white fish.

Over the years it had become a local custom in Cellardyke that on a suitable day each summer some of the fishermen would take their wives and families across to the May Island for a picnic. There would usually be dancing to violin music. On 1st July 1837, five boats heavily laden with happy people set sail. Tragedy was to strike, however, when the *John's*, only 33 feet in length and with 65 people on board, ran on to a skerry whilst attempting to enter the small harbour on the east side of the island. The overloaded boat foundered, and thirteen people, mostly young children, were drowned.

That was to be the end of the custom, and at the enquiry that followed it was said that the fact that only four sets of oars were being used instead of six, was a big contributing factor to the disaster. Perhaps there were so many people on board, that there wasn't enough room for more oars to be used.

In the year 1841 Cellardyke saw yet another disaster. The sailing fishing boat the *Lord Melville* was lost with all hands in the waters around the Firth of Forth. Five years later, on 23rd April 1846, the brand new boat *Nancy* was also lost with all hands just fifteen miles from the May Island. On 3rd November 1848 the *John's and Mary* also went missing with all hands. It was assumed that she had been in collision with a sailing brig from the Baltic. On 10th May 1865, the *Helen* was also lost with all hands.

These disasters and the many others which had occurred over the years, were to cost Cellardyke woman Agnes Birrell Reid the loss of twenty of her closest relatives. They included two husbands, two sons, two sons-in-law, two brothers, three brothers-in-law and many other close connections. What a long saga of mourning that must have meant for that poor woman.

The year of 1848 was to see the happening of a very important event. It seems that herring buyers from England who had already been buying fish at Newhaven for some years, now appeared in the East Neuk. One such English buyer, stepping over the gangway with his herring kits, was heard to remark, "Anstruther! I never 'eard of it till last night." Even though they still had to get their fish purchases by steamer to the railway link at Edinburgh they were managing to buy fish cheaper than elsewhere, and they were to put some stability into the local market for fish for the very first time. So much so, that it caused one of the local herring Skippers to remark that "they are the life of the shore, they English chaps."

I don't think that the local fish merchants and herring curers would have been best pleased with the appearance of all this new competition, and one of them was heard to say sarcastically that he thought the strangers would be "taken in!" I don't think that forecast could have materialised though, because very soon 80 to 100 waggons of "caller herring" were being delivered daily to just about every town in England and even across the channel to Paris. The shellfish trade was also benefiting from this influx of new buyers, with lobsters soon doubling in price.

It was reported that in August 1855, another successful fishing took place at the Lammas herring "drave" in the Firth of Forth, with Cellardyke having 130 boats attending, with boat after boat laden to the gunwhales with herring. This is quite an amazing statistic. We also read that by about 1857, the very first half-decked boats were now being built in the area, which would surely have provided shelter and accommodation of a kind for their crews. Nevertheless in 1856, Alexander Dick was lost at sea like his brother before him, and in 1859 another seven men were to lose their lives.

It's not well documented, but it's obvious to me from looking at the huge upsurge in the numbers of boats in the local fleets about this period, that after remaining more or less static for so long, fishermen must now have been starting to enjoy some favourable changes in their fortunes. My guess would be that the arrival of the railway over the borders, and the influx of new buyers resulting in better distribution of fish to the English markets, would have been the factors that were making the difference. It would have meant that profits were now being made, and that people could see a future in building new boats.

It also seems that by 1860 the general pattern was that the herring shoals had now returned, and on 21st August, 200 boats tacked to the pier with an average fishing of 180 baskets per boat. Two years later on 16th August 1862, 140 boats arrived at the piers with an average fishing of 200 baskets per boat. This was very good fishing indeed by any yardstick!

Another event marking a very important milestone in Scottish fishing history was to take place later in that same year of 1862. It would appear that a crew from the town of Fisherrow on the south shores of the Firth of Forth had successfully made the long journey south to take part in a late autumn herring fishery that was being carried out from Great Yarmouth in Norfolk. That following year, they were accompanied by yet another boat. The Skipper of the Cellardyke boat *Hope* had heard some news about these Fisherrow boats attending this fishery, and in 1863 he also decided to make the long journey south. It was reported that they had to endure some ridicule at first, on account of the fact that the gear they were using was not as efficient as that of the other boats that were fishing there. They must have been able to adapt quite quickly, for they made a profitable voyage. Anstruther itself had 38 boats registered at the port that year.

Amazingly it is recorded that this wasn't the first time that East Neuk boats had fished from Great Yarmouth. It seems that about 22 years previously several Fife boats had fished there in the summer, but that fishery had only lasted for about ten years or so. This new autumn fishery in East Anglia was to be very different though, and would gradually attract more and more boats each year. Although it was getting on towards winter, and becoming dangerous for these small sailing boats to be making that long journey south, eventually it was to lead to the dawning of a completely new fishing era. In time it would affect the lives and the fortunes of herring fishermen and all the attendant ancillary workers from all over Scotland, for almost the next 100 years or so. It was sometimes known as the English fishing.

Former Cellardyke fisherman "Auld Wull" Smith, reported that in his last two years as a fisherman in his father's boat in 1863 and 1864, the local inshore fishery had "fallen off" and the larger boats were now having to go further afield to seek herring. Some of the smaller boats were to get out of use. There were no engagements to herring curers on offer that year, and everything was sold on the day's price. For his summer's fishing at either Montrose or Arbroath, he earned eight pounds. He reports that in that same year, after the hired men had left for their homes in the Scottish highlands and even as far away as the Western Isles, herring arrived unexpectedly in great numbers at the "Auld Haikes" just off Kingsbarns. Some of the local men quickly made up full crews amongst themselves and managed to earn as much in that one single week as they had done in the previous two years!

We also learn from fisherman William Smith's book *The Lights and Shadows of a Fisher Life* (1885) that it was announced during the opening ceremony of Cellardyke's new Town Hall that the fishing industry was now starting to expand even more rapidly. By 1868, Cellardyke itself now had 150 boats manned by 450 men and boys. The fortunes of the white fish fishermen in this area must have also been showing some general improvement, for it is on record that on 9th January 1869, 41 local line-fishing boats landed 50 tons of haddock which sold for a total of £500 or 10 shillings per hundredweight — a very creditable amount. Most of them were bought by the curers to be turned into "smeekit haddies" or smoked haddock, this process had being brought into the village by a local grocer named Robert Taylor about 50 years previously. They would all eventually go to Glasgow.

In 1873 it was reported that local fisherman John Wood sadly was lost ten days after his wedding, and the story of the annual autumn herring fishing voyage to Great Yarmouth and Lowestoft in 1875 also makes very grim reading. Eighty-two boats from the East Neuk villages were attending the late autumn fishing there that year, and although the weather had generally been very good for the first three weeks or so after the boats had arrived, they had found the herring to be very scarce. The weather then became very unsettled and on one bad night, the Fife crews were much saddened by the news of the loss of local fisherman James Gardner. The fishing had somewhat improved towards the end of the voyage, but by 18th November some of the boats had already left for home. The remaining crews were becoming anxious to join them, and had also started to prepare for the long passage north. Some boats had taken on board extra ballast for the journey in the shape of a few tons of small gravel stones, and some had loaded barrels of cured herring for various merchants at home, for the same purpose.

The fishermen of those days wouldn't have had access to any sort of sophisticated long-range weather forecasting whatsoever, and would only have had their barometers and their experience to base their decisions on. On top of that, they might well have been easily influenced by the very fact that they wanted to set off for home before the further onset of winter. Whatever it was, on the very next day on their passage north to Fife, a tremendous gale sprang up with disastrous consequences. It resulted in three boats from St Monans, the *Quest*, the *Beautiful Star* and the *Thane*, and two from Cellardyke, the *Janet Anderson* and the *Vigilant*, being lost with all hands. Thirty-seven local fishermen lost their lives in that single gale, leaving nineteen widows, and seventy-two orphans. One St

Monans women was to lose her husband, her son, her two brothers, a brother in law, and a cousin. Another woman lost two sons, a son-in-law, two grandsons and a nephew. A disaster fund was set up to provide a pension for the families, and seemingly the landed gentry in the area and many others, contributed generously.

The *Beautiful Star* of St Monans had been a brand new boat, and this was her very first trip to the English fishing. A monument in her image was erected in the town of King's Lynn by the local citizens there, and dedicated to all the men who had lost their lives and are buried there. It is now very much part of the local folklore.

Four of the boats that were almost the last of the local fleet to leave for home on that fateful day, decided to turn back for Great Yarmouth when the weather started to freshen. Conditions had deteriorated quickly to such an extent that they were lucky to reach shelter safely, and even then not without loss of life. A twenty-two-year-old Cellardyke fisherman named John Watson was lost overboard when one of the boats broached whilst running before the gale. A heavy sea broke over the boat, and carried away the mizzenmast and sail and everything else, and tore the remaining mainsail to shreds.

The leading boats that had left Great Yarmouth and Lowestoft with the first group to set sail, were now so far on their journey home that they had no option but to try and keep going. The wind had been very favourable from the south west when they had first set off, and the boats were all making a good passage. It wasn't until some of them had passed Tynemouth, and making for the inside passage of the Farne Islands, that the wind started to come more from the North. Some of them that were able to, managed to turn and run for shelter to either Scarborough, North Shields or Amble.

The Brothers, skippered by James Stevenson, was one of the last to sail. They had just come in from the previous night's fishing, and had been encouraged to leave Lowestoft for home in a hurry in the company of the *Excelsior*, *Vigilant* and the *Dolphin*. They all encountered the gale early on, and *The Brothers* was lucky to be guided in towards Boston to a safe anchorage by the crew of a Grimsby smack which itself had lost some of its sails. They managed to get the good news of their safe arrival telegraphed home. *The Dolphin* managed to make it safely back to Lowestoft, and the *Excelsior*, after battling the storm all night, made it to Grimsby, but not without loss of life. How the *Vigilant* and her crew met their fate is not known, but she was lost with all hands.

The story of the boats that had got as far north as the Farne Islands and could get no further because of the weather, is well documented by fisherman William Smith who was a crew member on one of the five Cellardyke boats present that day. They had managed to survive the storm, and all of the boats were able to find shelter in the lee of the Holy Island where they lay at anchor for almost a week. Two of them had grounded on a sandbank on the way in, but managed to be refloated. It was a place where none of them had ever been before, and they were given lodgings and well looked after by the local people. How they all managed to find their way into a safe anchorage in that kind of weather without really knowing exactly where they were, is nothing short of a miracle.

Looking out to sea they could see two other boats running south before the storm with their sails down, and trying to find shelter in the lee of the Farne Island itself. They both managed successfully to get their anchors dropped, and at the first change in the weather in a day or two they got underway again and were the first boats to arrive home. One of the Skippers had written a message saying what had happened to them and put it in a bottle and dropped it into the sea. The message was eventually picked up on shore, but the boats had already arrived safely home before it was conveyed to Cellardyke.

Another Cellardyke boat, the *Waverley*, Skipper William Watson, found shelter in the village of Burnmouth situated between Berwick-on-Tweed and Eyemouth. They had been guided in by the local fishermen there, and had then been given ropes and anchors to make their boat safe. They were also given food and shelter until the storm died down.

The very next year, in 1876, the boats started the winter herring in the Firth of Forth early in the new year. They were joined by many stranger boats from the north. The fishing was good and the prices were good, but in the month of March tragedy struck once again. Skipper James Anderson of Pittenweem was knocked overboard just off Anstruther and was drowned. Later that month on 21st March, Cellardyke fisherman David Doig was also lost overboard. The crew had been having a brief rest shortly after reefing the mainsail when the boat suddenly lurched.

There were now as many as a hundred boats in the Cellardyke fleet which were surplus to requirements in the winter, and had to be hauled up from the water before the onset of any bad weather. This left just sixty of the bigger boats to go south to the English fishing. By this time though there are reports of steam traction engines being used, but the heavy task was still to take several weeks to complete. Many of these boats would not be refloated again until 15th June on the following year to go to the summer fishing from Aberdeen.

By 1878, the local fleet in St Monans had grown to 135 boats. Pittenweem had 82 boats, and Anstruther and Cellardyke had 200 boats between them. Crail also had 32 boats. The weather in the early part of that year was so bad that the boats had great difficulty in getting to sea, and it was reported that never had so many boats suffered so much damage to their sails as they had done in that particular year. The local winter herring finished in February almost before it had got started, and in March many of the boats were forced to make the long journey north to Lerwick in the Shetland Isles.

We learn that once again, later on in the autumn of that year, 101 boats from the East Neuk area made the journey south to attend the herring fishing from either Yarmouth or Lowestoft. 56 boats sailed from Cellardyke, 27 from St Monans, and eighteen from Pittenweem: not much different from the tragic autumn voyage of three years previously. Some had thought that the disaster of 1875 would deter many from going south, but that wasn't to be the case. The local fleet left for Great Yarmouth and Lowestoft on or about their usual time of

20th September.

That year, before leaving, the Cellardyke men had made a most unusual decision. They had decided for the very first time to leave most of the boats that were usually hauled up on the shore for the winter, floating in the harbour. The fleet made a splendid passage south, but did not start the fishing immediately when they arrived because there was very little herring to be caught. After a few weeks' fishing, things began to improve, but this was soon marred by an accident involving a young fisherman from Cockenzie.

His boat had just come in from sea, and the crew were about to land their catch in the market at Lowestoft. There was a heavy swell running and the boat was banging against the pier. This young man sprang ashore with a cork fender and was trying to prevent this happening when the boat gave an unexpected roll and trapped his head between a mooring post and the boat. He was killed almost instantly and fell into the harbour with his blood turning the water red. His body was recovered, and nearly 1,000 Scottish fishermen attended his funeral on the Sunday.

Only a week passed before yet another tragedy was to happen. Andrew Lyall, brother-in-law of the Skipper John Watson, was lost overboard and drowned from the yawl *Cyprus*, whilst they were making for the shore in a heavy gale. The boat had been struck by a heavy sea which covered the whole deck, and when it cleared, Andrew Lyall was missing. Only two days later on 28th October another Anstruther fisherman was lost when 42-year-old married man John Duff, one of the crew of the Cellardyke boat *James and Martha*, was drowned in Yarmouth river. His body was recovered several days later when it was caught by hook by boys fishing from the quay.

The very next month, on 4th November, the *Polar Star* also arrived in Lowestoft and reported yet another tragedy. The boat had also been engulfed by a huge wave and her Skipper and owner Andrew Watson had been washed overboard from his post at the helm. He was also only 42 years old and had left a widow and five children. The remainder of the crew had been lucky to have survived the gale.

The fleet had again left for home on 16th November, about their normal time, but much the same thing again happened as had happened in the unfortunate year of 1875. They had only gone about 40 miles on their journey home when they were forced to turn back because of bad weather. They sailed again two days later on 18th November, but the weather was still bad, and two boats were yet again lost. The *Useful* from Cellardyke was lost at Bulmar, and a St Monans boat was lost at Amble. This time mercifully there was to be no loss of life, and both boats were said to have been insured. It was also reported that John Montador from Cellardyke had been lost at sea off Stonehaven, as his brother had been thirteen years before.

On 14th October 1881 the well-documented Eyemouth disaster took place. The fleet of mainly line-fishing boats were caught at sea when a very heavy gale suddenly sprang up and 167 men from the Berwickshire port were tragically lost on that terrible day, leaving 91 widows and about 300 orphans. It was thought that over 200 men in total were lost around the coast in that one gale. That same year in May the Pittenweem boat *Isabella and Jane* disappeared off Aberdeen, and was presumed lost with all hands. Her rudder was all that was later salvaged from the water.

Also in that year the boats that had sailed to Great Yarmouth were much hampered by stormy weather, and were very seldom able to go to sea. It appears though that when they did get to fish they got good catches and good prices, a very rare occurrence indeed from a fisherman's perspective. The fishery was to end as being one of the best seasons since the boats started to go to the south fishing. The average earnings were to be about £300 per boat. Incidentally it was the normal custom when the boats arrived for the south fishing that each man would receive an advance of a shilling from their respective fish salesman. It was a lot of money in those days, and was always known as "getting their arles". I suspect the fish salesmen would always find a way to reclaim that money long before the season ended!

In April 1882 another two young local men lost their lives at sea off the East Neuk coast. Alexander Gardner (26) of Cellardyke was knocked overboard by the sail when entering Anstruther harbour, and Andrew Easson Scott (33) of St Monans was knocked overboard by the helm.

We also learn that the following year, on 18th November, when most of the local fleet had decided to end their fishing at Great Yarmouth and Lowestoft, and commence the long passage home to Fife, some of the boats encountered very heavy squalls and sadly another St Monans fisherman, John Butters, was lost from the *Grace Wood* while attempting to take in the jib.

Also in 1883 the statistics for Cellardyke recorded that there had been a further increase to 203 boats manned by 650 fishermen, and the boats were now being built in a larger size. This was a remarkable increase in the fleet, and now made Cellardyke the second largest fishing community in Scotland next to Buckie. Where they all managed to find berths in that small harbour beats me: I am sure that more than a few would have had to seek refuge in Anstruther. It must have been quite an impressive sight seeing all these boats leaving the various village harbours with their brown tanned sails set. That year 120 Fife boats attended the south fishing, and it was considered a great success with the average earnings being about £280 per boat. Nevertheless, it was still recorded that as usual some of the less fortunate boats and crews had hardly managed to clear their expenses.

Cellardyke fisherman William Smith noted that the local winter herring fishing in the following year, 1884, was the best on record, with the landings for the area being about double that of the average for the previous twenty years. We also learn that the local boats were now being built up to about 50 feet in length and completely decked over. I notice from about this period that at last the records were beginning to show that the terrible loss of life of the past was becoming less and less of a regular occurrence.

I have often wondered why the fishermen of that early period took so many years to build bigger and safer boats and why it took so long for them to accept larger boats that were fully decked over. Perhaps in spite of all the dangers that they faced, they still considered that they didn't need bigger boats as long as they were still making a living from the smaller boats that they had. It could well have been that the increase in the capital cost for bigger boats was simply beyond their limited means.

Maybe it was just the fact that bigger boats would mean much bigger sails that would not be so easy to hoist by hand. Although they were very efficient, it was the handling of these dangerous dipping lugsails which had been the cause of so many fishermen losing their lives in the past. Lowering those big sails and keeping control of the yards whilst the tack of the sail was passed around the mast and back on to the stem head again, wasn't an easy task in any conditions. Maybe it was simply just the case that bigger boats needed more water to float them, and the local men were always very reluctant over the years to accept any less of a tidal window. It was always a very important factor when bad weather was imminent, that they could get into shelter as soon as possible. Maybe they just still preferred hauling their herring nets from open boats.

Maybe it was just simply the fact that the local harbours in those early days, especially Cellardyke, were just not very suitable for bigger boats. Once they had dropped their sails to make their entrance, it was always considered that any boat larger than 30 feet was too big to be rowed easily. In addition, they would have always had to take into consideration the fact that because some of the boats would have to be hauled up on shore in the wintertime without the help of machinery and traction engines, weight and size would have always been a big factor.

As I said at the beginning, I have just attempted to retrieve a very much shortened version of local fishing history from all of these years for inclusion in my own story. Although it seems that much more detailed information is available from my mother's home village of Cellardyke than from elsewhere, I'm sure that I haven't nearly covered all of the events and the many disasters that happened. It is very easy for me to visualise though, that over that long number of years, the fortunes of all the East Neuk fishing villages and their fishing families, would almost certainly have always run on very parallel lines. I hope that it will remind people of the great dangers and loss of life that befell fishermen from this area during that long period.

I am very grateful to have learned so much for myself about my own heritage, and the history of fishing here in the East Neuk. I am most indebted to George Gourlay's outstanding work without which I'm sure much of the information about the story of fishing in this area in the past would have been lost. I also gained much from William Smith's book, based on his personal experiences as a fisherman in the mid eighteen-hundreds. Other more recent sources of information include Harry Watson's excellent book on Cellardyke; Peter Smith's various publications on the East Neuk fishing industry, and Aitken Fyall's history of St Monans. Full details of these works are provided in my acknowledgements.

The Modern Era

IN MY OPINION, the "modern era" of fishing really only got under way about the late 1880s. By this time the railway had already been running in the East Neuk for about fifteen years or so, with all the benefits that it brought with it to the area. Harbours had been much improved, the May Island light had been improved and electrified, and by 1887 it was reported that occasionally it could be seen from as far as 47 miles out to sea. The Bell Rock lighthouse, built by Robert Stevenson on the dangerous Inchcape reef and the scene of many shipwrecks in the past, had been completed in 1811, and had been around for a few years by this time. Its presence must have been very reassuring to fishermen returning from far out to sea, and a most welcome sight when entering the approaches to the Firth of Forth.

Steam-powered fishing boats were starting to be built, and the latest sailing fishing boats were now being built ever bigger. Anstruther itself was now reported as having seventy-seven fully decked boats, with some of them over sixty feet in length. This enabled them to fish away from their home ports, with the crews being able to live fairly comfortably on board. So much so, that they were now venturing as far to sea as two hundred miles to the east of the May Island in search of fish. "Half o'er, half o'er to Norrawa" (Norway) as they used to say. In the third week of May 1886, 62 boats arrived in Anstruther with a magnificent haul of more than a thousand halibut, 3,000 ling, 18,018 cod, 458 skate and 1,900 saithe.

St Monans harbour chock-a-block with sailing boats.
Photograph courtesy of the Scottish Fisheries Museum, Anstruther.

Ten years later, by about 1896, the normal sailing fishing boats of the day were now being built up to about seventy feet or more in length. These were now quite big boats, and well capable of withstanding all but the very worst of weather. They were also starting to be equipped with steam boilers to drive their capstans, which made it far easier for the crews to raise the sails and haul their nets and their great-lines. These boats which I have just described are in fact exactly the same type of boat as the Scottish Fisheries Museum's carefully preserved and renowned artefact, the "Fifie" sailing boat *Reaper*. She was built in Fraserburgh in 1902 and has already celebrated her centenary, and can be found berthed in Anstruther harbour close by the Museum itself.

When the First World War broke out in 1914, St Monans was still considered to be a very prosperous fishing village and by this time had built up its fleet to over 70 of these seventy-foot sailing boats. They normally carried eight of a crew, and it was nearly always necessary to hire men from the West Highland regions and as far away as Ireland to make up their full complements so that they could attend the summer "draves". When all the boats flocked home at the outbreak of war, it was said that the two basins of the harbour could not accommodate them all, and some of them had to go to Anstruther and other harbours to seek berths!

I include this list from 1914 compiled by Master Mariner Captain Robert Reekie of St Monans, who in his early youth had been a fisherman. He had been a close friend of my father, and after joining the Merchant Navy had risen to became the commodore of a shipping company based on the River Tyne. The family boat of the Reekies had been the *Prestige* ML118. Captain Reekie also included a list of the streets in St Monans where each Skipper owner lived.

Name of Boat	Name of Skipper	Address of Skipper
Promote	Robert Scott	Miller Terrace
Vesper	David Smith	Miller Terrace
Clan Mackay	Robert Mackay	Miller Terrace
Ann Cook	Alexander Fyall	Miller Terrace
Chalcedony	David Hutt	Miller Terrace
Renown	John Hutt	Miller Terrace
Vigilant	Tom Adam	Miller Terrace
True Vine	David Marr	Miller Terrace
Gleaner	John Marr	Miller Terrace
Ethel	Robert Lowrie	Miller Terrace
Good Design	Tom Guthrie	Miller Terrace
Chrysophase	Tom Morris	Miller Terrace
Endeavour	John Cargill	Miller Terrace
Jessie Mathers	William Mathers	Elm Grove
Lively Hope	John Allan	Elm Grove
Celandine	Alexander Innes	Station Road
Agnes Irvine	Alexander Irvine	Braehead

The Modern Era 21

Lizzie Cameron	John Cameron	Braehead
Elspeth Smith	James Smith	Braehead
Mary Duncan	George Duncan	Braehead
Sceptre	John Thomas	Braehead
Protect Me	Robert Marr	Braehead
Verbena	John Fernie	Braehead
Jessie	John Ovenstone	Braehead
Agnes Innes	Andrew Innes	Braehead
Oceanic	Tom Innes	Braehead
Mayflower	Andrew Innes	Braehead
Dayspring	Alexander Davidson	Braehead
Lily of the Valley	Andrew Gerrard	Braehead
Hopeful	David Lowrie	Braehead
Rejoice	Alexander Davidson	East Shore
Annie Mathers	Chapman Mathers	West Shore
Trust On	David Irvine	West Shore
Auricula	John Gillies	West End
Brighter Dawn	Tom Fyall	West End
Grateful	Tom Mathers	West End
Vine	Alexander Balfour	East Backgate
Ebenezer	George Davidson	East Backgate
Hazel	James Allan	East Backgate
Frigate Bird	David Allan	East Backgate
Star of Hope	John Mayes	Hope Place
Fragrance	William Guthrie	Hope Place
Golden Queen	James Allan	Hope Place
Ocean Queen	Robert Reekie	Hope Place
Emblem	David Smith	Hope Place
Alice	Philip Smith	Coal Wynd
Watchful	Alexander Aitken	Coal Wynd
Harvest Moon	William Gowans	Coal Wynd
Marjory	Charley Mackay	Coal Wynd
Johan	John Allan	Coal Wynd
Sunshine	James Innes	Coal Wynd
Children's Trust	Robert Reekie	Coal Wynd
Tina Wood	Robert Wood	Coal Wynd
Celtic	James Mackay	George Terrace
Maggie Reekie	David Reekie	George Terrace
Lizzie Duncan	John Duncan	George Terrace
Children's Friend	Andrew & Peter Scott	George Terrace
Honey Bee	John Allan	George Terrace
Barbara Wood	William Wood	George Terrace
Elizabeth Young	David Young	George Terrace
Alert	John Smith	George Terrace

Provider	Andrew Smith	George Terrace
Carmania	Robert Smith	George Terrace
Linaria Alba	James Innes	George Terrace
Pansy	Robert Reekie	George Terrace
Condor	James Lowrie	George Terrace
Celerity	John Mayes	George Terrace
Helen Wilson	William Wilson	George Terrace
Chrysolite	Tom Tarvit	George Terrace
Gratitude	William Ovenstone	Rose Street
Clematis	Alexander Allan	West Backgate
Bounteous Sea	Alexander Reekie	West Backgate
Vineyard	David Gowans	West Backgate
Jessie Dunn	Robert Dunn	Virgin Square
Violet	William Reekie	Virgin Square
Prestige	Alexander Reekie	Virgin Square

From that list, *Vesper*, *Watchful* and *Johan* were all sunk by German submarines though their crews were all mercifully allowed to take to their small boats. *Prestige* was contacted by one of the submarines, but not sunk. For reasons of security, her name was changed to *Coronilla* before she returned to to sea again.

Memories

I REALISE NOW that I should have started to record my own story a long time ago, when it was still possible to record some of this history before it was all lost forever. I personally knew many of the Skippers and crews from my own childhood who had actually worked on these boats, and who had served much of the earlier part of their fishing careers under sail. They would have been able to pass on many of the tales of their own experiences. I'm afraid it's far too late for that now, but nevertheless I intend to try and go back as far as I can remember, and retell some of the stories that I have heard told so many times.

A good number of these men that I do recall would have been able to remember well the good fishing years that took place just prior to the First World War. These same men that I knew would also have remembered the years around that time when about 120 fishing boats were reputed to have left the village of St Monans annually, bound for the annual summer herring "drave" either from Aberdeen, Peterhead or Fraserburgh.

It is very difficult to imagine now, but in the St Monans before my time many of these earlier fishing boats would have been built at the yard of Jock Robertson which was situated almost in the very centre of the town. It was located at the very top of the Coal Wynd, or Forth Street as it has now been renamed, where it joins with Miller Terrace. I can't find out exactly when Robertson's yard closed, but I can just remember many years later this property finally being converted into the walled garden that it is now.

The biggest of the boats that would have been built at Jock Robertson's yard at that time would almost certainly have been no bigger than forty or fifty feet in length, with most of them being much smaller than that. Most of the smaller boats would have been clinker built. This method of construction is where the planks overlap and are fastened to each other with nails and washers hammered to form a watertight join. The more normal method of building the bigger boats was known as carvel built. Because the planks were thicker, they were laid on the frames edge-to-edge and then made watertight by forcing oakum between the seams with a special caulking chisel.

Jock Robertson's yard in St Monans was certainly not suitable for building the larger class of sailing boats when they evolved later, because for one thing it was situated at the top of a very steep hill, and quite a long way from the sea. Even with the medium-sized boats that they were building, they had to hire a steam traction engine on launching day to pull the new boat from the shed. It would then have to be turned around, and gradually lowered down the hill on rounded battens towards the slipway at the harbour. It must have been quite a performance before they eventually reached the water.

My father once told me that the small boys used to try and jump on to the decks of the new boats as they passed the high walls of the houses going down Forth Street. That was certainly all finished long before my time. Recently when I paced it out, I found out that the garden where Jock Robertson's yard originally stood is only about sixty feet long in any case. Towards the end of the nineteenth century, Jock Robertson must have realised that he needed a bigger yard much nearer the water, and moved his business to the west pier, to the site where the patent slipway stands now. Jock Robertson's business had been established about 1870, and it had been passed on to his son-in-law Walter Reekie about 1913. They were to build the *Rejoice* ML337. She was the last steam drifter to be built in this area and was commandeered right after her completion. She was sunk in 1920.

Incidentally, the Scottish Fisheries Museum's sailing boat *White Wing* is an example of yet another method of constructing a wooden boat. She is carvel built on the bottom, but her topsides are clinker built. I don't know the reason for this, but it seems that it was quite a common building method at one time. *White Wing* was built in 1915 on the Moray Firth at Cadger's yard in Gardenstown or "Gamrie" as it is more commonly known locally. She was built as a working fishing boat, and towards the end of her career, after being used in the making of a film, she was kindly gifted to the Museum by the film company. She has since been restored with loving care by the members of the museum Boat Club, and is still sailed regularly by them each summer season.

As I said before, from what I can gather it seems that one of the more important periods of prosperity in the history of the St Monans herring fishing industry was around the end of the nineteenth century. Many boats were being built for the village, both steam and sail. Even up to 1913, when a record year was recorded in Scottish Fisheries, confidence in the future must have still been very high. Things were to change dramatically in 1914 though, because it was to see the start of the First World War in Europe, with Germany being the aggressor and France and Great Britain on the opposite side. This was perhaps the most brutal war of all time, with millions of people needlessly losing their lives in the process, and it was to last until the signing of the Armistice on 11th November 1918.

The period after the ending of the war was a very good time in the fortunes of the local herring industry. I have heard it said that many individual fishing vessel owners and herring curers were able to make small fortunes around this time. Even by 1928, St Monans fishermen still owned ten steam drifters, and the East Neuk as a whole still had 59. This is generally accepted as being the all-time record number of steam drifters owned in the East Neuk area at the same time. The last remaining steam drifter in Pittenweem was a steel ship named *Chancelet*, owned by Adam Lawson. He was to replace her with a 53-foot motor drifter named *Argosy*. She went off to war service and never returned.

Around the time that I was born in 1930, I gather that many of the continental markets for cured herring had gradually disappeared along with most of the local curers and their staffs. Many people had already lost most of the money that they had made immediately after the war, and it appears that the whole herring fishing industry was now entering into a long period of decline once again. Although the total fleet was very much diminished, I suppose St Monans would still have been regarded as one of the more important fishing communities in Scotland, with a population of around 1,800 inhabitants.

My early memories were of quite a substantial fleet of fishing boats that were primarily engaged in either catching herring by drift-net, or catching cod, ling, skate and other white fish species mainly by great-lines. The occasional new boat was still being built, and it would also be fair to say that almost every man in the village was still either employed as a fisherman or as a boat builder, or at least engaged in one of the many ancillary trades connected with the fishing industry. Sometimes when I look at the harbour now compared to what I can just remember from seventy-odd years ago, it seems that very little has changed, except that now every single fishing boat has long gone, sadly along with all their old traditions and skills. So have most of the men that built them and sailed on them.

By 1939, the number of steam drifters owned in the town had dropped from ten to five, and the number in the East Neuk area as a whole had dropped to 24. That all tells its own story. Also by this time most of the converted sailing boats had come to the end of their useful working lives, and had either been sold away or scrapped altogether. Many of these graceful former sailing boats from St Monans were sadly to suffer the indignity of ending their days by being sailed on to the beach literally underneath the old castle to the west of the town. There they were simply abandoned and left to break up: there were no environmental issues to be addressed then, as there would be now.

Between 1929 and 1932 the whole world was firmly in the grip of a great recession, and it wasn't only the people in the fishing industry in St Monans that were suffering. According to all accounts, the rest of the country and indeed the whole world was faring no better, and times were equally as hard in every other industry. We are all very familiar with the stories of various currencies becoming valueless, businesses collapsing and mass unemployment, hunger marches, suicides and all the rest of the despair of that time, both here and in America. Looking back now, it certainly did not hold out much promise for my future prospects in life, or indeed the prospects of all those of my whole generation who had been born in the middle of that great depression!

I remember my mother in later years used to regale us with a story from those poor times. Apparently I had just been born, and my mother and father and I were living at 31 Forth Street or, by its old name, Coal Wynd. It was in the downstairs flat of the house which belonged to my father's uncle Alex Aitken, who owned the boat building yard in Anstruther. My father had just moved to the steam trawling industry at Granton by this time, and the trawler crews had just come out on strike for an increase in their wages. Things must have been getting pretty desperate for us as a family, when my father suddenly remembered something from when he was still single and still living with his mother and father at 20 Miller Terrace.

It was the custom for all the boys in every family of that time to hand over all of their earnings to their mother to save for them, or contribute to the running of the home. Somehow or other my father had managed to "retain" a five pound note from his earnings, and had hidden it somewhere in the house. Up he went to look, and lo and behold, the money was still there. Five pounds must have seemed like a godsend to himself and my mother at that time.

We lived in that same house at 31 Forth Street until 1934, when it seems that my father's fortunes must have changed quite dramatically. Now, only four years later, he was able to buy the house at 17 Miller Terrace, almost next door to his mother. The house cost £400, and at that time it must have represented a very considerable investment. I once read somewhere later, that when these terraced houses in Miller Terrace were first built, they were just single family dwellings, which was quite radical for the time, and were considered to be a superior type of fishermen's houses. They nearly all had fine adjoining net lofts, and I remember many of the prominent Skippers of the day living in our street. Having said that though, I do remember that when we moved in to our new house it still had no bath or electric lights, and this was all to be added later. This was to remain our family home until my mother died in 2002 aged 94, when the house was sold as a holiday home.

Funnily enough though, my earliest impressions of that very difficult period in history — and I could very easily be wrong — were that I don't seem to ever remember that there were all that many men actually unemployed in St Monans. In fact, although I'm sure I must have been far too young to totally appreciate the situation, I can't remember that there ever was quite that feeling of total desperation in the village at all. It's true that most people must have been poor, and some must have been very poor indeed, but I don't think anybody was actually physically starving as they might have been perhaps in a big city or elsewhere in the country.

Living in a fishing village during this period I suppose, would have meant that fish would have always been readily available, although there wasn't much of anything else. In fact I'm sure that there would be very few houses in the village that did not have a half-barrel of salt herring standing just outside the back door, or a rack of dried fish hanging up on the back wall. You have to remember also that on the landward side the village was bordered with fields of potatoes and turnips! Whatever way it was, the boats in this area were still going to sea and although they certainly weren't earning much money, or indeed any money at all, men had jobs and were being kept occupied, and their families were being fed.

Jim Tarvit told me recently that when his father and his uncle were tragically lost off the Shetland Islands in the Leith steam trawler *May Island* in 1936, his mother received ten shillings per week for a widow's pension, and four shillings each for his sister and for himself. This gave them a total of eighteen shillings per week, in addition to the one pound per month which she received from the Shipwrecked Mariners' Society, which his father had contributed to before his death. It wasn't a lot of money, but along with her earnings from mending her brother's nets and the sewing that she did, she always maintained that as a family she thought they were perhaps better off than most of the people in the village.

When I was quite a young boy running about the streets of St Monans a long time before the advent of television, I can remember that there would always be large groups of mostly retired fishermen standing at the top of all the piers or at certain street corners down by the harbour. They were all dressed almost identically in a kind of informal uniform. Thick dark trousers made of kersey cloth with a front-opening buttoned flap, and navy blue fancy patterned home-knitted jerseys or guernseys, with either a round neck, or sometimes two pearl buttons on the side of the neck to enable them to get their heads through. They would also all wear flannelette shirts and home-knitted woollen "long drawers".

This was the way that they all dressed, both summer and winter. They used to say that what kept out the cold, also kept out the heat. I don't believe that story for one minute, because I have witnessed the sweat running down their noses in mid-summer whilst they were working, and sometimes even if it was only from the effort of eating their lunches. Every man would also wear a similar type of flat cap, because it was *de rigueur*. To be different at that time was to be spoken about, and that was just about the very worst thing that could ever happen to a person in a small fishing village such as ours.

I suppose many of these men who were filling in their time standing around the harbour would literally be the survivors of the crews of the much larger fleets from around the turn of the century. That meeting down at the harbour each day was a kind of a social thing that they had been accustomed to doing all of their lives. Some of the groups would even include younger working fishermen who were at home between the various seasonal fishings. They were perhaps taking a break away from their net lofts where they and their wives would always have plenty of work to do getting their own stocks of nets or lines ready for the next fishing voyage. They would also be joined at the weekends by men who were working in the local shipyards, and who were catching up with all the local gossip. Maybe they even included men who had sneaked out for a smoke and a breath of fresh air, while their wives were left to put the bairns to bed. I'm sure it wouldn't always be much fun in these small overcrowded houses with the normal five or six of a family running around!

I remember that there would always be groups of men standing at the gable ends of the rows of houses which stretch along the shore to the West End, adjacent to where the slipway is now on the West Pier. There would also be men standing at the foot of the Narrow Wynd down by the Post Office. They would mostly all live in the west part of the town. The favourite spot of all would always be at the bottom of the Broad Wynd, or Station Road as it is known now, with groups of men gathered on whichever corner was most sheltered from the wind. There would sometimes even be sub-groups gathered on the same corner. There would also be men standing outside Walter Reekie's grocer's shop adjacent to the top of the middle pier or perhaps down beside the Harbour Office itself. There would usually be yet another group standing at the foot of the Coal Wynd, or

Forth Street as it has been renamed, again close to whichever gable end was the most sheltered. There would always be plenty of yarns to spin, and stories to tell.

In the St Monans of that period, the fishermen who used to gather around the top of the piers to meet with their friends, had this very curious ritual which was supposed to be peculiar to the village. They would always pace backwards and forwards in unison, taking the same number of steps almost as if they were counting, and always turning inwards towards each other, and continuing to tell the tales that I am sure they had all heard told a hundred times before. It was a fine way to keep warm if nothing else, and besides, what else was there to do when they would have had so little money in their pockets?

If they perhaps included boat owners, they would have been down each tide to keep a watchful eye on their boats when they were either grounding or starting to float in the crowded harbour. If the weather was really bad, they would maybe even be down during the night. I have heard it said often enough that sometimes in the winter in bad weather, the Skippers would be glad to see the tide receding, and their boats resting safely on the harbour bottom so that they could get off home to their beds.

St Monans harbour never ever at any time in its long history had a formal fish market, and the fish were always landed and displayed for sale on the open piers generally opposite where each boat was berthed. The retired men of the village would always be very interested bystanders at these regular fish auctions which used to take place most days, during the wintertime. Perhaps also a new boat could have been recently launched into the harbour from one of the two shipyards. They could always wander down to inspect the fitting out and perhaps offer some criticism or advice, which every ex-fishermen thought he was entitled to do, whether that advice was asked for or not!

After they had got all the latest news, usually in the morning, some of them would wander up to the top of Station Road and lean on the parapet of the railway bridge and watch the trains arrive. They could see from their high vantage point who was getting on or off, especially if was summer and visitors were arriving from the cities. Some of the people who were arriving might have regularly spent their summer holidays in St Monans for many years, and may have been old friends. The annual Glasgow trades "fair" fortnight in the 1930s, the 1940s and the 1950s was always an exciting time for everyone in the local villages, with both young and old eyeing up all the new "talent" arriving from the cities.

After the excitement of the latest train arrival was past, the retired fishermen would perhaps pause for a minute to sharpen their knives on the soft sandstone of the railway bridge. The bridge is long gone now along with the railway line that ran beneath it, but if you examine the parapet of what used to be the identical railway bridge at Anstruther Station adjacent to Waid Academy, you will still find to this day the grooves where the Anstruther fishermen used to sharpen their knives. Incidentally, the St Monans railway station and goods yard were formerly situated on what is now the small industrial site.

In those more innocent days, every proper fisherman worth his salt would always carry a knife in his pocket. They never knew when they might get the opportunity to help a relative to repair a damaged fishing net, or maybe when they were strolling in the country side, they would see a chance to cut a suitable bough from a tree to be used in the construction of a lobster pot. More to the point, they never knew the moment when they might be offered the gift of some fish from a boat unloading its catch, and it was just as well to be prepared!

The favourite daily walk for the retired St Monans fishermen of the period, along with their dogs, might have been to carry on up the country road towards Abercrombie farm, and then turn right down the main road towards Pittenweem. They could maybe then take a short cut through the fields and down the right of way known as the Sandy Kirn, and back to the railway station bridge again. If they wanted a longer walk, they would maybe even carry on towards the railway bridge over the main road. Just before they reached there, they would turn on to the Black Road and down over the railway line, which would take them to the Coal Farm. They would then walk back west along the main road to St Monans.

Down by the harbour was where everything generally happened in the village, and was the accepted meeting place. Even to the present day most people always seem to gravitate there by habit, although now as I write these lines, I notice that there are very few people standing around, and perhaps only for an hour or so in the mornings. The mould has definitely been broken, and the people who were brought up in the village, went to school together and then worked or sailed together all of their lives, are now becoming fewer and fewer. There is not much left to see in any case. The shipyards have long gone, and except for a few small yachts moored there, the harbour is now completely empty. Many of the houses bordering the harbour have been sold as holiday homes and are only occupied at the weekends.

I attribute the very start of this depopulation mainly to the young people of my own generation. From 1946 onwards, when I left school, many boys and girls of my own age moved away from the area to be further educated, and then to find work and pursue their careers elsewhere. As a result their own families who would normally have been the new lifeblood of the village, are now scattered all over the country. I often think about all of this and the many young boys that I grew up with. Hardly any remained in the area.

Most of the fishermen that I am writing about at that time in the early 1930s, would have been the survivors of an era in which the fleet was very considerably larger than it was by the time that I was born. They had all worked for the most of their lives as share fishermen, either as boat owners or as crew members, and sometimes the rewards for a good part of their life's work could have amounted to precious little. Fishing has always been a gamble, and in many cases for some of these men there would have been individual voyages during that time which had not been a success, and could easily have resulted in no rewards at all. Worse than that, in extreme cases — again because they were share fishermen — it was not unknown for crew members to even have to pay in to meet the expenses of the previous voyage. Can you just imagine expecting anyone to do that now?

A fishing boat is first and foremost a business like any other, and all boats certainly don't earn the same. There were some Skippers who would always do well even in the worst of times, and there were other Skippers who would fare badly even when times were good. That was how it was in the Thirties, and that is how it is at present, and that is how it will always be. Sometimes in the old days if a man had a berth on a "poor" boat, and by that I mean a boat that didn't earn much, he could be stuck there for many years because he owned his own nets or lines on board. It wasn't always easy to make a change, and at best he could only keep hoping that things would get better.

In the early part of the 1930s especially, working conditions were desperately hard for all drift-net herring fishermen and their wives and families throughout the whole country, and not only in St Monans. Most of the time all they would have had to sustain them would have been their faith and their pride in being fishermen. There must also have been a certain degree of optimism or expectation every time they went away on a new fishing voyage, or otherwise they couldn't have done it. Deep down though, I'm sure they must have all realised for quite a long time that things were not going to improve very quickly. I think it must have been far more than a job: it could only have been a way of life! It must have all been quite heartbreaking at times, and on top of that, goodness knows how they survived their retirement with so very little in the way of savings. There were definitely no private pensions then, and only the meagre state pension to live on. Also, looking back to that time, the population of St Monans was much the same, and I sometimes wonder where everybody lived. This period that I have described was just around the time of the completion of the first new council house project of 1934. Forty houses were built in the upper part of the town, and named Gourlay Crescent after the local Provost. Many of the families who moved into them would enjoy decent housing for the first time in their lives.

Looking back to that era between the two great World Wars, the boats themselves were certainly not very sophisticated. In St Monans especially, with the exception of the steam drifters, most of the boats that remained were the very last of the larger sailing boats that had been built around the turn of the century. They had nearly all been converted to motor round about 1914, only a few short years after some of them had been built.

One of the very last of these old former sailing boats that I can remember as a boy still fishing, was the *Elspeth Smith*. Alex Smith, who was the Mate and part owner, was to describe in later years how the decision had been made by his family to abandon the use of sails and fit a new motor. Apparently the mainmast had split near to the top, and this meant a big decision had to be made. Either the mast had to be shortened to cut out the split, or a completely new mainmast had to be fitted altogether. Cutting the mast was probably not an option, because it would have meant that the mainsail would now have to be much smaller, and the boat would not have sailed as fast as was required. More radically, they could opt for the installation of a new motor. After much discussion the family finally took the big decision to fit the new engine and, believe it or not, it was said that the cost worked out marginally cheaper than the new mast would have been!

As was the custom in St Monans and throughout the whole of the Scottish inshore fishing industry, the boats were usually family owned. With so very little income coming in, you can well imagine that the Skippers and crews had to be very thrifty and resourceful indeed in order to survive and keep their boats in a seaworthy condition. Herring fishing voyages were all mostly seasonal, so in most cases, the owners and crews would do practically all their own maintenance in the time that they were laid off between fishing voyages. I have to say that it was a tribute to their industriousness that many of these boats were still fishing after 40 years or more.

The annual refits and engine overhauls and the painting of the boats were jobs that were always undertaken by the crews as part of their duties as share fishermen. None of them would have been trained originally as motor engineers because marine engines were very much in their infancy at that time, but by necessity they all soon became very skilful. They learned to overhaul their own main engines, steam boilers, steam capstans and everything else for that matter, only employing engineers or carpenters as a last resort to do any work they were unable to do themselves. Even then, in order to keep down costs, I have heard it said that some Skippers would go up to the yards and ask for a specific tradesman by name, one that they knew by experience would do a good job for them as cheaply and in as short a time as possible.

Bearing in mind that there was no patent slipway in St Monans in those days where large boats could be hauled out of the water, all work on the hulls had to be done on the beach at the top of the harbour during a spring tide. The fishermen of St Monans were fortunate because their harbour always had what I would call a good beach, both in the east and the west basins. Although it was mostly mud, it was quite firm mud with perhaps a bit of sand mixed in, and there was never any danger of anybody getting stuck. Those beaches were also quite flat and didn't have steep shelves, so there was never any chance of boats taking what was known as a "bad lie" when they listed down. Also, because the beaches were quite flat, the ebbing water would take much longer to leave the boats, and this was just ideal. It gave the crews much more time to scrub one side of the boat's bottom and have it painted long before the incoming tide reached the boat again. No power hoses were available in those days, and I can remember whole crews with their long white rubber thigh-boots busy hand-scrubbing with long hard brushes. They would manage to do one side one day, list the boat over the other way when she floated, and then do the other side the next. Even the larger steam drifters were all painted in this manner. Tidal harbours didn't have many advantages, but this was one of them.

The East Neuk fishing fleets working from the tidal harbours of St Monans, Cellardyke and Anstruther in the winter, and also Pittenweem before its harbour was deepened, always used to do a lot of damage to their keels, especially when the wind was blowing from the south-east and there was a heavy swell running. These harbours are all terribly exposed to the wind from that direction, and because they are all relatively shallow, the boats were invariably trying to get out or in before there was really ever enough water for them to float properly. For instance if the crew discovered that a piece of the iron strip that ran along the bottom of the keel had been torn off and was tearing the nets whilst they were being hauled, the boat would be beached. When the tide ebbed they would dig away the mud to reveal the bottom of the keel. The local blacksmith would then be summoned, and he would hammer out a replacement strip there and then, and it would be brought down and fitted.

I remember over the years seeing many not inconsiderable jobs being done on these beaches: new stems or sternposts being fitted, new planks put in; new rudders; perhaps even a new tube for the propeller shaft, or perhaps a transducer for an echo-sounder when they developed later. They would always have to be very careful of course to ensure that whatever job they started, they could manage to finish before the next tide came in. I can remember boats from many other fishing villages around the Firth of Forth coming to the beaches in St Monans harbour to have their repairs done. Because there are always two tides each day, six hours to come in, and six hours to go out, it was simply amazing the scale of the repairs that could be tackled on these beaches.

I'm sure there would have been many anxious situations when a job that they had expected to finish easily, would meet with an unexpected snag. There certainly was an art in doing repairs on these beaches, there's no doubt about that, but I'm sure they took it all in their stride because they had always done it that way, and in any case there was no alternative! Coupled with that of course, the beach was free and convenient and nearly always available, and that was very important indeed. Some difference from trying to maintain large fishing boats in the present day with all the costs involved!

The painting of the boats at the start of each season was something of the romantic and something of the picturesque, with the brave new colours being in line with most of the Scottish fleet. The hulls would nearly always be painted black, and the anti-fouling paint on the bottoms would be red. The two colours would be separated by a broad white waterline running the whole length of the boat, and widening out to a kind of shark's mouth towards the bows. The registration letters and numbers were painted twice along each boat's side, towards the bows, and towards the stern. It was always white lettering with blue shading painted on a black background. It was colourful, but also practical because it made them easier to read. The names of the boats, which were usually the *pièce de resistance*, would usually be carved out on detachable boards and painted in gold gilt lettering and then mounted on each bow.

In my young days in St Monans, this would nearly always be the handiwork of a local Skipper named Tammy Gay. He was a man who had perfected the art of painting names and numbers on boats, and he was always in great demand. His unique style always made the St Monans fleet instantly recognisable in any away port, even if it was crowded with other boats. Another of Tammy's specialities was the beautiful scroll work on the fronts of some wheelhouses. When an owner

Memories

had got his numbers painted on by Tammy Gay, it would be left on for years, only being touched up each year by the best painter in the crew. In addition to that, some Skippers would have their own preferences. The tops of the varnished masts on the St Monans boats usually featured a white band and a blue band close together. This was supposed to bring luck. If it were in the case of a steam drifter, their long funnels would all be painted in the distinctive colour bands that their owners preferred. Incidentally, Tammy Gay was also a very talented artist in his own right, and many of his fine paintings, mostly on board, are prized possessions around the village.

I remember also before the start of the Second World War hearing that there would be quite a few tradesmen who would sometimes become fishermen from time to time. They would take berths on the boats if work was slack at the yards, or perhaps if they thought that they would maybe be better off at the fishing for a few months. Some of them would work as fishermen for many years, before going back to their trades. They must have been an invaluable help with the maintenance.

One person that I knew who did that was a man called Davie Smith, who lived in Hope Place opposite the Bowling Green. He was, as they used to say, not the same Smiths as we were, but he was a good friend of my father, and then later a good friend of mine. He was a member of the Close Brethren religious sect who held their meetings in the hall opposite our family house in Miller Terrace, and Davie always had the reputation of being one of the best joiners in the area as far as fishing boats were concerned. I remember him once telling me that when he worked in Miller's yard, after a new boat was launched he and his work-mate would start at the front end of the fish hold, and work all the way through to finally fitting out the crew cabin at the after end or maybe the front end of the boat. Admittedly the boats were not nearly as lavishly fitted out as they are now, but it must have been quite a task just the same, if you bear in mind that everything would have to be made by hand. Davie was a most meticulous man and especially careful with all his tools. When I was a boy I was always making something from wood, and I could always count on being able to borrow anything that I needed from him. I can always remember him telling me that during his lifetime, his biggest mistake had always been that when he was working as a joiner, he should have been a fisherman, and when he was employed as a fisherman, perhaps he would have been better off being a joiner. Such is life!

There were always two shipbuilding yards in the St Monans of my young days. There was the yard of Walter Reekie at the west end of the harbour where the present slipway now stands and which had produced many fine fishing boats of all sizes, and whose reputation was second to none. In charge of the yard was Jimmy Butters from Pittenweem. He was the foreman and master boat-builder.

In the East Harbour was the yard of James N. Miller and Sons, who had a proud history of building fishing boats and yachts going back for over 200 years. The man who ran the boat-building section of that yard in my young day was the brother and partner Tammy Miller, who lived up beside us in Miller Terrace.

Miller's also had a large engineering section run by senior partner and brother Willie Miller OBE JP. In addition to holding the agency for Kelvin diesel marine engines, they were also responsible for many innovations in fishing equipment. Both these yards had branches in Anstruther at one time or another, and the Reekie yard at Anstruther was still going strong in my young day under the stewardship of foreman Tam Parker. They were building boats on two slipways leading into the outer harbour just to the eastward of the present RNLI lifeboat shed.

Jim Tarvit has recorded in his recent book on the history of the steam drifters that five wooden steam drifters were built in St Monans by Robertson at his yard on the west pier. This was in addition to building quite a few of the very last of the big "Fifie" sailing boats. Walter Reekie, the son-in-law of Jock Robertson, who took over the yard about 1913, was to carry on the yard under his own name for another thirty-five years after that, including all the war years, until his premature death by accident.

Around that same early period, Miller's yard in St Monans is recorded as having built ten steam liners and drifters between 1892 and 1900. After they bought over Jarvis's yard, they ceased building in St Monans and moved their whole operation to Anstruther, where they went on to build a further 19 steam liners and steam drifters under the Miller name. It is believed they built one further boat there, a wooden boat fitted with a motor engine, before they finally moved their whole operation back to St Monans again in 1912.

Apparently they were part shareholders in the patent slipway in Anstruther opposite the present Scottish Fisheries Museum, and now buried under the present car park. That was where all the steam drifters were built. One record of a steam drifter built by Miller's in Anstruther was of the *Venus*. It shows that she had been built in 1907 to the order of a William Smith and a Peter Murray of Cellardyke, and cost £2,600. She was known to have been fully repaid by 1914, including nearly £999 of interest on the loan. Miller's had ceased their boat building activities in Anstruther long before my time.

It would take a long time to give an account of the long history of Miller's yards, and all the fine fishing boats and the magnificent yachts that they had built between the wars, and perhaps I will leave that to someone else. What I do remember is that these two yards were very important employers of local labour employing men and women from all along the East Neuk. There were very few boys at that time from any of the local villages that did not receive an apprenticeship at one or other of these yards. Nobody had to go outwith the area to look for work, and in fact the reverse was more often the case. A lot of fine people actually came to St Monans to find work, took their place in the community, and lived the rest of their lives there.

Except for a few steam drifters, the majority of the St Monans boats in the early 1930s were nearly all seventy-foot wooden boats, most of which must have been well over thirty years of age by that time. They had all started life as sailing boats around the turn of the last century, and then had engines and steam

Memories 35

capstans installed later. Peter Smith, retired mathematics teacher and local fishing historian, tells us that in his researches he had discovered that the very last true sailing "Fifie" fishing boat to be built in St Monans for local owners, was the *Marjory*. She had been launched from Miller's yard in March 1906 for the Mackay family.

I myself can remember the *Marjory* towards the end of her days being berthed up in her usual place on the east side of the middle pier, up near the harbour-master's office. I believe that she was sold to the Buchan family in Peterhead, who fished in her for a while. I can also remember the *Marjory*'s very last Skipper. His name was Charlie Mackay, and in his prime he had the reputation for being one of the best fishermen in the village. Any man who sailed with Charlie even in the poorest of times was sure of a regular income. Jim Hughes of Pittenweem was to write later that Charlie had said that if he took a berth on the *Marjory* with him, he would have his own boat in a few years' time. He was correct, because Jim Hughes was later to build the *Emulate*.

Charlie Mackay lived half-way down the Coal Wynd, next to where two generations of Eastons had always had a paper shop and photographers. Like a lot of the fishermen of the time, particularly the Skippers, I remember Charlie always wearing his black cap with the shiny plastic snout, and decorated with black cord around the sides. I can also remember a similar boat, the *Celandine*, which belonged to the Innes family who lived in Station Road, being berthed in that area immediately after returning from naval service. I don't think that she ever fished again.

On the subject of the Easton family, the father Willie was one of the area's earliest photographers, and his studio was situated at the foot of George Terrace on the north side of the bend at the south end of the street. It was there that he was to record the history of generations of family groupings and wedding portraits of families from all along the East Neuk. Anybody who possesses a family photograph of that period can rest assured that it would have been taken by the camera of Willie Easton. Also all of these postcard-type photos of St Monans harbour from the sailing boat era were all from the same source. Sadly the studio was demolished around about 1950. Later on, a friend of mine, who worked for a local builder at that time, told me that he remembers when he was an apprentice, wheeling barrow-load after barrow-load of valuable glass negatives over to the refuse dump which was then situated where the caravan site is now. A whole history of our village recklessly destroyed. What a shame!

Another sailing boat that was among the very last to be built in St Monans, was the *True Vine*. She had been built at Robertson's yard in 1904 for a Skipper named Davie Marr, who lived with his wife Mary Barclay Marr at 34 Miller Terrace just opposite my own family home. I can remember Davie Marr very well as an old man. He was always a very prominent member of the Salvation Army in the village, and I clearly remember sitting on his knee as a boy. He used to sing that well-known hymn to me, "Mind your helm brother sailor, and don't fall asleep, watch and pray, night and day, lest you sink in the deep." He must have known that I was going to be a fisherman myself some day!

The thing that I find hardest to grasp as I write all of this, was the realisation that the last of these types of large "Fifie" sailing fishing boats, with no propulsion engines of any kind, were still being built long after my own father had been born. Indeed, the very last of the type, the *Marjory*, was completed only 25 years before my own birth in 1930. Even more amazing was my realisation that the Wright brothers in America had already made their first powered flight on 17th December 1903, two years before *Marjory* had even been built! It's very difficult to comprehend now that the men who were having these relatively large sailing fishing boats built at that time must have still been anticipating fishing under sail for the rest of their careers. This was even although there were literally hundreds of steam fishing vessels in use or being built during the same period.

I suppose the main reason that these fishermen were still clinging on to sails in spite of all the obvious disadvantages compared to steam power, must have been purely and simply a matter of economics. To build a steam drifter, there would first be the huge difference in the capital cost, and then inevitably there was the vast difference in the running costs. The sailing herring drifters were acknowledged to be quite profitable in their own way, and I have heard it said on more than one occasion that many of those fine substantial granite houses that many fishermen live in throughout the fishing villages and towns in Scotland, were mainly built from the earnings of sailing boats and not from the steam drifters. Whatever the reason, it certainly illustrates just how relatively short the history of the "modern" fishing industry really is.

Jim Tarvit records in his book on steam drifters that the very first steam herring drifters ever to be purpose-built were constructed at Leith in 1864. Apparently they were built as a pair. One was named *Forward* for Aberdeen owners, and the other was named *Onward* for Cellardyke owners. Although they were purely and simply just "Fifie" sailing boat hulls fitted with a boiler and steam propulsion engine, it seems that in the first instance they made excellent long-line boats. It was obvious that in time they would eventually more or less revolutionise drift-net fishing for herring. Mind you, it didn't happen overnight, and it really wasn't until the steam capstan itself had been perfected much later, and had become a regular part of the steam drifter's inventory, that they became a complete success. The end of the sailing boat era was now becoming inevitable.

One of the problems in the development of the steam capstan had apparently been with the pipe that carried the steam to the motor. The motor was on top, and it wasn't until the English engineering firm of Elliot and Garrood of Beccles and of Lowestoft had thought of the idea of carrying the steam pipe up through a hollow spine inside a vertically revolving capstan drum, that the steam capstan would become a complete success.

The very first new capstans and boilers that were fitted on the sailing drifters were positioned aft, because the fishermen still preferred to haul their nets from the stern as they had always done. It wasn't until progress overtook that idea, and the capstans were moved on to the forward part of the boats nearer to the bows, that they were now able to haul their nets with their heads to wind with greater efficiency and in greater comfort than before.

Alec Smith, Mate and part-owner of the *Elspeth Smith*, has recorded that the very first steam capstan and boiler to be installed in a St Monans sailing drifter was in around 1895. The boat was reputed to have been owned by leading local Skipper Jock Cameron. Naturally all the new sailing boats that were built during the next ten years or so after that would almost certainly have been fitted with steam boilers. This in fact was to be one of the main reasons why they were now able to build and operate sailing fishing boats as big as 80 feet overall, a much larger class of boat than previously. With the new steam capstans, in addition to hauling the nets and lines, they found that with the relatively small crews that they carried, they could now handle the bigger dipping lugsails much more easily.

Getting in and out of harbours if the wind wasn't favourable couldn't always have been an easy task in these big new sailing boats. Even after being a Skipper myself for forty years, I still honestly don't know how they managed half the time. How they ever sailed those big boats into those small crowded harbours and then manage to bring them to a halt without an engine, is very difficult to imagine. They would then have to berth them up without causing damage to themselves or to other boats, with those tall heavy masts catching every gust of the wind. It certainly couldn't have been easy. Previously they would always have been able to row out or in, but now as the boats got much bigger, this in itself would have become quite a task.

With the advent of the new steam capstans, in some cases it would be a little easier because they could now winch themselves in and out of some harbours. In St Monans, a concrete beacon known as Mathie's Monument had been constructed some 100 yards to the south west of the harbour and a heavy rope was strung from it to the end of the west pier. One or two sailing boats would raise steam, and by putting the rope round the capstan and letting it pay out over the stern again, they would winch themselves out to where they could hoist their sails to catch the wind. At the same time, they would maybe pull two or three other boats out behind them. These boats would then hoist their mainsails, and break away in turn when they were ready. Anstruther harbour, from the original harbour entrance further up the west pier, also had a rope stretched out to a rock opposite so that they could do the same thing. I believe Pittenweem also had a type of rope arrangement on the west side of the entrance channel for the same purpose.

Little were these men to know when they were building the last of those bigger sailing boats around the turn of the century, that by 1914, only eight years since the very last one had been launched in St Monans, they would all be installing propulsion engines that ran mainly on paraffin. Very soon, sails — except for the mizzen sail which was still vital to the working of the drift-nets and the great-lines — would very quickly become things of the past. It is recorded though, that quite unbelievably, a few of these sailing boats were never ever to be fitted with motors.

One interesting recollection that I have from that period is the way in which the new engines were installed on these former sailing boats. When you take into consideration the fact that there would have been no provision made for them in the original design, it could not have been easy. The favourite position adopted by most of them was right in the middle of the cabin where the crew lived and slept. Can you imagine that? I can always remember visiting the cabin of the *Elspeth Smith*, the boat that I so nearly joined as a boy cook when I left school, which had just such an arrangement. The table where the crew would take all their meals, had simply been shifted further aft to make room for the new engine and was now positioned over the gearbox!

I can remember hearing men that I knew, and who had sailed in boats similar to *Elspeth Smith*, recall later that it used to be a terrible experience with all the noise and the heat. If it was bad weather, and the hatches had to be tightly closed to keep the water out, the engine would soon burn up all the oxygen. After they had been sleeping in the cabin for some hours with the engine running, they said that they would wake up feeling as if they had been gassed. Coupled with that, I remember that the coal-fired cooking stove was also installed in the cabin. I even think that in some of the early installations when the boats were still hauling their nets by the stern, they might have also originally had the steam boiler for the capstan in the cabin as well. The heat in that small space during the summer months must have been quite unbearable. Talk about "Dante's Inferno"!

Some boats like the original *Carmania* which was owned by my father's uncle John Smith, had also started life as a sailing boat, but when they decided to install a motor, they chose another option. They had installed two engines, a 60-hp Kelvin engine driving the main propeller through the main stern tube, and another smaller 30-hp Kelvin engine driving a wing propeller which came out from the port side bilge. They had installed these engines forward of the fishroom in the bow compartment of the fo'castle. A much better arrangement I would say as far as living conditions were concerned, just as long as they managed to keep the propellers clear of the nets.

Another piece of information came to my attention recently, and, as Michael Caine would say, "not a lot of people know this." It seems that in 1899, Miller's of St Monans had built a "Fifie" sailing fishing boat named the *White Rose* for local owners, and by 1916 this boat had been sold on to Aberdeen owners, where she had later been fitted with a steam boiler and a 35-hp engine. She was then sold back to other St Monans owners, who later sold her on to Lowestoft, where she ended her days as a coal hulk in 1922.

The last big "Fifie" to be built in Pittenweem at Fulton's Yard was the *True Love* for the Anderson family. She had been preceded by the *Margaret Lawson* for Thomas Lawson in 1899. The *Margaret Lawson* was to end her days tragically on 3rd February 1937 after running aground at the Billowness swimming pool in thick fog while trying to find her way into Anstruther harbour. They removed all of the fishing gear on Bonthron's lorries and she very quickly broke up. The Skipper was by this time two weeks from his 73rd birthday. They contacted a Mrs

Memories

Mayes in St Monans and managed to hire her boat the *Celerity* which was lying idle due to a fatal accident to her husband, the Skipper/owner, and they then finished the winter herring in her.

During the Second World War I remember one of these large old former sailing boats being based at Anstruther, and being employed as an Air Sea Rescue craft. She was of a type known as a "Zulu", which had a heavily raked stern-post and had been much favoured by the fishermen from the Moray Firth area. Her name was *Humility*, and she was fitted with three propulsion engines: two 88-hp engines as wing engines, and one 132-hp main engine. All were Kelvin diesels, and she was reputed to have been very fast. I would imagine that she must have been very considerably over-powered, and if all the stories are true, I believe she occupied the beach for quite a lot of her time having repairs done to her hull. I think she might have from fished from Lerwick after the war. Incidentally, an identical example of *Humility*, the *Research*, is preserved in a specially constructed gallery in the Scottish Fisheries Museum in Anstruther.

I can remember my father telling me that as a youngster he had made the journey up to Peterhead along with my grandfather for the summer herring "drave" on the family sailing boat *Vesper*, fishing number KY640 and owned by David Smith. This would probably have been around 1910. They would sometimes be joined there during the summer by my grandmother and some of the rest of the family, who had travelled to Peterhead so that they could spend a few weeks beside their husbands. I'm sure it would not have been all holidays in Peterhead for my grandmother, because my father was one of a family of six boys and a girl. On top of that, more than likely there would have been a herring net or two to be repaired along the way. I can remember my father telling me that my grandfather and grandmother always used to lodge with the Buchan family. That would be the grandfather of John Buchan, the present Skipper of the Peterhead trawler *Pursuit*.

In writing all that I can remember about the St Monans of my childhood, maybe I should try and mention some of the more well-known and long-established fishing family names that were around the East Neuk at that time: families who had lived and worked there for countless generations. If you were to consult some of the old Nautical Almanacs, you would see that in St Monans, the names of the boat owners of the time are listed as Adam, Aitken, Allan, Anderson, Butters, Cameron, Cargill, Davidson, Duncan, Dunn, Easson, Fyall, Gerrard, Gowans, Gourlay, Hutt, Innes, Irvine, Lowrie, Mackay, Mayes, Marr, Mathers, Miller, Meldrum, Morris, Ovenstone, Reekie, Scott, Tarvet, Wood, and of course my own clan, the Smiths. I just hope that I haven't left anyone out.

In the same way, Pittenweem had their Andersons, Boyters, Bowmans, Horsburghs, Hughes, Lawsons, Woods, and Watsons. In Cellardyke, some of the fishing family names of the day were, Anderson, Barclay, Bett, Birrell (my grandmother's maiden name), Boyter, Brunton, Doig, Gourlay, Gardner, Henderson, Hodge, Melville, Moncrieff, Montador, Muir, Murray, Parker, Reid, Rodger, Smith, Stevenson, Stewart, Tarvit, Watson, and Wood. I think it would be fair to say that the Watsons would be the most prominent fishing family name in Cellardyke over the years. My mother's own family name was Corstorphine, and there were quite a few of them.

It is interesting to relate that the East Neuk herring fishermen of the mid-1930s had always been considered to be maybe just a little bit more fortunate than most at this time. This was due to the fact that they had this very important winter herring fishery, right on their doorstep in the calmer waters of the Firth of Forth. This fishing was always known as the "winter herring", and in my young day, I can remember the many stranger boats that would come down from the North of Scotland and from the West of Scotland and elsewhere, to join in.

I can also just remember that at that time nearly all the steam drifter Skipper owners in St Monans also owned smaller diesel engined 50-foot "Fifie" boats in addition to their larger boats. Skipper Willie Meldrum had the steam drifter *Lucy Mackay* and the motor boat *Economy*; Tam Gowans had the *Flush* and the motor boat *Godetia*; Rob "The Laud" Marr had the *Defensor* and the *Protect Me 3*, and Tam Adam, who was recognised as one of the foremost herring fishermen of the day, owned the steam drifter *Scarlet Thread* and also the motor boat *Vigilant*. Incidentally, the same Tam Adam, on being asked what he considered to be the secret of his success, had put it down to "perseverance and good gear." Probably true!

The steam drifters were totally unsuitable for working from these small tidal harbours in the East Neuk on a daily basis. They were of very deep draught, and required far too much water for them to float and manoeuvre. The idea of their Skipper owners in having these second smaller boats in addition to their steam vessels, would be so that they could mothball the bigger boats, and fish the four months of the winter herring in their "bauldies" as they were called. With their smaller draft and their longer tidal windows, and of course their very important low running costs, it certainly made economic sense.

When the winter herring was finished in March or April, they would then in turn lay these smaller boats up in tiers at the top of the harbour for the remainder of the year whilst they went off in the springtime in their bigger boats to prosecute different types of fishing elsewhere. Some of them would change over to the great-line fishing for white fish in the offshore grounds of the North Sea or perhaps to the early herring "drave" at Lerwick. Later on in the summer they would usually be fishing from Peterhead or Fraserburgh. This would occupy them until they went south to Yarmouth again in October.

One piece of fishing history worth mentioning was that Rob Marr, a former Skipper of mine when I had started as a boy, and always a very keen fisherman willing to experiment, had at one time decided to try and fully utilise his smaller "bauldie" *Protect Me 3* by towing her all the way through the Pentland Firth and round to Stornoway in the Minches behind his steam drifter *Defensor*. He presumably recruited some local crew there so that he would be able to fish both boats at once. I have no idea if the experiment was a success or if it was ever repeated.

There was also another story that I remember hearing told about the same Rob Marr. Apparently, when the *Protect Me 3* had been in the planning stage, he had gone up to Walter Reekie the builder, and told him that he didn't want her to be designed "like this" in the stern section under the waterline, and at the same time sucking in his cheeks, but "like this", and then puffing out his cheeks. It was a good description, and I am sure that Wattie Reekie knew exactly what he meant, and was able to incorporate Rob's ideas into the new boat! Incidentally, I spent a short season in 1946 fishing from Scarborough as the cook on that boat.

In addition to the winter herring fishing which played such a big part in the fortunes of the local fishermen during the period that I can remember, Peter Smith also writes in his book about another herring fishery that took place each year in the Firth of Forth long before my time. In fact, I can't even remember any of the older men that I sailed with when I first started my career even mentioning it, so it couldn't have figured very highly in their memories.

There was a late summer fishing which usually took place between July and September and was known as the "Lammas herring drave". It probably took its name from the annual St Andrews autumn Lammas fair. Each year was different, and for example in the week of 27th August 1860 it is recorded that the herring were so plentiful, that some boats were landing twice in a day from just off Pittenweem. The curers were sometimes unable to cope, and boats were directed to land elsewhere, and it was said that the year's total was greater even than the great year of the winter herring in 1936. Unfortunately, the last mention of any summer herring being landed locally from this Lammas "drave" in the Firth of Forth was in 1873.

I should also mention the former fishing village of Buckhaven to the west of Leven, or "Buckhind" to give it its local name. I think that at its peak it had a fleet of perhaps 60 large and medium-sized sailing boats. The "Buckers" were reputed to be good fishermen, but they usually fished for herring in the summer either from Berwick-on-Tweed or from North Shields, rather than going north to the Aberdeenshire ports. I can still remember the net-making factory operating there, but I don't think that I can remember ever seeing a Buckhaven boat and crew. Alas, the former harbour is now completely filled in.

I think that the cause of the decline of Buckhaven as a fishing port was that as coal mining developed in that area fishermen would start by taking jobs there between fishing seasons to supplement their incomes. They gradually discovered that more and more they were getting a regular wage working in the coal pits, when perhaps sometimes they weren't as fishermen, and they weren't then keen to go back to sea. Whatever it was, the fishing seemed to decline in Buckhaven far more quickly than it did further east along the coast.

The normal annual pattern of seasonal fisheries at different locations around the coast would generally start with the appearance of herring in the Firth of Forth in late January, and this fishery was always commonly known as "the winter herring". This fishery is very well documented by Peter Smith, but here's what I can remember for myself as a boy, or was told. After about 1936, and after surviving most of what was to be known as the hungry Thirties, there was no doubt that things were starting to improve a little in the fishing industry. Nobody seems to know exactly why, but as far as the herring industry was concerned my own particular theory is that the catalyst would certainly have been the fact that Germany was starting to re-arm in preparation for the Second World War. Because money was now beginning to circulate again, it was creating a new demand for cured herring.

There must have been a new optimism about, because for the first time for many years local fishermen were starting to think about building new boats again. It could have just simply been that many of these steam drifters and many of those former 70-foot converted ex-sailing boats that had been built around the turn of the century were coming to the end of their useful lives, and if their owners wished to continue their careers as fishermen, then most of these boats simply had to be replaced. Whatever it was, between 1936 and 1939 quite a few of the more progressive local Skippers in St Monans and elsewhere in the East Neuk, were starting to invest in this new kind of super "bauldie".

It was a definite reversal of the trend towards bigger boats. These purpose-built, smaller boats were of a new design, having a round "cruiser" stern as opposed to the traditional vertical "Fifie" stern. They were between 54 feet and 60 feet in length, with a much greater capacity than previous boats of those dimensions had ever had before, and some were fitted with full diesel National engines of up to around 100-hp. Some even had boilers and steam capstans fitted for hauling their nets, and for discharging their fish when the tide wasn't suitable and they couldn't run their main engines. These boats were all very efficient and were quite big enough to attend the summer fishing at Peterhead or Fraserburgh, or even to Scarborough, Whitby, or Great Yarmouth in the autumn.

The reason that the St Monans men were so relatively successful around this time was partly because these "bauldies" were to prove to be the right size of boat for the job. At least for a while! I think I can recall all of the names of this new generation of boats that were built in the late 1930s along with that of their Skippers. They were, *Boy John* (Jimmy Davidson); *Carmania 2* (John Smith); *Deo Volente* (Eck Hutt); *Girl Christian* (Tam Gerrard); *Myosotis* (Peter Fyall); *Procyon* (Dauvit Fyall); *Star of Hope* (Tam Ovenstone); *Vesper* (John Cargill), and *White Heather* (Tammy Gay).

Each year in January, before the "winter herring" fishing got started in earnest, they would shoot their nets every night in the hope of getting enough herring to be used as bait for their great-lines. They would leave harbour on Sunday nights after midnight, and go down mostly off Crail or to the May Island and shoot their drift-nets. If they were lucky enough to get a good catch of herring, they would make for the harbour to get the best price possible. If they didn't get enough herring to justify going to the harbour, they would be off as quick as they could to the nearest hard ground where they would shoot their great-lines, using the few herring that they had caught as bait. They would try and get the lines hauled again without wasting too much time, and be in harbour in time to catch the morning market with their fish. This all depended on the state of the tide of course, because the East Neuk harbours are all tidal. Their catch would be mainly cod, ling, and skate and because their economies were so small, with very little earnings, they could meet their expenses and manage to give their crews some kind of return.

As the fishing developed into the New Year, the main shoals of herring would set in to the Firth of Forth to spawn, and although they would continue to work their long-lines as well as their drift or anchored herring nets, by now it was only herring that they were concentrating on. Some years some of the St Monans crews were reported as earning as much as a £100 per man for their winter fishing. A small fortune at the time, and I have no doubt that sometimes they must have been the talk of the whole country.

In the good years, the main shoals of herring would appear literally overnight and always on or around 7th February. They would come inshore each year in their millions to spawn not so very far from here on the north shore of the Firth of Forth. They would congregate either on the "Auld Haikes", which is a stretch of hard bottom just offshore between Crail Golf course and Kingsbarns Golf Course, or on the "Hirst", which is almost directly off Crail harbour or out between the Fife shore and the May Island. They would be accompanied by thousands of sea birds of all kinds, and people would observe them from the shore because they had been watching for the signs. The cry of "herring in the haikes" would soon get around the East Neuk villages.

Boats would then arrive from all over Scotland to take part in this fishing, and it would last until almost April, with the boats landing their catches fresh every day in the main markets, either in St Monans, Pittenweem or in Anstruther. Anyone of my generation can look back to their boyhood, and remember all the hustle and bustle, and the towering stacks of empty "Klondyker" fish boxes and barrels stored all around the harbour areas in all of the villages, ready to filled with herring and then being loaded on to lorries or horse-drawn carts to be taken to the railway goods yards. Anstruther was always by far the main port, and I can remember the herring being transported from the harbour either by lorry or horse and cart up Rodger Street, along the High Street, around the Buckie House corner and then up to the goods yard in West Anstruther with a trail of herring spawn all the way. They would be taken away by train to the customers inland, or perhaps to be loaded on to steamers in Methil for export to Eastern Europe.

I mentioned before that St Monans harbour never at any time had a formal fish market building as such. Long before the days of boxing fish at sea became established, the rows of cod and skate would all be laid out neatly in scores according to size on the piers, awaiting their turn to be sold by the fish salesmen auctioneers. It was mostly done on the middle pier if possible, and I can remember it all as a boy. This would be the pattern all through the winter until the end of March. It was an unforgettable scene every day, although it finished a long time ago and will never be repeated.

As far as fishing for "winter herring" in the Firth of Forth was concerned,

1936 was generally reckoned to have been the absolute peak year, with the greatest number of boats catching the greatest number of herring. I can just remember that in those immediate pre-war days, I used to do all right from the winter herring fishing as well. Although by this time, my own father was an established Skipper of a steam trawler sailing from the port of Granton, and was not involved in the local fishing, my father's uncle, John Smith, was the Skipper and owner of the 58-foot motor boat *Carmania 2* KY66. She was relatively new at that time, having only been built at Aitken's of Anstruther in 1936 replacing a boat of the same name which had been built as a sailing boat. He was perhaps one of the best fishermen of his day in St Monans, and as a favourite grand-nephew what this meant for me was that I would sometimes get to "go with the money."

On Saturday, after the week's work was finished, the Skippers would all go along to the fish salesman's office, and collect the money for their boats' catches. After all the week's expenses, such as fuel, food, harbour dues and salesman's commission had been deducted, he would then take off the boat's share, and the remainder would be divided up amongst the crew according to the amount of gear each man owned on the boat. The ratio at that time, including the Skipper, would be one share for your labour, and one share for every share of the gear that you owned. Each man's money would then be tied up in the corner of a big red handkerchief and that's where I would come in. I would sometimes get to deliver it to each crew member's house on a Saturday afternoon. If it had been a good week, it was the custom for the boy or girl, who was "gaun wi' the money" to be rewarded with a tip of some kind!

There was also the "scranning"! We boys would usually hang around the boat of a relative, gathering up any loose herring that had fallen from the top of the baskets and dropped on to the decks when the crews were unloading their catches. We would then thread them on to a piece of string, and go around the houses trying to sell them. I can remember that we would get the fish lying in some funny places. In the bearers, under the top rails, in the rubber tyres that were used as fenders, on top of the wheelhouse, and perhaps even in the lifeboat. There was another way we could scran some herring. In return for doing some work about the boat, such as cleaning out the accommodation, or perhaps cleaning the herring scales from the wheelhouse, or wheelhouse windows, or for running messages for the crew, some herring would maybe left in a basket for the "scranners".

I seem to recall that our market was fairly limited though, and very few people would be willing to give too much for a herring in a small fishing village like St Monans during the season. Everybody seemed to know of somebody who could get them a few herring without having to pay for them! Sometimes we would walk to one of the surrounding farms to try and get a market for our fish, but I think perhaps there were many times when we would end up either having to give them away, or dispose of them in some other manner.

The drift-nets that were used in the winter herring fisheries were made of white cotton, and because the fishermen had discovered by experience that white

Memories

nets fished far better than brown nets in the Firth of Forth at this time of the year, the twine was left untanned. The nets still had to be preserved though, especially if they had been catching a lot of herring, and every third or fourth week, on a Saturday, after the usual hard night's work was over, they would have to be dipped in boiling alum instead of the more normal boiling bark or cutch. Before they finished for the weekend, they would have to separate each individual net from its neighbour, and "fake it up" into a neat bundle. In the case of a steam drifter, where they had the facilities to do this, the nets would then be dipped into a vat filled with boiling alum that they carried on board especially for the purpose. This was one chore that every herring fisherman absolutely hated, but I'm afraid with cotton nets it simply had to be done or the nets would have soon rotted.

In the case of the crews of the motor boats in St Monans, the nets would be hoisted on to a lorry, and driven up to Wullie and John Tarvet's yard on Station Road next to the old Congregational Church, now the site of the sheltered housing complex at Abercrombie Court. The Tarvets had installed six big wooden vats, which had been specially made for the purpose, and also an old steam boiler with a pipe leading into each tank to boil the water in order to melt the alum. Each boat would be allocated its own vat, and I can well remember seeing the nets being dipped into the boiling solution, with the steam flying everywhere.

It was not uncommon for the men to be still aluming their nets late on a Saturday night if there had been a big demand for the use of the facilities, or if they had spent all day landing a good catch of herring. Sometimes they would then take the nets to the outskirts of the town where they would loosen them from their neat bundles and hang them on any unoccupied fences to dry. On Monday morning, they would have to be all bundled up again and transported back to the boat. They would then be unbundled one more time, and linked together before being "set down" into the hold ready for sea again. What a task!

The Tarvet brothers must have been very enterprising businessmen, because they also ran a garage with petrol pumps from their premises on Station Road. They also provided the whole village with one very important service. Very few houses in the early 1930s, if any at all, would have had electricity, and if they owned a wireless receiver, it would be powered by a wet accumulator which would have to be recharged every so often. Everyone must have owned a spare one, because I remember that I would sometimes have to take our glass accumulator to the garage and exchange it for one that was fully charged. I can remember the rows and rows of accumulators with people's names printed on them.

Fishermen's wives would have had to play almost as important a part in the herring fishing at that time as the men. Maybe even more important! On every boat, each fisherman owned his own share of the fishing gear, and the Skippers would more than likely have two shares or perhaps more. In addition to looking after the house and the family the wives and mothers would also have to mend the nets. Some of the Skippers' wives, because their husbands had two or more shares of gear in the boat, would not be able to cope with all this work, and would have to employ other women to help them.

Skipper's wife Lizzie Mayes handing out hard biscuits to onlookers
when the *Carmania* was about to set sail for an away fishing.
The boy at the front is the author aged about six years.

I'll never forget my father's Uncle John's wife. She was truly an amazing woman. She was always known in the village by her maiden name of Lizzie Mayes, and I suspect she knew more about herring nets than most fishermen. She was a very clever woman and she would have all the spare nets ready for the various stages of the herring season. There would be "hard nets" when they fished best, or "soft nets" or "narrow nets" or "wide" nets, all descriptions of the size of the mesh, or the general condition of the net. Perhaps that was why my Uncle John was such a successful fisherman, and the *Carmania* such a successful boat. If all the stories are true, she was said to be almost as good at mending them, as he was at tearing them, and he was reputed to be pretty good at doing that!

It was well known to every Scottish herring fisherman at the time that the Firth of Forth winter herring fishing was a notorious graveyard as far as the destruction of herring drift-nets was concerned. The fishermen had to contend with crowded fishing grounds, strong tides, and most of the herring would be found in the relatively shallow waters around Crail and Fife Ness. It's usually the case that the best fishing is obtained where there is the most danger to the fishing gear, and the winter herring fishery in the Firth of Forth was no different! Some Skippers simply could not take the risk of shooting their nets in certain places, even although they knew there were plenty of herring to be found there. In fact there was so much gear destroyed at the East Neuk winter herring fishing that it was sometimes the case that Skipper owners who normally put in two shares of nets during the rest of the year could not afford to do so in the Firth of Forth. It was not unknown for them to offer their hired men — these were men who did not normally own gear — an opportunity to "put in gear" for the winter. Big deal!

Tearing drift-nets was such a regular occurrence that almost every household in St Monans at that time owned a unique type of wheel barrow which was specially designed to carry one or two herring nets from the boat to the house or *vice versa*. They had a single big iron wheel at the front with two shafts at the back and two wooden legs to keep them from overturning when they were set down. They were usually branded with the owner's name, and always kept nicely painted. They usually lasted for years. They were a very important part of a fisherman's equipment, and as so, were always a very acceptable wedding present! Nearly every fisherman also owned what was known as a hand barrow. They were simply two shafts with cross-struts between and used for the same purpose. They had to be carried between two men, and they were a very important part of the process when the herring nets were being tanned or dipped in alum.

It must have been heart-breaking for the wives of herring fishermen when the local winter herring fishing was in its heyday. There would hardly be a day when there wasn't a net being brought home to be repaired. If there were unmarried sons living in the house who were fishermen with gear then it would be much worse. Helped by any daughters or grandmothers, she would have had their nets to mend as well. Everyone was involved, and most of this work would have to be done in the living room in front of the coal fireplace, with only the light from a single gas mantle, while looking after the family at the same time.

The fireplaces in the local fishermen's houses were always known as black-lead grates, and had to be polished every week with some concoction called Zebo which came in a tin, and which, with the help of much elbow grease, brought up the fireplace nice and shiny. All the cooking was done on this coal fire and the kettle on the side always seemed to be boiling. I remember my grandmother telling me that when my mother and all her brothers and sisters were still in the house, she had to get up early each morning, get the fire going, and sit and toast endless slices of bread for them all. Incidentally, the "fisherman's cottage" in the Scottish Fisheries Museum contains a fine example of this type of fireplace.

I remember my own mother telling me that when she was a young girl in her mother's house in Cellardyke in the early part of the last century, and her father and three brothers all fishermen, her mother would just be glad to see Saturday night and the nets finally all mended. She would at last get her chance to sweep out the cuttings of barked twine from the waxed-cloth floor. Mercifully the boats didn't go to sea on Sunday, so at least they got a short break and a chance to catch up.

I also remember my mother telling me that in Cellardyke around that time, there was an Italian man named Cappuchi who apparently was quite a "character".

He owned an ice cream shop in the town along with a horse and cart, and for a small fee he would transport damaged nets from the boats to the fishermen's houses, and then back again when they were repaired. I have also been told that sometimes my grandmother used to get so frustrated with all this work, that she used to declare that that damned horse would stop at her house whether it had a torn net for her or not, simply from sheer habit! One story about Mr Cappuchi was that his horse and cart had gone over the pier into the harbour and both had to be fished out. It was reported that horse and cart survived!

To be fair, this pace of life didn't go on for the whole year round, and neither could it have done. The fishery usually lasted for the three winter months of January to March, with the peak being in mid-February. The very seasonal nature of herring fishing usually meant that fishermen had a lot of downtime, and the drift-nets could generally be repaired at a more leisurely pace. These days are far removed now, and very soon there will be no one left who can even remember them at all! Worse than that, maybe soon there will be no one left who is even interested in remembering them!

The start of the Second World War in September 1939 meant great changes

Ring-netters berthed in Anstruther harbour.
Photograph courtesy of the Scottish Fisheries Museum, Anstruther.

in the fishing industry's annual pattern, with large numbers of local boats, particularly the steam drifters, being requisitioned for war service, and also many local fishermen were being called up for the armed forces. This vacuum, however, was soon to be filled by a large influx of mostly smaller type varnished boats from the Clyde and the west coast, known as ring-net boats. They all used a very efficient new fishing technique which had been developed and perfected there over a long number of years.

These type of boats from the west coast had made the journey through the Forth and Clyde canal many years before, as far back as 1929, to try and establish a foothold into the prolific winter fishery in the Firth of Forth that they had heard about. They had based themselves at Granton at first before fetching up in St Monans where the local fishermen made it clear that they were not welcome. They were forced to leave without fuel, water or bread. They were made welcome in Pittenweem however, and, in 1930, 74 ring-net boats arrived in the Firth to try their luck. By 1932 and 1933, they were also being made welcome in Anstruther, where they hadn't been before.

Two of these ring-net boats would fish as a pair, and by steaming around trailing a long length of piano wire kept vertical by a heavy lump of lead on the end, they would detect a shoal of herring by the fish impacting on this wire. Some men became so expert with this "feeling wire", that they could almost tell to the basket what the catch would probably be, and they became much sought after crew members. If they thought that the signs were right, they would then quickly encircle the shoal with the large net. If the "ring" was a successful one, then the two boats would come alongside each other to allow one boat's crew to transfer to the other boat that had caught the fish. This was sometimes a dangerous manoeuvre jumping from boat to boat, especially in bad weather, but both crews would be needed on board the boat whose net had been used to catch the herring. This would be in order to handle the large net and get the catch on board.

Some of these pair teams were so successful that their Skippers, usually brothers, became legends in the history of the west coast herring fishing. Their reputations were well-known from the Minches in the North, to the Clyde and all the way down to the Isle of Man in the Irish Sea. Even on the east coast, they were known from the Firth of Forth down to Whitby and Scarborough in the south. Some of the Pittenweem fishermen who adopted this new method, particularly my friend David Wood in the *Hope* and his brothers, and also some members of the Watson family, would in time manage to become equally proficient as their west coast teachers.

In 1942 the ring-net landings in the Firth of Forth reached their peak, with the ring-netters catching herring almost non-stop in the daylight hours, bearing in mind of course that it was wartime and the boats were not allowed to fish in the dark in any case. Alec "Mackie" Watson once told me that when he was a boy just starting with his father, they would leave Pittenweem as daylight was breaking, and they would not have very far to steam before they would hear the sound of the herring playing on top of the water. In a very short time they would be back in harbour with their holds full up with herring. The Teviotdale family and the Smith families from Arbroath would also secure their place in the history of the ring-net fishing in the Firth of Forth, and they fished very strongly in their boats *Floreat 2*, *Floreat 3*, *Vigilant*, *Orion* and *Jeannie Smith*.

In 1943, after the success of the previous year, the decline started for some reason, and by 1945, unbelievably, the fishing would become a total failure, with no herring to be caught in this area ever again! Many reasons were put forward to explain why this should have happened, and of course it was inevitable that ring-net fishing would be allocated the largest part of the blame. Maybe the St

Monans men had been proven to be correct fifteen years earlier when, along with so many others before them, they had opposed the use of the ring-net in the Firth of Forth. Who knows? One thing that no one can deny is the fact that for whatever reason the herring have never ever returned. You can understand why so many local fishermen just returning from war service were so very bitter about the situation. They had fished these winter herring in these local waters every year from the time they had started work as fishermen and now when they were fortunate enough to have returned from the war, and anxious to join in the annual klondyke, the herring were gone.

Maybe it could have been another developing technique that could be blamed for helping the herring to change their habits. Seine-netting for white fish on the bottom was just starting to become popular in this area, and there was no doubt that these towed nets were destroying a large amount of the herring spawn and that couldn't have helped the situation. Maybe it was just a natural cycle that had occurred, and perhaps like the salmon, the herring were being fished elsewhere in the open seas long before they reached the Firth of Forth. We have learned that these famines had happened on many occasions long before that. Whatever the cause, I'm afraid we shall never know now. By this time the war had continued for almost six years, and for most people in Europe, there had been far more important things taking place than the catching of herring.

There was always a lot of quiet, religious fervour about the St Monans of the 1930s when I was growing up, hence the nickname given locally of "the Holy City". A lot of this fervour would surely have been imported to the village by fishermen who attended the traditional summer herring fishing locations at Peterhead and the north-east each year, because it was about this period that people were breaking away from the traditional Church of Scotland and other established churches, and were forming even stricter religious groupings. My father's uncle, John Smith of the *Carmania 2*, was one of those who formed the Plymouth Brethren, or the Open Brethren as it was known in St Monans, and his brother, my father's father, David Smith, was one of those who then broke away from the Open Brethren to form the Close Brethren. Sadly this sect can now no longer find a congregation, and ceased to exist in St Monans many years ago. Their meeting hall in Miller Terrace directly opposite what was our family home, has now become a joiner's workshop.

In my childhood, from about eighteen hundred or so of a population in the village at that time, I can remember that there were eight very definite different denominations. There was the "Auld Kirk", which of course is the Church of Scotland; the Free Kirk; the Congregational Kirk; the Plymouth Open Brethren; the Close Brethren; Duff's Brethren, and the Salvation Army. There was also a regular meeting of Pilgrims. As far as I can remember, they all had a congregation of some kind. Funnily enough though, there were no Baptists in St Monans although there were Baptist Kirks in Anstruther and Pittenweem. There were also no Roman Catholics either at that time, although there was a chapel in Pittenweem. It wasn't until two families arrived from Ireland some time after the

Second World War to find work on the various hydro-electric schemes that the situation was to change.

As a youngster, I can recall what Sunday meant for myself and my family. The Old Kirk Sunday School usually took place before the morning Kirk service, so we would attend there first. On the way home we would then all attend the Congregational Church Sunday School in their meeting hall on the Station Road. In the afternoon, most of us would then go to the Open Brethren Sunday school, which at that time was held in a large wooden hut at the foot of George Terrace, and is still there to this very day after being used as a joiner's business. On Sunday nights I would usually attend the Open Brethren meetings there with my father's uncle and aunt. On top of that, I would almost certainly be at the Salvation Army hall at least one night a week, especially during the winter when it was cold out on the streets. With five of us in the family, and my father away at sea most of the time, I'm sure my mother wouldn't have been sorry to see the back of us for a while anyway!

Having said all that, I don't think that what I did each Sunday was anything out of the ordinary. I think most of the youngsters in St Monans at that time, would be doing much the same as I did. No lines of demarcation with us. We embraced every religion that was on offer. Remember at that time there would hardly be anyone in the village who owned a car, and so the highlights of our social calendars were always the annual Sunday school trips and the Christmas parties. To get there you had to attend each Sunday school. We weren't all that daft! I think everyone of my generation will speak fondly of the Open Brethren Sunday School trips in particular. They were generally acknowledged to be the best. Besides that, as far as I was concerned personally, going to the "Meeting" at night with my father's Uncle John, did my chances of "gaun" with the *Carmania*'s money on a Saturday no harm at all.

On Sunday afternoons in the summer, after Sunday school, if my father was at home and the weather was good, we would sometimes get all dressed up in our best clothes for the traditional Sunday walk. In our case, we would cross the moor park from Miller Terrace where we lived and where the football pitch and the caravan site are now, and then walk east along the main road towards Pittenweem. Opposite the Coal farm, we would turn left up the Black Road and over the railway line towards Balcaskie estate. We would then enter the estate from the main road through the "white gate" and on to the "maister's walk" with the rhododendrons overhanging the whole length of the path. A great occasion on the Sunday walk would be if we were to meet any of my uncles and aunties with my cousins, doing the same walk but from the opposite direction. It would be a great opportunity for the adults to exchange all the news and the bairns to play for a while. I used to look forward to those walks. More innocent days!

During the week, especially in the winter evenings, the meeting place for all the village boys, would normally be Brattisani's billiard hall which was situated in the square halfway down the Narrow Wynd. It had three full-sized tables and a "wee" table crosswise at the bottom of the hall. You weren't allowed to play on the big tables until you reached a certain age!

My father's Uncle John and his wife, who was always known by her maiden name of Lizzie Mayes, lived in St Monans in the big square house at the crossroads at the top of Broad Wynd — or Station Road as it is known now — and George Terrace. It had a huge garden, and it was aptly named "Barron Hall". I'm sure it must have been one of the foremost fisherman's houses of the day. It also had a large net loft separate from the main house, and I remember that there would usually be women working in there. Underneath the loft, there was another storeroom which held all the messenger ropes and the canvas buoys. All were easily accessible from the street, for ease of transporting the gear to the boat. I seem to think that there was also a coal-fired boiler in the yard, which was used to tan nets from time to time.

One of my best memories was that as one of the leaders of the Plymouth Open Brethren, my Uncle John would usually invite people back to "Barron Hall" for supper after the Sunday night meeting. This sometimes used to include Peterhead fishermen who fished from St Monans each winter, and who stayed in the village with their families, and who were also part of the hierarchy of the Brethren. After supper they would usually discuss the service further, as well as the merits of the various preachers on the night. There were no formal ministers in the Brethren movement, and the sermons were all given by members of the congregation. They were mostly fishermen, and some of them certainly knew their Bibles well and were very good preachers indeed. Because I used to often go to the meeting with my uncle and aunt, I would be invited for supper as well. I can't remember, but I expect "sole" pies from Jimmy Ferguson's baker's shop would always have featured greatly on the menu.

That brings to my mind the story that my friend Willie Morgan, the former Skipper of the Peterhead boat *Sundari*, has often told me. When he and his brother were boys and their father was fishing from St Monans, he used to ask his mother if they were going out for their supper on Sunday evening. If she told them that they had been invited to the Fergusons' home, he used to tell me with a big grin on his face, that they were always sure of a good feed. Jimmy Ferguson certainly made a big impression on somebody!

Looking back now, I'm sure my own mother must have been considered very lucky at that time compared to a lot of other women in the village. My father was now sailing from Granton as the Skipper of a large steam trawler fishing for white fish, so they would have had a fairly regular income compared to most at the time. This also would have meant that she would have had no herring nets to look after. Mind you, with eventually five of us in the family, I'm sure that nowadays that would be considered more than enough in itself.

My early memories of my mother seem to be of coming home from school on a Monday, and her out all day slaving in the washing house with the coal-fired boiler. She was either at the glass-ribbed scrubbing board, or the "dolly" barrel, which was used to pound the dirt from the clothes, or turning round the wringer or the big wooden roller mangle by hand. After all that there would be almost

Memories 53

certainly be a meal to be cooked and then a big sinkful of dirty dishes to be faced. There were no automatic clothes washers or dish-washers at that time, and the fishermen's wives of the day certainly did not need aerobics classes in order to keep fit. My mother died on 21st November 2000 at 94 years of age, so she must have survived all that hard work remarkably well. Mind you, she did eventually have an electric automatic washing machine, which could well have been the very first in the town. I can remember that it was a Hotpoint, and I can distinctly recall helping her to puzzle out how to operate it!

As boys, if we weren't playing football on the moor, we would usually be found hanging around the harbour. I'm just old enough to be able to remember vaguely some of the last remnants of the large fleet of converted "Fifie" sailing boats or "the motor boats" as they were always known in St Monans, just before they were all broken up. It was great, just after school in the winter, going down to watch them all going to sea just before darkness fell.

Some of the older "Fifie" boats that I can remember from that time had names like the *Lively Hope*; the *Condor*; *Celandine*; *Celerity*, the *Elspeth Smith*; the *Ruby*; *Annie Mathers*; the *Brighter Dawn*; the *Marjory*, and the *Clan Mackay*. Incidentally, the *Clan Mackay* was the last big "Fifie" to be built in St Monans. At 68 feet in length she was not quite as big as most of the other former sailing vessels. She had been designed to be able to fit into the locks on the old Forth and Clyde canal in the same way as the old Clyde steam "puffers". Some of the smaller Fife "bauldies" that I can also recall were the *Celtic*; the *Express*; *Faithful*; *Paragon*; *Providence*; *Protect Us*; the *Protect Me*; *Diligence*; *Vigilant*, and the *Godetia*. The newer St Monans-owned cruiser-sterned motor boats at the time were the *Carmania 2*; *Procyon*; *Boy John*; *Deo Volente*; *Girl Christian*; *White Heather*, *Vesper*; *Mysotis*, and the *Star of Hope*.

It's funny, but after forty-eight years at sea myself I can still remember the sounds and smells of these particular engine exhausts spluttering in the water as the boats passed the end of the middle pier. I can also distinctly remember the special taste of the sweetened condensed milk that all the boats carried in their stores in those days, and which we boys would scoff wholeheartedly if we were ever given the chance. There were also the steam drifters, the *Kimberly*; *Flush*; the *Scarlet Thread*; the *Lucy Mackay*, and the *Ocean Angler*. She was scrapped in 1938, but was replaced the following year by the *Defensor* before being requisitioned for war service.

Friday night after school was usually when we got to go to sea, or "aff" as we called it, on a relation's boat, but only after a lot of pleading, and only if the weather was fine. I remember one Friday night in particular, going to sea in the *Carmania 2* which, as I said before, belonged to my father's Uncle John. She had only been built in Anstruther in 1936, so she must have been only two or three years old then, and was one of the new generation of cruiser-sterned fishing boats that were now being built. I must have been about eight or nine at the time, and I remember on that occasion going into Anstruther to land our herring in the morning. It must have been because of the state of the tide, because I can recall sailing round to St Monans in the afternoon after there was enough water to get in there.

The boats at the winter herring in those days did not carry a designated cook, and it was the custom for every man to bring his own food for the night. Each man used to carry his food in a special wooden "kit", and I can remember them queuing up at the coal stove after the nets were shot to boil their eggs or whatever their wives had put in for them. Some funny smells I can tell you: it's little wonder that I was always seasick! Somehow or another at that age I suspect that the real reason that we wanted go to sea in a cold January or February evening and spend the night without any sleep, was not so much because we enjoyed it, but more because your friends were doing it. There was always that little bit of status in letting people know that you had been "aff". Incidentally, *Carmania 2* must have been amongst the very earliest of the boats of that type that had a separate galley on deck connected to the wheelhouse, and set apart from the crew accommodation. This was to become normal from then on.

When the Second World War started in September 1939, it was to change many things in the fishing industry and in St Monans. Most of the newer fishing boats were requisitioned by the Royal Navy to be used as fleet tenders, and some of the steam drifters were taken over as mine sweepers. Many fishermen were to accompany their boats into this service, and others were called up for the armed forces. Many different tradesmen from all around the East Neuk and elsewhere were now being recruited to make up the workforce that was now needed in either the yard of James N. Miller & Sons, or at Walter Reekie's yard, to build the warships that were required for the Royal Navy.

I can just remember that the standard sizes that the Navy required for liberty and other general purpose boats during the war were all based on fishing boat hulls, and were sized 50 feet, 61.5 feet, 75 feet and 90 feet overall. I remember that Reekie's yard in St Monans built mainly the 75-foot and the 90-foot type. They also built the 110-foot transom-sterned motor minesweepers at their Anstruther yard on the site alongside the lifeboat shed. It must have been a busy period. Nearly all of these fine boats were eventually to become successfully integrated into the fishing fleets of Britain after the war was finished.

Miller's yard in St Monans was the one that I remember best because it was at the east end of the town nearer to where we lived. Being international yacht builders pre-war with a big reputation, they specialised in constructing the lighter-built 112-foot fast motor torpedo boats and fast motor launches for the Royal Navy. I remember hanging around the shed door and seeing the workforce building these boats two at the same time, side by side, with a new building method. They were built of double diagonal teak planking which must have been completely new to the work force at that time, and were clinker-fastened together with copper nails. The frames and the bulkheads were cut from prefabricated sheets of very thick plywood. I can't remember if they ever completed and launched two of them simultaneously, but it must have been quite a sight if they ever did. It is recorded that they built 29 of these boats altogether. It wasn't surprising that eventually, with all that fine wood available, nearly every boy in the village would soon own a sledge or a wheelbarrow or even a canoe, made from the very finest quality teak!

Another perk for us boys I can remember, was that the labourers would sweep up the wood shavings from the shed floors and take them to the edge of the outer harbour wall and dump them into the sea. Along with the shavings they would also sweep up all the cuttings from the copper nails. The sea would take away the shavings and everything else that floated, and after the tide had gone back we would endeavour to get down first to gather up the copper. We then sold it back to Miller's for a few pennies as scrap. I suppose in our own way we were helping the war effort!

Apart from these war years one of the busiest periods in Miller's long history of boat building must surely have been in the early 1960s. "Young" Jimmy Miller, who had taken over from his father and his uncle as the principal of the yard, had designed a unique type of cruiser-sterned yacht based on a fishing boat hull, and named the type "The Fifer". They were built in two size lengths of 33 feet and 36 feet, and when they initially displayed the prototype in 1958 at the London Boat show, it was with great success and they immediately secured a large number of orders. They eventually went on to build ninety of these "Fifer" yachts in total.

I was told recently that at one period they were building as many as seventeen of those yachts at the same time in a kind of production line system, and also because the fishing industry was on an upward spiral, they were also building simultaneously up to six fifty-foot fishing boats in the two big sheds on the piers: four in the east shed, and two in the old Walter Reekie shed on the west pier, which by this time Miller had taken over.

Twenty-three boats being constructed at the same time. Quite remarkable! I was also told that in the years 1961 and 1962 they had completed eleven or twelve of these "Fifers" in each of those years. They used to hire in a large crane, and it was not unknown for the firm to launch as many as seven of those yachts into the harbour on the same day. They certainly must have been close to being one the leading builders of leisure craft in the whole country.

Apparently one of the reasons why this building program had been such a success was that at the time there was some sort of tax concession available, and that was why so many of these high-earning stage and screen stars made the journey to St Monans to take delivery of a "Fifer" type yacht. This was to include Michael Bentine from the famous comedy group the Goons, who had a smaller 26-footer especially designed and built for him.

It wasn't too long before some of the other traditional fishing-boat builders around the coast eventually got in on the act, and started to build similar types of yacht based on their fishing-boat hulls for exactly the same market. Sadly, orders then became harder to get, and the final "Fifer" cruising yacht was built around 1975. It had been a good time for the yard and for the St Monans workforce.

Less than a month after the official start of the Second World War the first German aeroplanes to bomb the mainland of Britain arrived over the Firth of Forth on 16th October 1939. Two squadrons of Spitfires from 602 Squadron were scrambled to intercept the Junkers 88 dive-bombers, whose targets were the naval ships in Rosyth dockyard, and five German planes were shot down. I can remember all us youngsters rushing out from St Monans primary school to see one of the bombers crossing the area with smoke streaming from it and being pursued by the Spitfires before it crashed into the sea. All the Spitfires were to return safely. I was to learn in later years, that one of these Spitfire pilots on that day was named Hector McLean, and that he was later to lose a leg in the Battle of Britain.

I remember also very well from that time in the early days of the war, that Crail aerodrome was home to the Fleet Air Arm, and the base was known as HMS *Jackdaw*. I think the main purpose of the base was to train pilots to drop torpedoes on enemy warships. The planes based there were mainly Swordfish, Albacore and Barracudas, and anyone who was around at that time will surely remember that during their training many planes would accidentally be lost in the waters of the Forth. It seems that after releasing their torpedoes, they would sometimes hit the water with their wing-tips as they veered away. I remember hearing reports that as many as seven planes were accidentally lost in a single day. Some of these planes were occasionally forced to crash-land in fields in the East Neuk, and it didn't take us long to get up there on our bicycles when we heard the news, to see if we could salvage anything.

Many of these pilots who were stationed and trained at HMS *Jackdaw*, were the same pilots who flew the Swordfishes which disabled the German battleship *Bismarck*. They managed to put its rudder out of action with their torpedoes and enabled it to be sunk by the British Navy. After it was disabled, they probably could have gone on to finish what they had started, but they were ordered by the Navy to back off. The *Bismarck* had just sunk the *Hood*, the pride of the fleet, and the Navy wanted their revenge by sinking her themselves. Although they only did about ninety to a hundred miles per hour and were almost sitting ducks, no planes were lost on that occasion.

Anstruther was the wartime base for a fleet of requisitioned steam drifters whose main job was to recover these practice torpedoes after they had been dropped. I suspect they would have to rescue more than a few pilots as well. Two small tugs were also based at Anstruther harbour, and used as recovery vessels for crashed planes. They carried divers on board, and would bring the recovered planes into the outer harbour at high tide where they would be salvaged when the tide ebbed. Shortly after the hostilities had finished and the war had ended, HMS *Jackdaw* eventually became known HMS *Bruce* for a while, and took on a new role as a boys' training establishment for the Royal Navy.

I remember another incident from that time very well. One winter's night in St Monans during the Second World War, a few of us boys had been down on board the ex-sailing-boat *Lively Hope* for a heat and a cup of tea and to visit a crewman from Stornoway who was living on board. The boat had apparently not been given a big enough list towards the pier and had fallen over when the tide went out and had stove in her side. Because of her great age, she was not considered worth repairing. This fine old boat was towed to the beach on the west side of

Newark Castle and left to break up.

This must have been around 1941, because David Smith, an uncle of mine who was married to my mother's sister, sailed on this boat. He had been a former crew member with the *Carmania* for many years before the war started, and she had been requisitioned for war service. The *Lively Hope* had been owned and skippered by a very fine, upstanding man called John Allan, who, I remember, used to live in Elm Grove. She was one of the last of the remaining "Fifie" sailing boats to be converted to motor, so she must have been about forty years old by this time. It was sad to think that she had to end her days like that.

After losing his boat, John Allan was later to purchase a small thirty-two foot "Fifie" seine-net boat from Port Seton named the *Mary*. She was powered by a 30-hp Kelvin diesel, and Ena Gibbons told me that her father John Gowans, who was the engineer on the boat, has it that on their first day's fishing they landed so many fish that they almost cleared off the payment on the boat. It must have been very much beginner's luck, because seine-netting would have been fairly new to all the crew at that time, and I'm sure none of them would have had any experience in that method of fishing before the war started. They were all drift-net herring fishermen and great-line fishermen, and because most of the young men were away on war service, they would all have been relatively old men at that time. I remember being allowed to go out to sea for the day in her, and we worked in the Firth of Forth, just off Pittenweem, probably at the grounds they called the "Fluke Hole". The boat had absolutely no instruments in those days, except for a compass. If the visibility was good, then they could do a fine job navigating from the landmarks on shore.

The way they prosecuted the seine-net fishery at that time was a long way removed from the manner in which it was to be done later. They had no automatic rope-coilers then, and the winch was mounted fore and aft instead of thwartships. What they would do was this: after they had set the gear on the bottom in the form of a large triangle they would recover the starting buoy and simply tow until the ropes were almost closed. They would then throw out the ropes from the stern guides and heave over the broadside till the net came up. They didn't work long fleets of ropes, and they were coiled by hand. It seemed to work, because good hauls were sometimes taken by that method. My memories of that day spent on the *Mary* though, were of very few fish each haul, and the cod-end being lifted on board by hand.

I'm sure it would be the wives and daughters who must have been happiest of all when the fishermen changed over from being herring fishermen to becoming seine-net fishermen. Most of that crew were too old to be called up for war service anyway, but for perhaps the first time in their lives some of the wives were now free from the endless drudgery of mending torn herring nets.

It was about that time at the start of the war that a lot of older Cellardyke fishermen found themselves unemployed. The Anstruther drifter fleet had all been requisitioned almost immediately the war started, and there were no jobs for the men who hadn't gone with the boats. By the same token, a few of the St

The author's father's family. Father is in the centre of the back row.
There are four Skippers in the group.

Monans boats couldn't muster crews because the young men had been called up, and some of them were hired out to Cellardyke crews. One such boat was the former "Fifie" sailing boat *Annie Mathers* which caught fire and sank off Scrabster whilst returning from a fishing voyage to Stornoway in the Outer Hebrides. I was later to sail as a crew member along with Willie Mathers, one of her former part owners!

My own father, Robert Smith, was the result of two well known St Monans fishing families coming together. His father, my grandfather David Smith, had come from a family who had always been boat owners, and who had in time owned sailing boats, motor boats and steam drifters. His mother, my grandmother Mary Bruce Aitken, had also come from a boat-owning family. In fact her own father had named a new sailing boat after her, using her initials M.B.A. Apparently when the boat was being launched someone had asked what did the letters M.B.A. mean, and some wag had replied that it stood for "Muckle Bold Aitken". Of course from then on, her father was always known by his nickname of "Bold Aitken". I remember being told that although her own grandfather owned several boats and several houses at the same time, it was said that he could neither read nor write. The Aitken family had the wooden steam drifter *Camelia* built by Miller's in Anstruther in 1907. Whilst I am writing this, the thought occurs to me that I can hardly think of any man by the name of Aitken still remaining in St Monans. Most of the decendants of these fine fishermen either moved away during the

Memories

war or soon after, and never returned!

My father and all of his five brothers, my uncles of course, were fishermen or had been fishermen at some time in their careers. Two of them were later to become carpenters. The youngest brother, Bruce, after only one voyage to the herring fishing in the Minches to the west of Scotland, left to serve his apprenticeship with Walter Reekie's boatyard in St Monans. He eventually became a qualified marine architect, and worked at Rosyth Dockyard. He was later to train as a woodwork teacher, and taught in Dunfermline, eventually becoming Head of the Technical Department there. My Uncle Philip, one of twins, was to serve his apprenticeship with their own Uncle "Eck" Aitken, who had started Aitken's boat yard in Anstruther next to the Scottish Fisheries Museum. He was later to take over the yard along with Eck's son-in-law Murray Hutton, and to rename it Smith and Hutton's.

I remember that uncle, who was of course really only my father's Uncle Eck, once telling me that he had cycled back and forth the three miles from his home in St Monans to his yard in Anstruther, every working day in all weathers, for over fifty years. I can just remember him myself coming across the Moor Park on his bike after dark, with the carbide gas lights burning.

When Uncle Eck Aitken had first started in business he had employed a man named Fulton, who had formerly owned the shipyard in Pittenweem, as a consultant. They went on to earn a huge reputation for their boats, and built 32 of them between 1927 and 1938, with sixteen being for fishermen from the Hull and Bridlington area. Some of these boats were still around many years after they had been built. They were about mostly around 50 feet in length, and all of the "Fifie" type. The Fisheries Museum, which now owns the property that the shipyard stood on, has a complete record of every single one of these boats that Aitken's built.

The other twin brother in my father's family was my Uncle Willie, who was also a fisherman and a partner in the cruiser-sterned motor boat *Procyon* KY181, built at Walter Reekie's yard in St Monans in 1938. He was later to work at Smith and Hutton's in Anstruther with his twin brother Philip for the latter part of his working life, but more about Willie later.

My father's oldest brother was David Smith. He had been the Skipper of his father-in-law's family boat, but like many other herring fishermen at that time, he had been driven by poverty to Granton to sail on the steam trawlers there. He was also to become a trawler Skipper, but he didn't return to fishing after the Second World War had ended. He was to finish his career working for the government as Skipper of boom defence boats, and later as the Skipper of a surplus ammunition dumping ship.

The second oldest brother of my father's family, was my own Uncle Eck. He was to marry a Peterhead girl, and like so many other north-east herring fishermen at that time he joined the trawling fleet in Aberdeen. The family eventually moved to Aberdeen, where they made their home. He was to become a very successful trawler Skipper, and eventually became a partner in a trawling company, owning several steam trawlers.

Smith and Hutton's yard in Anstruther was to build 51 fine boats, including my own first two boats, *Argonaut*, and *Argonaut II*. They also built the long-liner and drift-netter *Silver Chord* for well-known Cellardyke fisherman James Muir MBE, in which he was to win the Madame Prunier Trophy. This trophy was presented annually at a grand dinner in London to the Skipper and crew of the vessel which landed the largest daily catch of herring each season at the East Anglian autumn fishing. They also built the successful long-liner *Verbena* for his brother John Muir.

The *Brighter Hope* was built for John Gardner and Jim Tarvit in 1955, one year after my own first boat had been completed, while the largest boat that the company ever built was the 100-foot purpose-built motor line-boat *Radiation* for Skipper Alexander Gardner, who was John Gardner's brother. This boat was built to mainly fish at Iceland and the Faroe Islands and was designed by my uncle, Bruce Smith, the brother of Philip her builder. After a long and successful career, she was eventually taken over by the Scottish Fisheries Museum, and part restored at Tayport harbour. She was eventually sold to the Orkney Islands, and was sadly to sink in Scapa Flow. The firm of Smith and Hutton, which has been closed since 1977, went on to build many other fine fishing boats, and has now been incorporated into the Scottish Fisheries Museum. After a lot of refurbishment, it is now known as the Old Boatyard, and is open to visitors to the Museum.

It's interesting to note what was happening in the late 1920s and the early 1930s when the herring fishing had all but collapsed. Eyemouth fishermen were finding their way to the North Shields trawler fleet, fishermen from around the Firth of Forth, from the East Neuk of Fife and from Newhaven and Port Seton and so on, were getting berths on trawlers in either Granton or Leith, and fishermen from all along the Moray Firth, and from Peterhead and Fraserburgh, were flocking to Aberdeen, either to the trawlers or the steam great-line boats. There was even a small fleet of trawlers based in Dundee at that time, working mainly around the Bell Rock Lighthouse, and many Arbroath fishermen were getting work there. They were all exchanging one hard life for an even harder one, and possibly as precarious as the one they had just left, but people had to survive. Some men at that time saw their future in the merchant fleets, and some even joined the whaling fleets.

My own father, who had started as a herring and line fisherman like nearly everyone else in St Monans at the time, used to tell me how he first got into steam trawling. In those days, the custom was for all the young folk from the neighbouring East Neuk villages, to flock to Anstruther on Saturday nights, and almost certainly none of them would have had too much money in their pockets to spend. There were two brothers though, Michael Davidson and Bobby Davidson from St Monans, who had followed their elder brother Charlie to sail on the trawlers from Granton, and there they were, millionaires for the weekend, flashing their pound notes about. That definitely convinced my father where he thought his future lay.

Memories

Incidentally, my father — who himself in time became one of the leading trawler Skippers in the country, and who was awarded the MBE in 1943 for services to the fishing industry — was during his career Skipper of the trawlers *Cramond Isle*, *Starbank*, *Walter Paton* and finally *Cairnburn* of which he was also a part owner. He used to regard the above-mentioned Charlie Davidson as the finest trawler Skipper that there was in the North Sea during that era. Charlie had been unbeatable as a Skipper over a long number of years preceding the Second World War and immediately after. The ship that I myself can remember him being associated with was the *Contender*. She had been built for the long-established firm of T. L. Devlin, one of the most famous Granton trawler-owning firms of the past. This ship had been built specifically with Charlie Davidson in mind, and he fished in her very successfully until he retired. There is a photograph of the *Contender* in the Scottish Fisheries Museum.

Charlie Davidson must have been a great hero of my father's, because I remember him telling me that when he was first a young Skipper himself, and was returning from a particularly quick trip at sea and feeling quite pleased with himself, it was only to meet Charlie and the *T. L. Devlin* sailing down the Firth of Forth in the opposite direction. Charlie had made an even quicker trip and had landed his fish on the previous day, and was now off to sea again.

Many modern young Skippers, accustomed to present-day practices, will be very surprised indeed to hear that one of the many stories about Charlie Davidson was that in all the years that he was a top Skipper, both summer and winter, nobody was allowed to control the winch but himself. The reason was, of course, that no one else would heave up the gear quickly enough to satisfy him. At the first turn of the winch by the watchkeeper, Charlie Davidson would jump from his bunk and run down on to the deck dragging his oilskins on as he went, and open the winch throttle full up. No matter how tired the crew might have been, heaven help anybody on the *Contender* who wasn't at his post when the otter boards came up. He must have been a very hard man indeed! That was one of the reasons that my father used to often say to me, "You'll never really be a trawler Skipper until you've sailed with Charlie Davidson!"

He was to be correct on two counts of course, because I never did get to sail with Charlie Davidson, and although I was myself to become a very young First Mate at around twenty years of age, I never quite became a steam trawler Skipper either. As I will tell you later, I'm sure it did me no harm. In fact, on reflection, it was probably very lucky for me that I didn't, or maybe I wouldn't have been so keen to branch out on my own when I did, and I probably wouldn't have had the successful career that I have had.

In those days in steam trawling, and I can remember them well myself from when I joined Cairnburn in 1947 as a young boy, the Granton custom was different from other ports. You weren't awakened by the watch in time to take tea before you heaved in the gear. Oh no! When the trawling watch was finished, the watchman would run down on to the deck and run the winch with the drain taps from the cylinders wide open to allow the water to run out and be replaced with steam. The driving clutch was then engaged and the boat was always thrown over the broadside no matter what the weather conditions were like. The Granton trawlers towed on the brakes only in those days. The warps were knocked out of the towing block and the winch started to heave. The crew were supposed to hear all of this happening and get on deck as quickly as possible. The amazing thing was that you always did, no matter how tired you were.

I remember myself as a seventeen-year-old deckhand on watch all alone on deck in wintertime in the dark of the night on this 147-foot long steam trawler, and running down onto the deck and preparing the winch before starting to heave in the gear. Talk about health and safety!

Jobs on trawlers were hard to get in the late 1920s and if you did not have a relation, or knew somebody who was already in the business, it was not so easy to get started. That was why I will certainly never ever forget the stories on that subject that my father told me more than once. Later on, I'm sure it was to have a big influence on what was probably the biggest decision that I would ever make in my life.

My father told me that when he had first gone up to Granton to look for work, he simply could not get a berth no matter how hard he tried. He then moved down to North Shields to try his luck there. After a week trudging around the docks with no success, he decided to come back to Granton. Again there were no jobs to be had, and he was beginning to despair when he heard that there was a boat in nearby Leith, just about to sail, and that they were looking for a deckhand. Unfortunately, there was another man hanging around who was also looking for a job, and he had heard this news at the same time. They both rushed up the pier, and jumped on the first tramcar that they knew would be going to Leith. The problem was that neither of the two of them knew where this trawler was berthed. My father was the lucky one, because it was he who found the ship first and got the job. The ship belonged to a small firm called Flockhart's.

I remember him telling me another story, about how later he was to get his first Skipper's job. He had been working as a deckhand only for a few trips, learning all he could about the trawl net and the steam trawling method which was still all very new to him, and there they were lying in Leith docks and about to sail. The owner of Flockhart's firm was a man called Johnny Flockhart, and he came on board and asked my father if he had a Skipper's ticket. On being told that he did, he then said that he wanted my father to take the boat to sea.

My father told me that at the time he was not very keen, as he felt he did not have enough experience in trawling to do himself justice. Remember that in those days there were no radios, no Decca navigators, no GPS receivers or video plotters with recordings of other people's information that budding young Skippers could acquire by fair means or foul. Everything had to be learned the hard way, by experience! To cut a long story short, the owner persuaded my father that if he had confidence in him, why did he not have the same confidence in himself? The owner must have been very desperate to find a Skipper on that day, and my father eventually was persuaded to take the ship to sea on that trip. Alas,

Memories

the owner's confidence in him had been misplaced, and he was very soon back to being a deckhand again. His time would come later!

This period in the very late 1920s, during which my father was trying to establish himself in the steam trawling industry, must have been hard, and there were certainly no fortunes to be made in fishing at that time. Skippers and Mates were always paid on a percentage of the gross sales, and I remember him telling me that if a Skipper did not earn himself more than one pound per day, he would probably be sacked. It's not hard to imagine what the rest of the crew were being paid. The reason that men were so desperate to get trawling jobs at that time was that the herring industry had all but collapsed and boats were going away on various herring voyages with the crews perhaps coming home in debt and having to pay in to meet the expenses. At least on a trawler, a man would receive a guaranteed wage, small as it may have been.

One of the reasons that my father possessed a Skipper's certificate in the first place was in no small way due to the encouragement and teachings of a very fine man who lived in the village. His name was David Smith, and he was the Skipper of his family's boat. His navigation skills were completely self-taught, and it was he who used to coach all the young fishermen in their spare time between seasonal fishing voyages. I don't think he was a relation of ours, but he was a great friend of my father. I remember him when he was an old man and I was just a youngster, and thrilled to be playing draughts against him in the Old Men's Club. After perhaps a couple of moves, he would announce to me that he had played that game before, and that he had won. Needless to say, I thought at the time that this was amazing. I'm certain that if he had been born in another era he would surely have been a brilliant mathematician. I don't think his name was ever very high on the scroll of fishing glory though. Perhaps he was much too clever!

There was one classic story from around that time about the Cellardyke steam drifter that had just returned home from a Yarmouth herring-fishing voyage. The Skipper's wife was waiting anxiously on the pier along with the rest of the women, to see if there was going to be any money, and asking her husband how they had got on. "We're clear," he announced with some pride, meaning of course, that they weren't in debt on the voyage. "Aye," said she, "but you were clear before you went away!" As always, trust a wife to get right to the bottom of the matter! I don't think it would have been very funny for the people that were involved, but it certainly illustrates just how bad things were in the herring industry at that particular time.

Incidentally, there were certain people on a steam herring-drifter at that time who did receive a guaranteed wage, albeit a small one. The chief engineer was paid £3 per week, and the fireman £2.50 whilst they were away on a fishing trip. In addition to his normal duties of sharing the watches in the engine room with the chief engineer looking after the engine, and keeping steam on the boiler, the fireman would also have to assist with the hauling of the nets, and the landing of the fish. Sometimes, if a fireman was perhaps an older man, and had no interest in ever becoming a fisherman owning his own nets, or simply just because he did not even possess a set of oilskins or seaboots, he would maybe arrange to exchange jobs with the cook. The cook's job, when the drift-nets were being hauled, was to take up station down in the fore-part of the ship, and coil the heavy, freshly-tarred messenger rope that ran along the underside of the nets into the huge forward compartment that was set aside for the purpose. The cook was usually a young boy learner who would be desperate to get on deck with the men in any case and become a real fisherman.

There was one story about a St Monans steam drifter that was making the long passage home from Yarmouth after attending the herring fishing there. Because they had been delayed by bad weather, it was now getting near to Saturday midnight and they still had some miles to go before they reached St Monans. The Skipper informed the fireman that he was paying him off, leaving the chief engineer alone to take the boat the last few miles home. This was to avoid having to pay the fireman any wages for the Sunday. Hard times!

There is another story about a steam drifter returning from an unsuccessful voyage. This time it was a Cellardyke ship coming home to Anstruther from fishing at Stornoway in the Outer Hebrides. The fishing had been very poor, and the crew were not anticipating much for their shares, if indeed anything at all. The fireman, who was on a regular wage, small as it was, announced to the assembled crew that if there was one thing that he liked to eat for his breakfast, it was a "smokie and an egg." The rest of the crew just looked at him in amazement. Bearing in mind that they were expecting to be paid practically nothing when they returned home, they just might have a slim chance of getting a smoked haddock, or possibly even a chance of getting an egg, but I'm certain that there was absolutely no chance of getting them both on the same plate at the same time!

My mother, whose maiden name was Agnes Birrell Corstorphine, was from Cellardyke, and she and my father would probably have met in Anstruther on the usual Saturday or Sunday night promenade along Shore Street down by the harbour there. This would have been about 1927, because I remember when I was growing up in the 1930s in St Monans, there were about nine or ten former young Cellardyke women who must have all married and moved into the village around the same time, possibly between two or three years of each other. They were all almost exactly my mother's age and eventually had families that were all around my own age. Unless it was purely coincidence, I've always thought that there must have been some pattern in the fishing at the time that caused this to happen, because it never ever happened again.

The funny thing about all those married women in St Monans was that none of them was ever referred to by her married name as I can recall. They were always known by their maiden names. Jessie Tarvit married carpenter Rob Aitken and her two sisters Jean and Lizzie married fishermen Rob Wood and Wullie Gowans respectively. Annie Gardner came to St Monans to marry Jock Mathers who owned and ran the local fish and chip shop. Elsie Hodge married into the Fyall fishing family, and has just celebrated her 100th birthday, and Mimi Keay

Memories 65

married into the Tarvet garage family. Aggie Gardner was my mother's close friend, and our next door neighbour in Miller Terrace for more than fifty years, and she had married local Skipper Jimmy Adam.

There was also Annie Wallace who lived in Miller Terrace and was married to carpenter Willie Doig, and their neighbour Annie Strachan who was married to fisherman Jockie Mayes. My own mother, Agnes Smith, was to be known by her maiden name of Aggie Strachan or Corstorphine, until the day that she died. They had all come from Cellardyke, and taken their place in the St Monans community and had all become staunch supporters of the "Auld Kirk".

A classic story of around that time was supposed to be that when a young St Monans man met a Cellardyke girl for the first time, the first question that he was supposed to ask her was, "Does your father own a standard steam drifter?" I'm sorry to relate that my grandfather on my mother's side did not own a steam drifter! Although he and her three brothers were all fishermen, they all worked on other people's boats. Mind you, on reflection, things were sometimes reputed to be so bad that if all the stories of the times were true, some of the people who owned steam drifters, and I include my grandfather in St Monans from my father's side amongst them, would perhaps have been better off if they had never ever seen a steam drifter.

One story goes that the Barclay family from Cellardyke, who owned the drifter *Bene Vertat* in 1938, had laid her up because of the poor times. Even although everyone had a fair idea that war was imminent and that their boat would probably be requisitioned and provide them with a steady income, they were forced to sell her to St Monans, because they found that even the cost of the harbour dues for her lying there were too prohibitive. Incidentally, Jimmy Barclay, one of the sons, was to later become one of the leading trawler Skippers in the Granton trawling fleet, and my father's great rival.

The start of the Second World War in September 1939 was to see many changes in the East Neuk fishing villages, particularly in the fishing industry. Most of the young men were being called up for war service, and most of the boats had been requisitioned for naval service. Many people were to lose their lives in the conflict, and many of the young men who returned had seen another side of life apart from fishing and did not wish to return to the industry. That's probably why, for example, in 1945 my mother's two brothers George and Tom, decided to stay on at Rosyth dockyard, where they had got good jobs with regular wages. They were crewing the MFVs which acted as liberty boats for the warships when they were in harbour. They would find it very hard to give this up when they could remember all the hard work and the uncertainties of fishing, and the poor times they had experienced in the years leading up to the war.

My mother's third brother, my Uncle John, had met a girl from Gardenstown near Banff whilst he was away at some herring fishing, and she was there working as a herring lassie. They eventually got married, and he moved north to Gamrie to make his home there and to carry on as a fisherman. I remember meeting him in 1946 when I attended the first post-war summer fishing at Fraserburgh. He was a part owner on *Convallaria*, a new Banff 70-foot motor boat.

Incidentally, fifty years later my wife and I attended the funeral of my Uncle John's wife Barbara in Gardenstown in January 1996. She was aged 98, and had surely seen a lot of changes in the fishing industry in her long lifetime. Although sometimes towards the end of her life she didn't have a lot going for her, she always managed to maintain her great sense of humour. When I used to visit her when I was in the Banff area she would always have a funny story to tell me about her days as a "gutting quine". I remember in particular her telling me about the first time she had left home as a young girl along with her two sisters, to work for a herring curer. They had joined the passenger steamer at Aberdeen to make the sea journey to Lerwick, and apparently the weather had been so bad that all the girls had been seasick except her. At least, that was what she told me!

In those days, the herring girls used to work in teams of three, two gutters and a packer, and they would be hired or "engaged" by a curer for the season. They were always paid by results, so it was important to get a good team together, and she always worked along with her two sisters. There were no rubber gloves available in those days to protect their hands, so they did the best they could. Each morning before they started work, they would wrap up each individual finger with a "clootie" tied on with old recycled knitting wool. These "clooties" were simply made from any suitable old materials that they could cut into strips like bandages. I remember her telling me, that during the winter when they were having a spell at home, they used to occupy their time making up all their "clooties" ready for the next season's trip. Nothing was ever wasted.

The annual work pattern for the herring girls was exactly the same as that of the boats and their crews. They would start at Lerwick in the early spring, and then they would follow the boats to the summer fishing at Fraserburgh or Peterhead from May until the end of August. There would maybe even be a short spell at Whitby or Scarborough in August and September, and then eventually finishing at Great Yarmouth or Lowestoft in November and December. They mostly lived in the "huts" adjoining the curer's yards, and they had to cook and look after themselves. When I started my own fishing career thirty years later, I can remember girls not much older than myself just like my aunt had been in her early working days, working away, gutting herring out in the open in all weathers, with their sleeves rolled high above their elbows.

I can also remember these girls quite clearly at the Yarmouth autumn fishery, whilst they were waiting for herring to be delivered to their curer's yards, strolling down to the quayside arm in arm in rows across the piers. They would sometimes be singing, and be down to visit a herring drifter where possibly one of them might have had a father or a brother or perhaps a boyfriend on board. They would also sometimes come down in pairs to a relation's boat at the weekends to make the Sunday lunch for the crew. I think they were like the rest of us, they were glad to sit down and enjoy a decent meal in peace after a hard week's work. They were a tough, hardworking breed, and for the most part always seemed to be happy enough with their lot.

Memories

I'm afraid that the trade of curing herring, with all its skills and traditions and infrastructure, has long gone. It was about 1958 when the herring finally disappeared from the East Anglian grounds, and the boats stopped making their annual voyage to Lowestoft or Great Yarmouth. It was to mark the end of what had been a way of life for a lot of people for a very long time indeed.

My mother's oldest sister Annie from Cellardyke had also married a St Monans fisherman, and she followed the herring fleets around the various fishing ports to work either as a gutter or as a packer for a time when she was young, but my own mother didn't. I suspect that one of the reasons that so few of the East Neuk girls of my mother's era did likewise was that, unlike their contemporaries from the north-east ports, there was always plenty of secure regular employment for young women to be had at home. At that time in the late 1920s, Cellardyke had several busy oilskin manufacturing factories. Carstairs's, Black and Martin's and Watson's amongst them, and they were quite famous businesses. My mother was one of the dozens of local girls who worked there, and they made all kinds of oiled canvas waterproof clothing for the fishing industry. They also made the famous "Sou'wester" hat. This was a special type of waterproof hat that practically every fisherman used. It had an extended flap at the back, which was supposed to prevent salt sea water running down the wearer's neck in bad weather.

These two factories were also to also introduce many other new products which would influence fishermen's waterproof clothing and fishing methods. The most famous product of all from Cellardyke was surely the patented canvas buoy, the invention of which was credited to Black and Martin's factory. These buoys were used mainly for the flotation of herring drift-nets, and they were made in all sizes and sold to fishermen all over Great. Britain and elsewhere. They were very successful and hard-wearing.

They were simply canvas panels sewn together to form a balloon shape, and then seized on to a wooden base with treated twine, and then partly filled with tar to make them waterproof. They were inflated by removing the tarry plug from the hole in the wooden base, and simply blowing them up by mouth. It was not unusual to see a fisherman going around with a big smudge of tar on his face, especially if he had been overhauling his gear. I don't think aftershave was in vogue for the fishermen of the East Neuk in those days.

The above-mentioned canvas buoys were a huge success, and they were to be the standard floatation for all kinds of fishing gears for many years, until they in their turn were superseded by moulded rubber floats which needed no maintenance. Previous to all of that, the bladders of various animals, mainly cows and dogs, were treated and used as flotation for herring nets. Drift-net herring fishermen traditionally took great pride in maintaining their gear, and their canvas buoys were no exception. They would usually be painted gleaming white every season, with the alternate panels usually painted in contrasting colours. Then they would add the fishing letters and numbers of the boat that they were sailing on. There was usually great competition amongst the fishermen on each boat, with each man trying to make his own buoys look the best.

Another big employer of female labour in the East Neuk, but a generation later on, was the new bus depot in West Anstruther. This was to be the very earliest bus service running locally between Leven and the Tay Ferry at Newport, and was established about 1928. It had been started by brothers Tom and Martin Gardner, who belonged to one of the best-known fishing families in Cellardyke and their original depot had been at the present site of the Scottish Fisheries Museum. It was a great success, and they were to remain in business for many years until they were later taken over by Alexander's, a much larger company.

The food that local families lived on in my childhood days was usually very simple, with everything being basic and home-made. Everybody was very much in the same boat, and processed food was almost unheard of! The culture of supermarkets and pre-packed meals lay at least fifty years in the future, and as for wine, I don't believe that I can ever remember seeing a bottle of wine in my mother's house. Because my father was a successful trawler Skipper he must have been earning a better wage than most, and on the whole that must have meant that as a family we must have been a little better off at that time. It still seemed to mean that we had to have home-made soup nearly every other day. It would either be scotch broth which was always known by its local name of "kail", or lentil soup, or perhaps potato soup made with minced beef. The boiled beef that was used to provide the stock for the broth would always be removed from the pan and eaten with potatoes as a main course. Inevitably it would be either rice or Cremola custard to follow. My mother was quite a baker in her time, and we always seemed to get our fair share of that.

In the East Neuk, Saturday usually meant for everyone mince pies from the local baker's, and everyone had their personal favourites. I also seem to remember that Sunday in our house sometimes meant roast beef and Yorkshire puddings. I suspect that eating habits were about to change not long after that though, with quite a few different foods being developed by necessity during the war years. We had all heard the old stories about peas being fished from the soup pot and served cold in a paper "poke" as a delicacy. I think in my young days we had perhaps moved on from there and I don't think I would have regarded eating cold peas as much of a treat. One curious thing about the eating habits of the fishing community in St Monans at that time was that there was never high tea. You got a cup of tea when school came out, but you had to go home later on in the evening for supper. Just like the grand folk!

We ate a lot of fish, especially when my father was at home. It was the custom that every crew member on a trawler was allowed to take home a certain amount of fish each trip for personal use, with the Skipper and Mate usually being allowed a halibut. I can remember my father's favourite meal on his first day at home from sea as if it was yesterday. It was always the same. Boiled pure white halibut and boiled potatoes, with a jug of melted butter on the table to pour over them.

This allocation of fish to the crews after each trip was always known in Granton as a "pauchle", or a "fry", but I suspect it amounted to a lot more than that on many occasions. I do remember once hearing one deckhand boast that

Memories

his "fry" was as much as he could "stagger up the pier with." I don't think he was entirely jesting either, and on a lot of occasions I think it would probably have been filleted and sold on to provide some extra revenue for excursions to the pubs.

My father used to bring his "fry" home in a special type of bag that all the trawler fishermen used at that time. It was made from woven straw, and was always known as a "pauchle bag" or a "bass". I remember that he would usually arrive home to St Monans on the three o' clock train from Edinburgh, and my mother would be waiting with some of us to meet him at the station. When we got home he would select the fish that we were keeping for our own use, and my job was sometimes to deliver the remainder to my grandmother and to some of his old uncles and friends in that bag. My mother would have the bag washed all ready for him going off to sea on the next trip.

Mentioning the railway again and going to the station to meet my father, reminds me of a day that I will never ever forget. It must have been about 1942 or so, and well into the war, because I remember that at the time I was about twelve years of age, and attending Waid Academy. Luxury articles were well nigh impossible to acquire during wartime, and the only type of bicycle that could be bought, if you were lucky enough to locate one, was almost a frame with wheels and pedals and absolutely no extras.

My father had a deckhand on board the trawler with him at that time, and he had mentioned to this man that he was searching for a bicycle for me. This man then said that he had been a keen cyclist before he had become a fisherman, and that he had had a bike standing in his mother's house for years, and that she was fed up threading her way past it, and was always urging him to get rid of it. A deal was made and for the princely sum of £3.50 my father would get the bike for me.

That afternoon when the train arrived at St Monans station, and we went to the goods van at the rear of the train and the guard handed out this bicycle, my eyes almost popped out from my head. It was just unbelievable. It was a Raleigh racer model complete with badge, the finest make that you could get at that time. It had white mudguards and cable brakes and electric lights driven from a chromium-plated dynamo. It also had three-speed gears and a speedometer. Can you believe that in the middle of a war where even all the metal railings from every house had been cut up for scrap, my father had managed to locate a bicycle like that for me! An item like that was just simply unobtainable, and wasn't I just a lucky boy to get a bike like that. I used it for many years, and I cycled between St Monans and Anstruther to the Waid Academy almost every afternoon from then on.

In the small fishing villages of the East Neuk in the 1930s, the local bakers all seemed to play a very big part in everyone's lives, and St Monans was no different. Incredible as it is to believe now, we had five different bakers' shops in the village as far as I can remember. There seemed to be one on every street corner. We had Jimmy Ferguson at the foot of Miller Terrace, and Willie Ferguson on the corner where the Broad Wynd and the west Backgate meet. The Home Bakery was further down at the harbour, and Alec Reekie (Sandy Baird), was in the East Backgate (East Street). Redpath's or "Reppets" as he was known locally, was at the West End. Along with all the vans and horse-drawn carts that came around the village from the neighbouring towns, goodness knows how they all made a living. Perhaps they didn't really.

Each baker was best known in the village for his specialities, and I can well remember on a Saturday morning being sent by my mother to a certain baker for his bread, another baker for his scones, another for his pies, and so on. Sunday breakfast in our house when my father was at home, usually meant bacon and eggs with pork sausages, and always accompanied by a fried scone. Pork sausages were practically unobtainable in wartime, but, if you knew someone . . . ! In our case they were supplied by my uncle David Morris who had a fishmonger's and poulterer's business in St Andrews.

Jimmy Ferguson, who had his business at the foot of Miller Terrace, was our local baker. In addition to the fresh hot rolls every morning, the bakehouse was where you would get all the latest gossip. All the local news of who was getting married, or who had just recently passed away — something that you don't get in a modern supermarket.

I think it would be true to say at that time no self-respecting "simininser" would dream of starting off his day without the customary two or more warm morning rolls with the butter running out of them. I can almost taste them now. Worrying about cholesterol certainly wasn't a factor then, and it was also long before the days of sliced bread. It's hard to believe that from all of those bakery businesses that we had in St Monans when I was young, there isn't a single one left today. How sad!

Jimmy Ferguson was one of the leaders of the Plymouth Open Brethren along with my father's Uncle John Smith. Jimmy Ferguson's son John didn't follow him into the business, and it was later to be owned by John Guthrie, who was followed by his son Billy, and finally his grandsons, until it closed down in 1996. Jimmy Ferguson and his wife Mary were a very fine couple and according to some of the stories I've heard, they were more than good to a lot of the fishermen's families during the hungry 1930s, particularly when the boats were away at Peterhead for the long summer herring "drave", or maybe at Yarmouth in the late autumn. A lot of the families would have little or no money to visit the baker's too often, and it was said that the Fergusons would present them with cakes or other stuff that was unsold to help tide them over. They would also allow many of the wives to "tak oan", (credit) and stop their families from literally starving. They certainly practised what they preached!

The Fergusons' speciality at that time was known as a "sole" pie, and these pies were unique. People came from all around to buy them. They were made in different sizes, but I remember them as being about 8" wide and 2" deep. The case was made of a thick short crust almost like savoury shortbread, with a very thick bottom, and they were filled with real steak and gravy. The reason that they were called "sole" pies was because they were fired directly on to the bottom of the oven, or the sole as it was called, and not on a tray or a dish of any sort. I'm sure you couldn't get them anywhere now if you tried. Certainly not from Jimmy Ferguson anyway, he's been dead for a long time now.

In those days, many years before church weddings with hotel receptions became fashionable, the grandest weddings were always held in the local Town Hall or perhaps the church hall. The young couple would usually be married in the Church manse, and one of the local bakers would do the catering. If it was St Monans, and it was the Fergusons who were doing the honours, and somebody who would normally have been a guest at the wedding was unable to attend, it was the custom for them to get a "sole" pie delivered to their house.

I can remember these weddings, and all us youngsters hanging around the Town Hall kitchen after the meal was finished. If there were any "chappit tatties" left over, the women helpers would come out with a big dish and dispense them to all and sundry. I'm pretty sure that we didn't get knives and forks to eat them with either. I'm also pretty sure that there wouldn't have been too many "sole" pies handed out! It was recorded that in Cellardyke it was the custom that members of the crews would receive a "sole" pie when they visited their Skippers' houses for the share-out after a fishing voyage. They probably paid for them somewhere along the line anyway.

In addition to the two shipbuilding yards in St Monans there was also a marine engineering shop and two blacksmiths. There were also quite a few other small businesses serving the fishing industry during my boyhood. It's difficult to see how they all gleaned a living. I can remember that there was only ever one butcher's shop though, and the owner, Geordie Grant, came from Pittenweem. I can't ever recall hearing the name of another butcher being mentioned before that. His shop was in the building facing the harbour immediately on the east side of the foot of the Broad Wynd. It was always the Saturday gathering place for women buying their beef for the weekend, and I seem to remember that it was always quite a busy shop when I was young. I'm not quite sure if that was before or after the war, but obviously things were to change. It was later to see service for a while as an old men's club, before eventually becoming a private house again.

There were three banks, a Post Office and two shoe shops, David Black's at the bottom of the Station Road, and Eck Dunn's down the vennel from Virgin Square. There were five bakers, three plumbers, seven grocers, two newsagents, two garages, two drapers and gents' outfitters, and at one stage, three fish and chip shops. Sometimes on a Saturday night, I would be sent up to Wullie Summers's draper's shop at the top of George Terrace for a new cap for my dad. I can just about still remember his size! There were also two house painters and decorators, and two fish salesman's businesses.

What we didn't have, of course, was a doctor. If someone took ill, or if there was a birth to attend to, he had to be summoned from Anstruther. Dr Armour was our family doctor, and my mother used to tell me that if he was called out in the middle of the night he had to get his horse and trap rigged to make the journey along to St Monans. The village's very first chemist's shop was opened in December 1930, and seemingly it was a partnership between George Doig who was the chemist in Rodger Street in Anstruther, and chemist John Bett, who came from Cellardyke to run it. John Bett eventually settled with his family in Elm Grove in St Monans.

The opening of the Co-operative stores in Pittenweem and Anstruther in around 1932 must have done many of the small local shops a lot of harm. Coupled with the lure of their annual dividend pay-outs, they became very popular indeed. I suppose in a way these early Co-ops were almost the blueprints for the modern supermarkets. You could get all of your bakery, grocery, and butcher requirements and also all types of house furnishings under the one roof. Some Co-operatives even had undertaking departments and furnishing departments. I can still remember my mother's membership number of 4385 to this very day.

St Monans was a "dry" town when I was born in 1930 and was to remain so for many years. Seemingly a vote had been taken whilst the men were away, and the women had voted the village dry. There was no alcohol of any kind sold in the town, and anyone who wanted to have a drink had to travel by bus to one of the neighbouring villages. I can always remember when I was a small boy and coming home with my mother from Cellardyke after visiting my grandmother on a Sunday night, there would always be a few "travellers" boarding the nine o'clock bus at Pittenweem on their way back home to St Monans. In the other direction, the Victoria hotel in Elie was also a popular haunt.

There was never a cinema in St Monans at any time, but the famous "Empire" was in business in Anstruther for many years before I was born. There were also small cinemas in Pittenweem, Crail and Earlsferry. Films were also being shown in Anstruther Town Hall. I certainly can't remember my mother and father ever attending after I came on the scene. Entrance only cost about a shilling, but the patrons were charged a sixpence if they sat in the body of the hall. As I got a bit older, and the new modern "Regal" cinema was opened in Anstruther, I can remember we would cycle along there to see the latest "Tarzan" film, and try to imitate Johnny Weissmüller's famous cry on the way home

There wasn't a barber's shop in St Monans when I was a youngster, and it was the usual thing for nearly every household to possess a pair of hand hair-clippers. Either your father or some relation would cut your hair for you, or you went along to Anstruther by bus to the barber's there. Eventually John Creggan settled in the village and opened a shop in the East Backgate and I believe he did women's hair as well. That must have been quite an innovation. He later moved his business to Anstruther.

The highlight of the week for us in the 1930s was to go down to Ivy Easton's paper shop in Forth Street, or the Coal Wynd as it was called then, on a Saturday night with my mother. She would pay for the week's papers, and get a bag of sweets or some other treat. It was always a busy shop, and we would always meet some relation or other who would be in the shop doing the same thing. It was also a type of chemist's shop and served all our needs in that direction.

The virtual downfall of the fishing industry in St Monans and Cellardyke was no doubt due to the Second World War. Hostilities had ended in 1945, but it was some time before the herring fishing industry was to pick up the pieces and get back into the routine that it had been accustomed to before the start of the war. Many of the local fishing boats did not return from active service because their owners had either sold the boats, or for other reasons. As a result, there were not enough berths for many of the men returning from the war, and some of the Cellardyke men sought work in St Monans.

I remember as a boy overhearing quite a few vigorous discussions down at the harbour. Owners accused the young men of not returning to fishing, and the young men accused some owners of selling their boats and not considering what would happen to their crews. Many of the younger fishermen who naturally remembered all the poor times and all the hard work for very little reward, had little appetite for returning to fishing in any case. They were determined that they were leaving the sea and at that time many of them easily found other work elsewhere.

People were generally better off after the war, and many fishermen were determined that their families would lead a far different life from the one that they themselves had led. For almost the very first time, it was the boys and girls of my generation all along the East Neuk who were being encouraged by their parents to break the mould, and go on to further education and other work ashore, instead of going to sea. Who could blame them?

The exception to this trend locally was in Pittenweem. Many of the young men returning from the armed forces looked at things entirely differently, and very quickly took advantage of the various Government grants that were available at the time. They built up a whole new generation of new boats for seine-netting and herring fishing. Most of them were to do well, and this was to be the start of a very long period of prosperity for the village.

My Career

MY FATHER, who as I said earlier had been a successful trawler Skipper for the greater part of his career, saw things from a very different perspective than most people did. He had always actively encouraged me to become a fisherman ever since I could remember. As a result, my own career as a fisherman started at the age of fifteen.

After leaving school I had been offered a berth on two different boats. One was on *Procyon*, and the other was on *Elspeth Smith*. I chose to sail on the *Procyon* probably because she was the newer boat, and maybe because my uncle was a partner in the boat. I have always had a sneaking regret somewhere at the back of my mind that if I had joined *Elspeth Smith* instead, it would have linked me right back to the days of sail. She must have been amongst the very last of the big sailing "Fifies" that had been originally launched as sailing drifters, and later fitted with motors, and was still actively going to sea. This was 1946, and that would have made her about forty years of age at that time.

I joined *Procyon* KY181 as the boy cook instead, and in May 1946 we set off for Fraserburgh and the first summer herring "drave" since the Second World War hostilities had ended. *Procyon* was one of those so called dual purpose "super bauldies" that I mentioned before, and had only been built in St Monans in 1938 at the yard of Walter Reekie on the west pier. She was 54 feet in length by 18 feet in breadth, and was powered by an 88-hp Kelvin diesel, the normal size of engine for a boat of that length at that time. She usually carried a crew of seven men, and had been requisitioned by the Royal Navy almost immediately after she had been built. She had been stationed at Methil Docks as a liberty boat for most of her war service, and her own Skipper owner David Wood had been on board during all of that period. She had been well looked after, so she was still considered to be a relatively new boat.

"Dauvit Fyall" as he was known to everyone in St Monans, was very particular with his boat, and as the cook I was responsible for keeping the galley and all the accommodation clean. He was a fine man, and very patient with me. He had his own way of getting the best out of people. He gave me great encouragement, and showed me how to do everything properly, which was to serve me in great stead for the future.

His partner in the ownership of the boat was his brother-in-law, my Uncle Willie, who was my father's brother. He was the Mate and engineer and joint owner of the *Procyon*, and the two owners were as opposite as black is to white, to say the least. I would be being very kind to my Uncle Willie if I were to say that if Dauvit was patient, then he would have been impatient. My goodness, did he chase me around! For example, if I happened to go off to bed and leave the light on over the galley stove, he wouldn't switch it off in passing, oh no, he would awaken me and get me from my bed to do it. I very soon learned to switch it off when it was not required, which I suspect was the object of the lesson.

I remember my very first day as a fisherman as if it was yesterday, and in fact the very thought of it almost makes me blush. The boat was lying on the west side of the middle pier in St Monans harbour when I arrived on board, and Skipper Wood set me to work almost immediately cleaning the brass in the wheelhouse. The engine was running, and how was I expected to know that the little brass handle fastened to the side of the wheelhouse was the throttle for the engine. By moving it up and down when I was polishing it, it caused the engine to race and almost jump off the engine beds. After my Uncle Willie had run up from the engine room where he had been working, and explained to me in no uncertain manner how stupid I was, it was only to be a few minutes later when he was to be all over me again. I had turned and turned the brass reverse control wheel attached to the front of the steering wheel whilst I was cleaning it, until I had managed to engage the Kelvin in head gear and send the boat shooting ahead on its mooring ropes. Certainly a most uninspiring start indeed to my fishing career!

The main part of the cook's duties on a herring drifter were, in addition to cooking the meals for eight men, fetching all the stores whilst in harbour, and keeping the accommodation clean. Another of the cook's duties was to coil the heavy messenger rope that ran along the bottom of the drift-nets whilst the nets were being hauled in. This messenger rope was really a series of ropes belonging to each man, and lashed one to the other to form a continuous rope. It was also known as the bush rope in other ports.

A legacy from those thrifty pre-war days before everything had a depreciation value decreed that before setting off for the summer fishing this rope had to be pulled through a vat of soft tar before coiling it on board the boat in order to preserve it. Can you imagine the mess the cook's hands and arms got into every night after coiling this rope down! It seemed to me, that however long the fishing lasted, this tar would never ever dry. It was probably unnecessary to do it every year, but these old habits die hard, and some of these ropes might have been at least fifty years old.

After the hauling of the nets was completed, the cooks would then have to first remove the tar from their hands and arms with paraffin or diesel oil, before finally washing up with soap and water. Rubber gloves, which would have been ideal for the task, were just not thought of in those days. They would then have to start gutting and cleaning the herring for breakfast. Every morning it was the same thing: three herrings for each man had to be prepared and fried. Mind you, it was amazing how delicious they tasted after a hard night's work, even after sometimes being up to the knees in herring at times!

Another duty that fell to the cook was to be on the "guy" rope when the herring were being unloaded in harbour. This rope would be to steady the loaded baskets when they were going ashore from the fish hold, and then to pull back the empties for refilling again. If there was a pause in the landing operation due

My Career

to a new buyer appearing or for some other reason, that would be the cook's opportunity to run to the galley and attend to the preparing of the lunch.

I remember a story from that first season fishing from Fraserburgh in 1946. On board the *Procyon* at that time there was a crew member named Robbie Peattie, also from St Monans. He and my uncle Willie had grown up together and had been great friends all their lives, and had played in the same successful St Monans Swifts amateur football team together for many years. I was very fond of Robbie because he had this great sense of humour, and none knew better than he how volatile my uncle could be, and how to get him going.

One night we were hauling in the drift-nets. It was a very dirty night, and the boat's head was jumping up and down and some nets were being torn, and everyone was on a very short fuse. None more so than my uncle! When it was his turn to be on the foredeck, I can remember every command to me would be a snarl: "hang on", or "ease your hand" as the case may be. There I was, fifteen years old, tired, sleepy, sea-sick, with tears in my eyes, down in that poorly lit fo'castle; coiling that thick rope dripping with wet tar into its locker, thinking that the whole world was against me, and wishing that I had never seen the sea. Every time the boat's head would lift, the rope would surge on the winch and I would be lifted off my feet, and my fingers would be jammed against the deckhead.

The reason that I wasn't able to hang on to the messenger rope, although I didn't know it at the time, was that there weren't enough turns around the winch drum to grip it and give it more purchase. If they had put on the proper amount of turns, I would have been able to pull much harder and would have perhaps damaged the nets even more. Robbie Peattie, who was hauling the nets in the fore part of the fish room and who was not a net owner, and who knew all of this, quietly waited his chance to whisper through to me, "David, ask your uncle Willie for another turn on the barrel of the winch." Well, when I did do that, if I thought that I had seen him angry before, then this time I thought he was going to explode. So much for my friend Robbie!

I survived all of that, and I hope I haven't painted too black a picture of my uncle because it wasn't really as bad as that at all. He really looked after me, and it was all a very important part of the training. Incidentally, it was only he who ever shouted at me, he never allowed anyone else to do it. In later life, my Uncle Willie and I were to be the very best of friends, and had a lot of mutual respect for each other. We were to play many rounds of golf together over Elie Golf Course.

I mentioned earlier that the only reason people were able to survive the poor times in the fishing industry was simply by pure thrift, and although things had lightened up a bit by this time, old habits die hard, and the following story is absolutely true, even for 1946. Sailing on the *Procyon* that year as a crew member was a man called Philip Gay who was married to an Aitken. As I mentioned before, my grandmother had been an Aitken, and I think his wife might have been a niece of hers. Philip Gay lived in George Terrace where most of the Aitkens lived at that time, and he was a fine, upstanding, God-fearing man and very typical of the St Monans fishermen of the period. What I remember about

Philip was that each Saturday when he was about to take his weekly shave, he would get out his tin box with his shaving gear in it, and he would strop his razor back and forth on its leather belt to sharpen it. He would then get out his shaving brush and carefully unwrap the piece of newspaper that he had wrapped around it the previous week before he had put it away. This was so that he wouldn't have to use any soap again when he dipped it in his shaving mug. The soap from the week before would perhaps do several times. Now that's what I would really call thrift!

There is another story from the *Procyon* at that time. Bear in mind that it was just immediately after the war and food was still rationed. It seemed that the only place in the whole country where it was possible to buy pure white bread was in the Peterhead and Fraserburgh area. Each Saturday morning, just before the crews got on the specially-hired bus that was to take them home for the weekend, it was the cook's last task to run up to the baker's shop and purchase two loaves for each man to take home for his family. It was an enormous treat at that time after all the wartime scarcities, and we were always very careful to ensure that the bread was never allowed near to the boat in case it got tainted with diesel oil.

I remember one particular Saturday when we were to have a very quick meal of sausages before the bus arrived, and Uncle Willie volunteered to fry them while I had been ordered to the baker's to fetch the bread. For whatever reason, these wartime sausage skins would explode whenever they entered the frying pan, and would dispatch the hot contents of the sausages over your fingers with dire results. This of course resulted in Uncle Willie exploding as well, and the sausages all being steered into a big heap in the middle of the frying pan. Goodness knows how they were shared out. I wasn't caring much anyway, because in a short while they would all be off home, and then I would have the boat all to myself for the weekend.

One last tale about *Procyon*. It was almost impossible to purchase fresh eggs that very first summer just immediately after the war had finished, and the crew were rationed to one egg per man per week. If yours happened to be rotten, then hard luck! Powdered eggs imported from America easily filled the vacuum, and I must say that they were a great favourite with all the young cooks. You just mixed the powder with water to the correct consistency, and they were much easier to fry in bad weather than real eggs. This particular night I had decided that we would have scrambled eggs for supper after the drift-nets were shot, but some how or other I just didn't get the formula quite correct. As a result, the crew were left balancing bowls of yellow water on their laps!

Much later on in life, when I had acquired some sort of reputation for myself as a successful Skipper, I would sometimes meet former crew member Peter Gerrard, an ex-Skipper himself, down at the harbour at St Monans. Without fail, the very first thing he would greet me with when we met would be, "Aye David, remember yon time that you made the scrambled eggs for the supper?" I am sure that older fishermen like Peter, who had witnessed many generations of young boy cooks just starting off on their fishing careers, must have seen and eaten

My Career

many worse disasters than that over the years.

I also remember the many boxes of kippers that were supplied by the same Pete Gerrard and his friend Willie Mathers, who was always known by his tee name of "Palachie". They had both been boat owners pre-war, and were now just seeing out the twilight of their careers on *Procyon* before they retired. They were a pair of worthies, and between the two of them they knew just about everyone in the herring trade. They would disappear to the pub almost immediately after the herring had been landed, and always reappeared dead on time for lunch and their afternoon nap, along with all the current fishing news, and a box of kippers for supper. I don't know how they financed all of this, but I'm sure that they had their ways. As I said, a pair of worthies indeed!

That spring of 1946, the first year immediately after the Second World War was to see only four boys commence their fishing careers as cooks in the traditional way. We were the first boys to start fishing from St Monans since the war had begun in 1939. Sadly, only two of us were to continue, with the other two boys leaving the sea to do other things immediately after completing their first season. I suppose that, in a way, these were the early signs that the fishing in St Monans was going to decline.

After that first post-war summer fishing at Fraserburgh had finished, the boats now returned home and commenced seine-net fishing locally from their home port of St Monans. They landed their fish daily and the crew carried their own food so they didn't need cooks. I was now paid off, but I was lucky enough to find another berth right away. It was to be for a short season fishing from Scarborough and Whitby as cook on another St Monans boat the *Protect Me 3*. She was one of the smaller "Fifies" that I mentioned before, and had been built by Reekies in December 1927 for Skipper and owner Rob Marr who was always known by his nickname of "Rob the Laud". Rob had also previously owned the steam drifter *Defensor* and coincidentally my own father had sailed with Skipper Rob Marr many years before that when he was himself a young man. I always remember that we carried a ring-net on board for that fishing, but it was never used. They were drift-net men!

After that short fishing was finished I became surplus to requirements once more, but because my uncle Tom on my mother's side was the Skipper of a liberty boat at Rosyth Dockyard, I was able to obtain work with him as a cook during that winter. It was certainly easy work for me now just looking after the five man crew, and with no other duties. Perhaps it was too easy, because by the time the next spring came I was already champing at the bit, and eager to get back to fishing and to secure a berth for the summer herring "drave" again. I was very ambitious even then, and working on a liberty boat at Rosyth Dockyard certainly wasn't part of my future plans. Nothing was going to stop me from becoming a fisherman and eventually becoming the Skipper owner of my own boat. I had made up my mind about that a long time before. By this time though, the *Procyon* that I had sailed on the year before had been sold on to Moray Firth owners, and my next berth for the summer "drave" would be with yet another St Monans boat, the *Carmania 2* KY66.

This was the boat that I had always been associated with as a boy growing up, and had even been on board as a six-year-old when she was launched into Anstruther harbour from the yard of Alexander Aitken in 1936. The present Skipper of the *Carmania 2* was always known as "young" John Smith, and he was my father's cousin. He was the son of the man that I had always known as my Uncle John but who was actually my father's uncle, and who had had so great an influence on me in my very early days. The *Carmania 2*, like all the St Monans boats in the past, traditionally fished the summer herring "drave" from Peterhead, and this season was to be no exception.

This year however was to see the start of a very interesting experiment, and the first time that it had ever been done. In order to maintain the price levels that they thought they should be getting, the Peterhead fishermen's leaders at the time (and I seem to recall the name of one "Pow's Tam" of the *June Rose* as being one of the leaders) decided to split the fleet into two groups. They would be known as A-fleet and B-fleet, and I can remember it was just splendid news for us boy cooks. Three nights at sea in one week, and two at sea in the next. Great! I was reminded recently that somebody at the time had said about me, "Look at him, jumping over two boats at a time with the news that only one half of the fleet would be going to sea that night." It was probably true of course, but mind you, I have a sneaking suspicion that more than a few of the crewmen would not be displeased with the new arrangements either!

My friend Jim Tarvit, who was about the same age as myself, had just left school one year after me, and he was now the cook on board the *Golden Arrow*, a Cellardyke boat under Skipper Jockie Watson. We could always manage to persuade our respective Skippers to berth the boats alongside each other at the weekends. It was no wonder that I stayed away for sixteen weeks with never a visit home. It was a glorious summer, and I was having the time of my life when we weren't at sea. I sailed with the boat to Peterhead in May, and returned with her to St Monans in August.

George Mair who was originally from Portknockie and who was a partner in the *Carmania*, was the brother-in-law of my Uncle John. He was always known by his nickname of "Doddie Peem", and he lived at 11 Miller Terrace and so was almost our immediate neighbour. He was always quite happy to take my kitbag home to my mother with any clothes that needed to be washed. Mind you, my father was not at all pleased with this arrangement, and he passed on a message to me to say that if I didn't come home some weekend, I should stay away forever. I'm sure he didn't mean it, but I think he was worried that I might have met some local Peterhead girl and maybe ended up in Peterhead! Peter Buchan of Peterhead was maybe correct when he wrote later in one of his poems that "the stranger quines (girls) always seemed to be fairer than the fisher quines at hame."

The Skipper and the crew certainly didn't object to me staying on the boat whilst they went off home. It was ideal for them to know that the boat was being looked after during the weekend, the bilges were being kept dry, and they

My Career 81

certainly didn't mind coming back to the boat on Monday to find that a cooked lunch was all ready for them on their arrival. All the stores that were needed for the week would be on board, and the fresh water tank would be filled up. Probably as important as all of that was the fact that the whole fleet of herring nets which had been hauled on to the side decks to dry over the weekend would be "set" down into the hold ready for going to sea. There would usually also be one or two of the younger fishermen staying on the boats at the weekend who did not wish to go home either, and it was more or less expected of them to do this.

After the autumn of 1947 and that summer fishing at Peterhead had ended, *Carmania 2* would now start her usual winter-time pattern of seine-netting for white fish from her home port of St Monans and again with a smaller crew. Once more I found myself in the position of being surplus to requirements. This time the situation didn't bother me unduly, because now I was a year older, and desperately looking for a berth on a bigger boat to go south to the Yarmouth herring fishing.

I wrote to some of the salesmen's offices in Peterhead, and managed to get myself engaged as the cook on the wooden steam drifter *Easter Rose* PD191. What a coincidence! The Skipper of the *Easter Rose* was a man named Jimmy Strachan, commonly known in Peterhead by his nickname of "Pallets", and who, in addition to being quite a character, was also a brilliant herring fisherman. I could just remember Jimmy from his days during the war, when his forty-foot boat *King George V* was one of the Peterhead fleet of smaller inshore boats fishing from St Monans at the winter herring in the Firth of Forth. He had apparently engaged my uncle John, who was retired by this time, to come on board for a spell as a pilot.

The *Easter Rose* had been built at Inverness in 1914 for Burghead owners, and had latterly been owned in Fraserburgh before coming to Peterhead. She was getting quite old by the time that I joined her, and was getting very close to the end of her working life. I believe Jimmy Strachan had only bought her the previous year, and had a very successful year, being the top Peterhead boat attending the Yarmouth fishing. Apart from the Skipper, all the rest of the ten man crew were complete strangers to me. The boat had no electric lighting, only gas and oil lamps, and of course all the cooking was done on a coal stove. In addition to that, the boat was full of four-legged vermin. Mind you, at sixteen years old, all of that didn't bother me too much, as I had been desperate to get to Yarmouth to meet some of those young female herring gutters that I had heard about!

Speaking of coal stoves, I am reminded of an incident whilst I was on *Easter Rose*. It was always the unwritten rule of the steam drifters that when the coal bunker in the galley became empty, the cook had to ask the chief engineer for coal. He would then fill it up, and the cook would have to haul it up the ventilator in the ash bucket and carry it aft to the galley. I remember this one particular night, the chief engineer whose name I remember was Taylor, must have been in a bad mood, because when I requested the coal, he decided to be awkward and told me that I would have to go down into the bunkers and get it for myself. I was having none of that, and off I went to bed. When the crew turned out at midnight to haul the nets, of course the fire was out and there was no tea ready, the crime of all crimes. When I gave my side of the story, the Skipper ordered the chief to give me the coal. As a fully paid up member of the "cook's union", I knew my rights. The chief and I must have become friends again after that, because I remember later staying at his house whilst on holiday in Peterhead.

That was in 1947, and I may well be wrong, but I think it was reputed that almost one thousand Scottish boats were attending the Yarmouth fishing there. The confusion in that very tidal river every day was something to behold. This particular day we had arrived in the river along with hundreds of other boats with possibly about a mile or more still left to sail up to the fish market. All that Skipper Jimmy "Pallets" could see was a queue of boats all the way up to the market ahead of him, and with very little chance of him getting his herring sample on display in time to be sold in the all important "first pool". Being the resourceful man that he was, he spotted a butcher's boy on the pier with one of those bikes of the period, with the iron frame and the wicker basket mounted over the smaller front wheel. He steered the boat alongside the pier, and instructed the Mate to jump ashore and confiscate the bike.

After a bit of wrestling, the Mate secured the bicycle and off he went with his sample bound for the market. When he was almost there, the front wheel apparently went into one of the grooves in the road that held the railway lines, and he went head first over the handlebars, herring sample and all. The price obtained for the herring was always dependant on the condition of the sample, so he had to pick up the herring one by one and wipe them on his jersey, which was all he had. He was a kindly man by the name of Jock Rose, and he was always very good to me. He told me in later years, that he had never been so embarrassed in all of his life. I'm sure it didn't bother Jimmy "Pallets" all that much though! That year *Easter Rose* was not to be the best of the Peterhead boats, and I could easily have been the Jonah on board!

In December 1947, immediately after coming home from that trip to Great Yarmouth, I joined my father as a deckhand learner on the deep-sea steam trawler *Cairnburn*, registered number A419, and based at Leith. She was owned by my father in partnership with the firm of Craig Stores, who had their offices on the North Esplanade East in Aberdeen. She was now being managed for them by the firm of Thomas H. Scales in Newhaven.

Cairnburn had originally been built in 1917 for her Hull owners as the *Cape Trafalgar*, and she had been one of the top-earning boats there in her time. I believe she had once held the record for the number of trips made to Iceland in a single year. She was 147 feet in length with a speed of 11.5 knots, which was very fast at that time. She was a much bigger ship than the normal run of Granton trawlers, which had all been built to fish mainly in the North Sea. *Cairnburn* could hold almost twice as much fish. She had a long sloping square tunnel which ran from the fish hold through the centre of the main thwartship coal bunker straight into the stokehold. This was so that when they were fishing at Iceland, they could fill the fish room with coal for the journey out and could trim it down that tunnel to be used first. The fish room would then be well scrubbed out before fishing commenced. I never saw any coal being carried in the fish room whilst I was a crew member on *Cairnburn*, because she could quite comfortably carry enough coal for a normal North Sea trip without that.

The job of a coal-trimmer on a Granton steam trawler in 1947 must have been one of the hardest jobs that you could ever imagine. For many people it was sometimes the only way they could get started as a trawl fisherman. My heart used to go out to them, and I was very thankful that because of my connections I hadn't had to start like that. In those early years immediately after the war, the decks were generally running over with fish waiting to be gutted, and the two coal-trimmers would have to work on deck amongst the fish along with everyone else.

I seem to recall that most of them would be on their very first trip at sea, and they had come ill-prepared for the job ahead of them. Because they weren't skilled in gutting fish, they would be allocated the job of lowering the filled baskets of fish down into the fish hold and their soft, unprotected hands would soon be torn to pieces. In those days, nobody ever wore protective rubber gloves as they do now, and they probably would have been laughed at if they had.

After all the fish had been stowed below each haul, and if there was still some time left before the end of the tow, the deckhands who weren't required for the watches in the wheelhouse would get below and try to snatch some sleep. For the coal-trimmers, very often no such luck! In addition to having to wait to fill up the kettle for the next cup of tea, they would have to go down into the coal bunkers and shovel coal until they had delivered enough to supply the engineers.

The main thwartship coal bunker on a steam trawler was just a huge space situated between the boiler and the fish room and separated from the stokehold by a steel bulkhead. It stretched from one side of the ship to the other, and was filled to the deckhead with coal whilst in harbour. There were two trapdoors in this bulkhead to allow the coal to flow freely into the stokehold.

After the coal had stopped running naturally, the chief engineer or the fireman would summon the trimmers. With one man on each side of the bunker, they would have to refill the space caused by the coal sliding down. It was essential that they started to shovel the coal from as far forward in the bunker as possible, to build a "wall" which would create a pocket that would hold enough coal to let them get some time in their beds. It was always a temptation for a new trimmer, when he was tired and inexperienced, to try and take a shortcut by taking the coal from the wall. This was fatal, and would have meant that in the long run he would constantly be on call for the whole of the trip.

I was young and energetic, and because I was classed as a deckhand learner and had no trawling watches to keep, I was always able to do a deal with one of the trimmers. In exchange for their allocation of chocolates from the bonded stores, I would fill up their side of the bunker and let them get some time off for a sleep, and perhaps be glad that it wasn't my responsibility.

At that time almost immediately after the Second World War, with the fairly long absence of any great amount of fishing activity, the North Sea was fairly teeming with fish, mainly haddock, whiting and herring. There were certainly plenty of cod as well, but never to the same degree as the other species. We were to do well that year, finishing up with earnings I believe of £51,000. That represented quite a substantial amount for that period, and could well have been about the top grossing for the Granton fleet.

I remember the following year, in early 1948, and one trip especially that we had made to the west coast grounds during my second year as a trawler deckhand. It was just immediately before I was called to do my National Service in the Navy.

In the very early days of the war, huge numbers of the Granton and Leith trawler fleet had been sunk in the North Sea by German bombers, and the remainder had been forced to move to the west coast grounds for safety. They had based themselves at Oban, where their fish could easily be transported to Glasgow market, and also where they could get their coal supplies brought in by railway. Because of the constant presence of German submarines on the lookout for a soft target, they generally did most of their fishing in the North Minch grounds, so my father knew that area well.

Now we were fishing for hake amongst the Fleetwood trawler fleet to the north-west of the Butt of Lewis, and almost along to the Flannans. This was a new departure for him. The bottom was very hard where we were fishing, and because the Granton fleet generally worked on finer ground we really were not equipped with the proper gear. These Fleetwood ships were accustomed to being there, and whereas they all had heavy steel bobbins rigged along the bottom of their nets, we had to improvise with only a heavy grass footrope wrapped round with coir ropes, and cut up old car tyres.

We must have been very lucky, because I remember some big hauls of fish being caught. One I remember in particular, because it included 180 boxes of very large hake. Some boats got much bigger hauls than that, but were unlucky enough to burst their nets and lose the fish. The trawl nets that were being used then didn't have nearly the capacity of the nets being used now. We were still able to land some 640 boxes of hake on that trip, at the controlled price of £3.50 per box. I believe our catch of hake was some kind of record for Granton for the period. Naturally we returned to the same grounds the following trip, but I remember that this time it was a very different story. We were still not equipped with the proper gear, and after destroying all the spare nets in the boat, we were glad to leave the area with our tails between our legs, and finish our trip catching haddock and saithe at the Orkney grounds.

There is one story from trawling in the Minches during wartime that I remember hearing my father tell. He had just risen from his bed to haul the gear at the end of their tow, and Jock Allan from St Monans, the deckhand in charge of the towing watch, informed my father that he thought he might have seen a torpedo go close past the ship. Apparently Jock's eyesight was a bit suspect, so the story was quickly dismissed as nonsense. I can't remember all the exact details of the story as it's so long ago now, but later that day apparently some other trawler had the same experience, and all the fleet that were working there very quickly slipped their gears and ran to Stornoway for safety. The Granton trawlers used to have the end of their warps fastened to their winch drums with only a light lashing of rope instead of being shackled on, for this very purpose.

Even two or three years after the war was finished, trawling still wasn't without its dangers. Dragging up the occasional mine in the North Sea was very much part and parcel of the game. I distinctly remember hauling the net one haul and seeing two mines banging their heads together in the cod end. They were judged to be "safe" and lifted on board along with the fish and spent the remainder of the trip lashed down on the foredeck. Did somebody know something that I didn't know? I remember they were dumped over the side in the Firth of Forth just before we went into Leith harbour.

Later on in the summer of 1948 we started trawling for herring in the Fladdens, and I'm sure this would be because of the influence of my Uncle Alec, my father's older brother. He was a well-established Skipper in Aberdeen and was already catching herring along with a part of the Aberdeen fleet. They were all doing well, and so did we! One of the problems though was that we couldn't catch the herring when they rose off the bottom during the hours of darkness. It was very galling to watch the bigger German trawlers getting good fishing in the dark alongside us. We worked a large wooden kite on the headline of the net to give it the maximum opening height, but the net was really designed as a white fish trawl, and we didn't have the ability or the power to make the whole net lift off the bottom. We also didn't have the electronics to track the fish shoals when they rose from the bottom. We certainly caught plenty of herring during the daylight when conditions were suitable, and we were making a landing into Aberdeen every three or four days with 1200 to 1400 boxes at £3.50 per box. It was very big earnings indeed in those days.

There is one experience that very much sticks in my mind from those early days of herring trawling, strange as it may seem to young fishermen now. Trawl nets up to that time weren't fitted with halfling beckets to split up big hauls into manageable lifts. You have to bear in mind that no one in Scotland had ever seen a splitting becket until the Danish Vinge trawls came along many years later. Getting big hauls on board at that time, meant that they had to be divided up by passing a rope under the bottom of the bag, sometimes not without a struggle. This was all right as long as the fish were floating, but I can remember to this very day that the first haul of herring that we got was of about 150 boxes. Before we got them on board, they had all drowned and they were hanging up and down, and now we had a problem. We just could not get them divided up, and we had no other option but to just put a becket around the cod end, and try and lift them all at once.

You have to remember that this was long before synthetic materials were being manufactured, and nets then were made from natural fibres of either manila or sisal. Also the "Gilson" wire from the winch to the masthead for lifting the fish on board, was only a single ply of wire. After breaking a few beckets and wires, and also breaking tackles that had been hanging there since the ship's Icelandic days, we finally got the fish over the rail only to see the cod end containing the big haul completely explode. Looking back to that time, I am amazed at how naive we all were concerning fishing gear, especially when I think back to how easy it was to become later during my own career to handle catches of more than double that amount with the greatest of ease. Such is progress I suppose!

I reached the age of eighteen on 1st November 1948, and I was called up almost immediately to do my National Service in the Navy. At that time every young man in the country had to serve for a period of eighteen months in either of the armed forces, unless you served in certain reserved occupations. Some young fishermen got their call-up deferred for a time as they were perhaps the only person who could look after the engine on their father's boat. I think they only postponed the inevitable and eventually they were called up like everyone else.

I did my initial Navy training at HMS *Royal Arthur* in the village of Corsham near the Welsh border. It was whilst on my way there to report for duty, that I met my lifelong friend John Watson from Whitehills in Banffshire, another fisherman like myself. We met by chance on a London underground platform, and as neither of us had ever been to London before, it was very much a case of the blind leading the blind. We managed to reach our destination, and after doing our three months' training there, we luckily found ourselves being posted together back to Scotland to the same destroyer, HMS *Ulster*, based at Rosyth dockyard.

That was to be a very happy year in my life. Between playing football for the ship's team several days each week, and dancing at the Kinema Ballroom in Dunfermline almost every single night, National Service passed quite quickly for me. HMS *Ulster*'s main purpose was as part of a boys' training flotilla. Every eight weeks or so, the ship would get a new batch of boy entrants to the Navy to finish the sea-going part of their training. There would be about fifty boys in each group and they would come either from HMS *Ganges*, HMS *Raleigh* or maybe from HMS *Bruce* at Crail. These were the Royal Navy's three shore-based boys' training establishments in the UK. HMS *Bruce* had formerly been a wartime Fleet Air Arm airfield. These boys were looked after by four petty officers, who were responsible for their further training and these POs had their own separate mess deck down aft, adjacent to the boys' mess deck.

Whilst I was working as an ordinary seaman on deck one morning I had a stroke of luck. One of the petty officers came up to me and told me that he had been watching me, and that he had a job for me if I wanted it. I asked him what the job was before I volunteered, and he told me that it was to look after him and his three fellow Chief Petty Officers as a PO's messman. After having been a cook on a steam drifter for two years, that certainly sounded very much like an easy billet for me, and it didn't take long for me to make up my mind. After a couple of weeks in my new job, and they had made sure that I was the right person, they then invited me to bring down my hammock and live in their mess along with them.

The job turned out just as I had expected, and I carried out my part of the bargain, and looked after them all very well indeed. They would have to rise up each morning much earlier than I did to attend to the boys, and when I got up my first duty would be to lash up their hammocks for them, and stow them away. I would then make sure that their tea and toast was ready for them when they came back. I kept the mess spotlessly clean and served them with good food. In return, they made sure that the rest of my Navy time was relatively easy. I was free to go ashore just as often as I wanted, with no watches to keep, and I could get home to St Monans any weekend that I chose. It certainly beat being in the jungle in Burma with the Army!

On top of that I was very lucky. The government had decided to move the goalposts, and had increased National Service from serving eighteen months to having to serve two years. I just missed having to do that extra six months by the shortest of short hairs. Having said that, like a lot of other people before me, I wouldn't have liked to have missed National Service altogether. It certainly introduced a taste of discipline into our lives, and certainly broadened all our outlooks. It's a great pity that they weren't able to keep it going, because I think the country's youth would maybe have been all the better for it, and many of the problems that we are seeing now maybe would not have developed.

By the summer of 1950 I was demobbed, and the fun was now over. This was now the start of the rest of my life, and it was serious. The control price for fish which had been set during the war, had now been lifted, and my father had made his first trip to Iceland expecting to hit the "jackpot" on landing. My Royal Navy time had counted towards my sea time, but I still needed another three months before I was eligible to sit the examination for my Mate's ticket. By this time the *Cairnburn* had now moved from Leith to Granton to be managed by the Ardrossan Steam Trawling Company there, and so I joined one of their steam trawlers the *MacGregor Paton* as a deckhand, to complete the rest of my sea time. Charlie Bell from Granton was the Skipper, and his brother Oliver was the Mate. I enjoyed sailing with them.

After I completed the required sea time, I enrolled in the Navigation class at Dundee Technical College. These were more relaxed times, and the course for a Mate's certificate wasn't nearly as long as it is now, mainly because there was no radar section included. I secured digs in Dundee, worked hard, and after only seven weeks at the college I got my Mate's ticket.

Back to sea again after that, and to my first job as Mate on the *Cairnburn*. I really didn't have enough experience overall for a Mate's job, and no one knew that better than I did, but my father insisted. He was the Skipper and also a part owner, so he signed on an extra second fishermen to help out with the mending of the nets, and I took on the job. Traditionally over the years it had always been the Mate's job in the Granton fleet whilst at sea, to ice and stow the fish in the fishroom alone. Now just after the war years, the composition of the fleet had very much changed, and instead of the traditional 115-foot long type trawlers holding about 700 boxes, there were now ex-Humber type boats as big as 150 feet in the fleet, and holding more than 1,200 boxes, and *Cairnburn* was one of these.

I was young and fit and I could certainly do the work of boxing the fish, but having said that, it was no easy task to cope. The Mate was always alone in the fishroom stowing the fish, and with the 14-man crews, the fish were gutted and put below very fast. Especially with the Granton practice at that time which some people will find very strange indeed: that the fish were stowed away in the fishroom unwashed after being gutted. It was thought that on these shorter trips, unwashed fish would keep better than fish that had been washed.

In those days, because there was no fish market in Granton, the practice was that the catch of fish would be boxed at sea immediately after being caught. This was long before any other deep-sea fishing boats were doing this. The fish were stowed in custom-made wooden boxes which were narrower and deeper than the present boxes, and were fitted with hinged opening lids along with coir rope handles. This was peculiar to these ports because all the fish were sold either locally in Newhaven or in Glasgow, and obviously they had to be transported there by lorry. By the time I started trawling though, dock cranes were now being employed to unload the fish, and they would be landed on pallets which contained ten boxes. The usual method was for three lorries to be standing side by side alongside the ship, with the fish being first landed on the middle lorry. Depending on the type and size of the fish, the boxes would then be lifted across and stacked on to the lorry for whatever market that they were going to.

That first summer sailing as a Mate, we were again trawling for herring on the Fladden grounds, and it was just around this time that my father who was only just forty-eight years of age, became plagued with ill health. I don't really think that he should have been at sea at all in his condition. I think he found that trawling for herring was easier for him, and as long as we were making money, that was why we were there. The bottom at the Fladden grounds was softer for one thing and there was very little damage to the nets. Some hauls I remember my father would not be able to rise from his bed at all, and I would have to haul and shoot the gear again. Not a good situation for me, because I was just on twenty years old and I had no real experience. Because this was long before the days of Decca navigators and other position-finding instruments, half the time I suppose I didn't really know exactly where we were except for the depth of the water. My father had to retire from going to sea shortly after that, and as the *Cairnburn* was over thirty years old and very much past her best, she was soon gone to the breakers.

I remember that sometimes we would get very big hauls of whitebait, especially during the night. They would be allowed to go back over the side again. We would also dine well on all the large prawns that we were catching. These were the days long before people had really woken up to the possibilities of a directed fishery for them, and all day long we would select the very biggest of the prawns from amongst the herring and we would tail them and clean them. During the night when the cook was off duty, one of the firemen would boil them in a huge pot, and then it was a case of seeing how many prawns you could fit on to one slice of bread and butter. Talk about gourmet dining: I seem to be able to still taste them yet. Crew members would also pickle them in vinegar in large jars and take them home for their families. At least that was what they said they did with them! I think most of them would have probably ended up in some pub in exchange for alcohol!

Another story about dining comes to my mind. The highlight of the Leith and Granton trawler officers' social calendar was the Skipper and Mates' annual dinner and dance, usually held in some fancy hotel in Edinburgh. There I was, about twenty years old, feeling swell, and all dressed up in my dinner suit and attending the event for the very first time. A prosperous-looking man came over to me and asked me if I knew who he was. I said that I didn't, but I suspect that he knew me, because he was a friend of my father. "I'm Joe Croan," he said. "I'm the man who makes successful Skippers. A good Skipper is like a good jockey. He's all right as long as he rides to instructions." I suppose if I had carried on in the trawling industry at that time, I might have eventually become one of Joe's Skipper jockeys.

My father was to go back to sea again later, and I am certain that they were the very first Scottish fishermen to pair trawl for white fish in the North Sea. The *Alorburn* and the *Maravane* were two ex-government 90-foot wooden MFVs belonging to Craig Stores in Aberdeen, the firm to which my father was connected through his partnership in the *Cairnburn*. The Spaniards were the masters of the pair trawling trade at that time, and George Murray, the managing director of Craig Stores, had gone down to Milford Haven with my father to purchase a new net. Unfortunately they didn't manage to make a success of the new trade, and I remember this net was eventually to hang from the store roof for many years after that.

I have always wondered why pair trawling didn't work out for them, but you have to bear in mind that at that time they had no power blocks, no radars to maintain their distance apart, no navigation aids and most important of all, no experience. This couldn't be got overnight, and after all the Spaniards had been learning this trade for a long time. Perhaps because his health was gradually failing, he didn't have the energy that he once had to make it into a success. It was to be very shortly after that his fishing career was to be finished for good, and he was only forty-eight years of age.

Soon after this, I joined Skipper Jock Watson as Mate on the Dundee steam trawler *Lynn Fenton* sailing from Dundee and sometimes landing into Aberdeen. This small trawling firm was owned by Len Fenton, the brother of Lord Provost Fenton of Dundee. He was a friend of my father and was himself a former Merchant Navy Captain. Apparently Jock Watson had been a policeman before becoming a fisherman, and it was his first trip as a Skipper. He was one of three brothers belonging to Broughty Ferry who were now all trawler Skippers. I would say that the *Lynn Fenton* was in far worse condition than the ship that I had just left. There was always some fault or other. I remember the very first time we arrived at Dundee Fish Docks to land our fish. As the Mate I was steering and as we entered the very small fish docks the engine refused to reverse. "What do I do now?" I asked Jock. "Steer for a soft bit between the piles," was his reply. I can still see Captain Len Fenton's face yet when he emerged from his office to see his ship embedded into the soft pier almost up to the length of the whale back, and not for the first time either, I was to learn later!

The boiler in that ship was on its very last legs, and for a steam boat the boiler was as important as the engine it was driving. During the short time that I was sailing on that boat I have distinct memories of the chief engineer crawling into the furnace to expand the tubes which were leaking and causing all the trouble. I used to go down into the stokehold to watch and help him if needed. The technique was lie over the broadside and to wait as long as possible for the boiler and furnaces to cool down, and this took ages. Pond boards from the deck would then be laid along the floor of the furnace and wet bags draped over them to lie on, with everything roasting hot. I used to warn him that some day his body would swell up and we wouldn't be able to haul him out. It was a common occurrence for him to have to do this every other trip, but certainly not for me thanks!

I had only been in Dundee for a few months when the trouble that I had been having with an in-growing toenail meant that it finally had to be removed and a skin graft put in its place. I also had more serious trouble that same year when a corneal ulcer developed in my eye. Because the drugs that are available now weren't available then, it kept breaking down year after year to my great discomfort and often took months to quieten down. Goodness knows what my prospective in-laws must have thought when I called as a young man wearing an eye-patch and my foot bandaged up. Eventually after nearly twenty years, when I was forty years old, I received a successful corneal graft from a donor at Dundee Royal Infirmary, and I have had no more trouble since then. With the help of contact lenses, I have enjoyed perfect eyesight.

Once I had got all my health troubles sorted out I joined the Granton steam trawler *Grace Paton* as the first Mate in 1953. The Skipper was Jock Dunwoodie, a local Granton man and a very fine person. I got on very well with Jock for the year that I served as his Mate on the *Grace Paton*. He was always recognised as being a west coast Skipper who preferred to fish in the Minches and around the islands of North Rona and Sulisker in the summertime. This was in the days before the Moray Firth seine-net Skippers were to take over all these grounds. We were doing quite well, and I was being well paid, and for me it was very a happy year. I was also getting ever nearer to my eventual goal of becoming a trawler Skipper like my father.

All that year, although I was doing well, something at the back of my mind was always bothering me. Most of the Granton steam trawlers were now becoming very old boats, and I could see more and more of them coming to the end of their lives each year and being scrapped and not being replaced. Modern diesel-engined trawlers were still quite a few years into the future. The *Cairnburn*, the ship in which I had started trawling and in which my father was a shareholder, had already gone to the breakers, and I always kept remembering my father's tales of his early days whilst trying to break into the industry. I could easily see myself perhaps struggling to retain a job, and maybe eventually being unemployed.

I finally made up my mind, and when I arrived home after one trip, I told my father that I was getting out of the trawling industry, and I was going to have a seine-net boat built for myself. I can always remember his reply to this day. He said to me, "You're getting out? You're not even in yet," meaning of course that I hadn't yet become a trawler Skipper! I told him that it didn't matter, because I had made my mind up. I was going to have a new seine-net boat built. "All right," he told me, "if that's what you want to do, we will go ahead, and I will take a third share in the new boat with you. This will be a share for your brother John." The other shareholder was to be Alex Keay from Cellardyke, who was much older than me and married to my mother's cousin.

I don't think I fully realised it at the time, but this must have represented a huge gamble for my father, and an unbelievable demonstration of faith in me. I was only twenty-two when we started to plan the new boat, and I didn't even have a Skipper's ticket, and yet here he was, finished with the sea for three years and unable to work because of ill health and only fifty years of age. With a young family of five of us still in the house, and no pensions of any kind in those days, and yet he was still willing to risk a fair bit of his savings going into business with me. All the more particularly as I had never even seen a long line shot, or a seine-net operated except on a day trip during the war as a very young boy. Here I was, proposing to have a new 72-foot boat built and take it away to sea as Skipper, with practically no experience of these new fishing methods, and absolutely no information of any kind on the fishing grounds that we were about to fish. I suppose it must be full marks for my father's confidence in me.

The first *Argonaut* was to be built with the help of the second Government Grant and Loan scheme which was at that time administered by the White Fish Authority. The steam drifter era was fast coming to a close, and many owners from all around Scotland were taking advantage of this offer, and building new motor boats of around the same size as our own to replace their old boats. The conditions of this aid scheme were such that the owners had to put up 15% of the total cost, and then there would be a grant of 30%. The remaining 55% would be in the shape of a loan from the Authority. It was an excellent scheme, and many young fishermen like myself were able to get their first start as boat owners because of it.

What it meant in real terms was that the new boat was to cost £13,300, and we had to find the sum of £1,995 to cover our 15%. It doesn't sound much now, but relative to the times, it was an awful lot of money. Because I was sailing as Mate on a steam trawler, and earning what were very good wages for someone of my age, I remember that I had managed to save up the substantial sum of £750, which covered exactly my portion of the down payment. Obviously inflation hadn't really got into its stride at this point, and many people observing my young age of twenty-two, and my obvious lack of experience, were heard to remark, "Poor laddie, he'll never manage to pay all that money back."

People normally expected to get their big start in the industry by taking other people's boats to sea, and then if they were successful, they might be given their own chance in a second-hand boat. I was proposing to start at the very top. The new boat was to be designed by the late Jimmy Miller of Miller's of St Monans, and the order to build her was placed with my uncle, Philip Smith, at the Anstruther yard of Smith and Hutton's.

The new boat was to be 72 feet by 20 feet, and because we couldn't get a 152-hp Gardner at that time, such was the demand for them, she was to be fitted with a 132-hp Kelvin diesel engine instead. She was launched in September 1953, and was named *Argonaut* by my mother. I wasn't even there to see her take the water for the very first time, because that was the day that I was in Aberdeen sitting the final examination for my Skipper's ticket. Those were very different days from what was later to become the normal in the industry. No bagpipes and kilt outfits and long dresses and hats for the ceremony, with a dinner dance to follow when a new boat was launched. Just lemonade and buns up in the drawing office along with the workforce.

The White Fish Authority surveyor of the time was Commander Cochrane, and he gave the assembled company a few words of wisdom. He advised the women to "mind the houses, and the men would mind the boats." These were very wise words, I would say, prompted no doubt by his presence being required on more than a few occasions in the past, to arbitrate when partners fell out caused mostly by wives interfering. It didn't happen in our case, I might add.

During the fitting-out period and some time before the boat was ready for sea I remember going along with my new crew by lorry to the beach just below the 10th hole at Elie Golf Course. In the time-honoured fashion we collected quite a few tons of the hard, round volcanic stones which are to be found there, as ballast for the new boat. This was still some time before the days when boats were to be ballasted by pouring concrete between the frames.

The new *Argonaut* turned out to be an exceptionally fine boat, and in the ten years that I owned and skippered her, I can honestly say that she never ever put a foot wrong. I certainly put that boat through the mill. The down-side was that the 132-hp Kelvin engine wasn't man enough for the job, and only four years after the boat was completed, we had to replace it with a 152-hp Gardner engine. We also decided at the same time to replace the wooden wheelhouse and galley with one made of steel. It was at this point that I was joined by my younger brother Robert who eventually became a partner in the boat.

Looking back, I suppose if I hadn't had what it takes to be a Skipper, then it could have meant financial disaster for everybody concerned. Fortunately that didn't happen, and *Argonaut* proved to be a very successful and profitable vessel, and her gross earnings in that crucial first year compared favourably with any of the new boats in her class. I will be eternally grateful to my late father for giving me my start in life.

We assembled a crew, and a very fine crew it was too, all experienced long-line and drift-net men except me, and I was supposed to be the one in charge. I can't remember who decided what type of fishing we should prosecute first, but I don't really think it was me. It was probably my partner and my father between them. Whoever it was, on reflection, it probably was the correct decision at the time. Instead of seine-nets, we decided to fish with great-lines and herring drift-nets just like the few remaining steam drifters which were still fishing from Anstruther.

Winning isn't everything. It's the only thing!

I WILL ALWAYS REMEMBER my first day as a Skipper. It was on 4th January 1954, and bait had been delivered by rail on Saturday from Newhaven market to Anstruther harbour where the boat was lying. It was a Sunday, and I had ordered the crew to report at 1800 hours that night. This did not go down at all well with the new crew. At that time, inshore fishermen did not go to sea at the weekends, and the favourite time for sailing was always after midnight, or "back o' Sunday" as it was known. Here was I on my very first day as a Skipper, breaking the long-standing unwritten rules by proposing to sail on a Sunday. I didn't realise that there was a problem. I had been sailing on trawlers from Granton for the last few years and it was all the same to me when we set sail. We had to leave at that time in any case, because Anstruther was a tidal harbour, and the boat would not have been afloat at midnight and we would have lost the next day's fishing.

It was a cold winter's night, and I can remember how, as the crew were cutting up the herring and squid on the foredeck, church bells could be heard ringing out all over the village calling the congregations to evening worship at the various churches. Isa, my girlfriend, later to be my wife, was standing on the pier waiting to watch us leave along with my youngest brother Albert, who was just a boy at the time. One of the crew looked up and asked her, "Do you want a bit of advice? Get out now before it's too late: this is only the start, and it will only get worse from here on."

My wife's parents had no connection with the fishing industry whatsoever, so at the time I don't think she really quite understood the significance of what he was trying to tell her. Whether she regretted not taking his advice I don't know, but he was definitely proven to be correct, it did get worse! Being the Skipper of the *Argonaut*, and her various successors of the same name, was to take over my life for the next forty years or so, to the exclusion of a lot of things and people that I might have made more time for. I'm happy to report though, that in the Craw's Nest Hotel in Anstruther on 15th January 2005, my wife Isa and I happily celebrated our Golden Wedding and fifty years of marriage together, along with our family and friends.

We sailed that night as planned of course, and for the next few weeks or so we worked on all the old-fashioned grounds around the Firth of Forth that retired Skippers would tell me about. Somehow or other we managed to earn enough to keep things going, and provide the crew with decent wages. We were more or less filling in time until the end of February, when the promise of better weather meant that we could sail to the offshore grounds of the North Sea along with the rest of the Cellardyke fleet. I was also gradually gaining more and more experience as a great-line Skipper in that much kinder environment.

Although I had just recently bought a fleet of brand new seven-pound long-lines to use when we went offshore, it was part of the folklore of the East Neuk that you needed to work very light lines in the shallow waters of the Firth of Forth to catch the most fish. I didn't want to buy another set of lighter lines so I went hunting around the villages trying to obtain second-hand lines from some pre-war fishermen. I remember locating and buying some of these old lines from a retired fisherman called Gowans who lived in Forth Street in St Monans and who had once owned a boat called the *Harvest Moon*. I'm sure that they could easily have been forty years old. I do know that it had been a long time since Mr Gowans had been to sea.

Anyway, when we were shooting these ancient lines for the first time, the man who was "steadying" the lines took hold of it when it was running out, and when it came tight it broke in his hand. That was the end of the light lines. They were all consigned to the rubbish dump, and the brand-new heavier lines were bent on in their place immediately so that we would have no more trouble.

Long lines were normally shot in strict rotation from the oldest to the newest, with the oldest of the lines going out first. The brand new lines would usually be shot last, and would be kept nearest to the boat and would be the first to be hauled back. It was not unknown out in the eastern North Sea for other foreign vessels to come across the dhan buoys of a great-line boat by accident, and start to haul the lines from the other end. They would be about twelve miles away and well over the horizon so that they couldn't be seen. The culprits at that time were usually Dutch herring lugger crews who were lying about after hauling their nets, and probably fancied a few fresh fish to supplement their endless diet of herring. It wouldn't have been so bad if they had rebaited the lines and paid them out again after taking off the fish, but that didn't normally happen. Every lost line belonged to some crew member, and would have to be replaced with an expensive new line along with the dhan buoys and an anchor.

Line fishermen in those days usually made up their own great-lines. New strings of line or "taes" of line as they were known in Fife, would be ordered and delivered from the rope factory in Gourock on the River Clyde, and each man would be responsible for turning them into a great-line. The end of each string would be taken from the centre, and carefully taken off its coil "against the sun". Each string in turn was then stretched out to its whole length on some suitable flat piece of ground, usually on an empty pier on a fine day. Standing about the middle of the stretched-out string, the line was now coiled from the centre towards one end which allowed all the turns to automatically run out. The coil was then turned over and the other half of the line was now coiled towards the other end which allowed the rest of the turns to run out. If this process was done correctly right from the start, the line would then handle properly for the rest of its life.

The long-lines that the fishermen from Anstruther and Cellardyke preferred were made up from the very best Italian hemp, and when new they were exceedingly strong. The strings were just beautifully made, with not a fault or a raised strand in their whole length. Each complete long line was made up of seven "strings" of sixty fathoms each (110 metres) spliced together to form a continuous line of perhaps 420 fathoms in length (760 metres). Each string weighed about 7 lbs, and this was also a measurement of the thickness of the line. Attached to each string at 21-foot (7 metre) intervals, were the 9-foot-long branch lines or "snoods" or "stroods" as the Cellardyke men preferred to call them. These stroods were then attached to the main string by a special rolling hitch which prevented them from slipping along the line.

Attached to the end of each of these stroods was a lighter piece of doubled cotton of about one foot in length locally known as a "tipping", and it was attached to the strood by a simple sheet-bend knot through the bight. Each of these tippings had a single hook attached to the two single ends which were drawn together with beating twine. After a single hook and tipping was knotted on to every strood, it gave a total of about approximately 115 hooks on each long-line.

The main purpose of this short piece of doubled cotton was to absorb the abrasions from the teeth of larger fish. If one strand were to be chaffed through, the other strand would normally be strong enough to raise a large fish up from the seabed. It was also meant to be disposable when it became damaged or if the hook itself suffered damage from the hard bottom. If the hook had been attached directly to the strood itself then through time it would have eventually become shorter and shorter as damaged bits were removed. It would have meant that the strood itself would then eventually have had to be replaced at much greater expense.

The purpose of having these exact measurements when setting up a great-line was that the men who were baiting the lines as they went out over the side, would have enough time to put a bait on each hook. They would not be taken by surprise by a strood that was much shorter than the rest. Secondly, a strood that had become too short could mean that when hauling, a large fish could have been accidently lifted from the water and if not properly hooked, the hook could have torn out and let the fish escape. Thirdly, by keeping the stroods that exact distance apart it ensured that the hooks did not accidentally foul their neighbouring hooks and prevent them from fishing.

The long lines used by the Aberdeen, Peterhead and Fraserburgh line fishermen, were set up more or less in the same manner as the Fife fishermen. The main difference was in the kind of hooks used. The Cellardyke men favoured number eight straight hooks, and the north-east men generally used the same size of hooks, but with off-set points. There did not appear to be any difference in the amounts of fish caught.

After a new line had been "set up", it was then carefully coiled into a large, purpose-made cane basket, with each hook in rotation being carefully stuck into a rope lashed into place around the rim of the basket. The line fishermen from the north-east of Scotland, who preferred to use the bent hooks, would have had cork instead of rope around the rim for this purpose.

During the fishing trip, each morning as the long lines were being run out they would then be knotted in rotation to the next one by a simple overhand knot. Depending on the weather of course, thirty-five baskets of lines were normally shot each day, making a total of approximately 4,025 hooks stretching to over twelve miles.

Although for the first few weeks of the new *Argonaut* we were working in the relatively sheltered waters of the Firth of Forth it wasn't an easy time by any means. We would shoot our lines just before daylight, and then, bearing in mind it was mid-winter, it would take us all day to haul them. The hauling rate on that shallow water, would generally be three to four lines per hour. We would then have to steam up the Firth to Newhaven Fish Market where we would land our fish direct for the following morning's market. We would sail again immediately, and spend the next few hours chasing around the upper reaches of the Firth of Forth looking for some ring-net boat who would sell us as much freshly-caught herring as we needed for bait. We would then steam all the way down the Firth again to the Dunbar area and perhaps the "Kirk Hard" grounds and shoot our lines once more.

Sleep was a very scare commodity, and after five days and nights of that, I can remember we were all pretty tired by the end of the week. I remember on one particular night we decided to shoot our lines all the way along the coast just off Kirkcaldy. One of the crew, who was an experienced line fisherman and had been accustomed to working far off-shore, just couldn't adjust to the smell coming from the local linoleum-manufacturing factories and still speaks about it to this day, fifty years on.

There has always been a saying in the fishing industry that you don't really know a man until you have sailed with him, and I'm afraid that was the situation between myself and my new partner. At the end of only that very first week's fishing, there was an incident which was to mar any relationship which we might have had from then on, and which certainly did not bode well for the future.

On the Saturday morning after that very first week's work with the new boat was finished, my partner demanded that I take him along to talk to my father, the third partner. He told him that for various reasons he was sorry that he had become involved in the new boat, and that he wanted released from the partnership. My father, who as I said before had been a very successful trawler Skipper before becoming ill, was accustomed to taking decisions. Without hesitation he told my partner, "Right, if that's what you want, then I will take over your interest in the new boat."

Now I wasn't too sure about all this bearing in mind my age, and the fact that I had only been a Skipper for one week, and also my inexperience at all these new jobs, and I told my father so. I thought that I would maybe need the help of my partner in the years ahead. I can remember my father's words as if it was yesterday. He said to me, "Please yourself, but I can tell you this much, if this is an example of the help you are expecting to get, then I pity you. If we take over the whole boat now, it will cost us only seven hundred and fifty pounds, but if you wait till later, and mark my words it will happen eventually, it will cost you four times as much." To cut a long story short, my father was right as usual, and after four acrimonious years working together, it did cost me as much as that when we eventually took over the boat. It was at this point that my brother Robert joined the boat as a junior partner.

Looking back, even to 1954, it was amazing just how primitive the manner in which new boats were still being fitted out was, compared to a new boat of the present day. We had only a small Stuart Turner auxiliary engine fitted to provide emergency power, and at that time the only generator was driven from the main engine by only a single belt. Usually the first warning that we would get that the belt had broken and the generator was no longer charging was when the lights went dim. Now we had the dilemma that if we stopped the main engine to repair the belt, and the starting batteries weren't fully topped up, we would maybe have to start the main engine by hand.

Even for hauling the lines, which was our main job, we unbelievably started off with a second-hand steam-line hauler which had been purchased from the owners of a small redundant Anstruther boat, *Winaway*, and had been converted by the local engineer to be powered by compressed air. It is hard to believe that we started out like this on a brand-new boat, but by this time I suppose no one was making the kind of line haulers that we required any more. I'm not quite sure, but I think that hydraulic equipment was practically unheard of on fishing boats then anyway, especially in the UK.

The most important thing about this set-up that we had was that it worked very successfully indeed for the next ten years or so that I spent as a great-line Skipper. The single-cylindered air compressor itself gave absolutely no trouble, and was driven from the winch shaft which extended forward to the fo'castle. With the benefit of hindsight it could still be a good system even today, but we would have had bigger compressors and a spare one already rigged up on site. We much preferred them to a hydraulic hauler anyway, when eventually they were introduced. They were far more sensitive, and we could feel right away if the line was snagged in the ground, or if we had hooked a very big fish such as a halibut or a big skate which required special treatment to bring it to the surface.

We had practically no navigational instruments of any kind apart from a compass and a radio. I may be wrong, but I think the *Argonaut* could well have had one of the very first radio transmitter receivers designed and installed by the new electronics firm of Woodson's of Aberdeen. We did have an echo-sounder though, which recorded the depth of water on wet paper, and this in itself was an innovation at the time. It was a Kelvin Hughes MS 24, and they were to serve the Scottish industry well.

No Decca navigators had been fitted on any boats in Scotland when the first *Argonaut* was built. The Decca system was a new development during the latter stages of the war, and fishermen had not yet realised their full value as fishing instruments. Very soon though, Peter Murray in the Anstruther seine-net boat

Boy Peter would become the very first in the whole of Britain to fit one, and it would ultimately revolutionise the face of fishing. For the very first time Skippers would know their exact position at all times, and their rental cost was about nine pounds per week. It seemed like a small fortune at the time, and it certainly deterred a lot of Skippers from following his example for quite a long while!

We did use the Consol bearing system which had been in existence for a few years by that time, but it was of fairly limited help. It consisted of two wireless transmitting stations positioned at Stavanger in Norway, and also at Bushmills in Northern Ireland. The signals that they sent out could be translated into a series of dots or dashes which had to be continually counted by ear, and were different depending on where you were on the grid. By taking a bearing on the station by direction finder, and consulting a special chart, you could estimate which sector you were in. Sometimes the signal could give you your latitude pretty accurately if you were working east in the North Sea.

You could get a cross-bearing of a kind by tuning in to the other station, but there was always a certain ambiguity about the result of the count and no two people would come exactly to the same conclusion. It was better than nothing at the time, and it was certainly very handy for locating the harbour after steaming in from the Norwegian sector, especially when you had nothing else. I can always remember that Aberdeen harbour lay on 42 dashes, or there again, it might well have been dots!

The Loran navigation system, which was to be developed later, was to be much favoured by the Norwegian fishermen but wasn't really adopted by the Scottish Fleet. In some ways it resembled the Consol system, only a special receiver did the counting for you. I think that quite a few Scottish Skippers eventually showed some interest in Loran with the introduction of more sophisticated receivers, but that was to be some time in the future.

I was very lucky in many respects, because I had only been a Skipper for about a year or so when practically the whole Scottish fleet woke up to the benefits of the Decca navigating system. There was a rush to install them, and we of course did likewise. It made a huge difference to a young Skipper like myself. Even experienced Skippers were having to learn the fishing grounds all over again from a different perspective.

The American military satellite Global Positioning System was later to change everything once more. Access to GPS was released to the world at the time of the first Gulf war, and because all the American allies didn't have the latest receivers, it was released at first with full accuracy. This was so accurate that it eventually even displaced the Decca system itself, which had faithfully served the fishing fleets for so many years. Later on, a hundred-metre random error was built into the system by the military for national security reasons, and customers were forced to fit receivers which automatically corrected this error.

When mid-February came on that very first year, the great-line fleet of steam drifters was now preparing for the start of their season. There were still five remaining in Anstruther at that time, and they had been tied up since they had returned from the Yarmouth fishing in December, so they were champing at the bit to get started. We got ready along with them. The new *Argonaut* and myself as the Skipper were very much the new boys, and the spotlight was on us. Everybody was waiting to see if the new 72-foot motor boat would be able to compete successfully with the steam liners out in the Norwegian sector of the North Sea where the line boats normally worked. After all, it had been some years previously that one of the more well known of the Cellardyke Skippers had tried to do it in a 75-foot ex-government MFV and pronounced that size of boat as being unsuitable for the task. I have no idea why that should have been the case, because, young as I was, there certainly were no doubts in my mind as we prepared for the season ahead.

We "set down" the normal 28 drift-nets with which we would catch our own herring bait each night, and after steaming to Aberdeen to take on ice, we all set off together for the Norwegian coast. That first trip went very well, and although we weren't the best boat, we certainly weren't the poorest either. I was proud of that fact, and I was still learning.

The second trip was to end up being even more successful for us. During that trip, an unusually strong gale had sprung up, and the boats were all dodging head up to the wind to keep out of trouble. Bearing in mind that this was long before the days of autopilots, this technique had been developed by the herring boats and the line boats over many years. What this meant was that we would hoist our big square mizzen-sail, and then set it right in the centre of the boat. It literally hung out over the stern and when hauled down absolutely bar-tight it acted as a rudder in the wind. We would then lock the steering wheel with the helm dead in the middle and by just maintaining headway the boat would keep exactly head on to the wind and the weather for as long as was required without anyone ever having to touch the wheel.

It was an amazing technique, and one which I'm certain helped to keep me and my crew safe from harm in all the bad weather that I was to experience in my long career. In fact, long after the herring days were over and we had long since been fitted with automatic steering, such was our faith in the practice that we still clung to the mizzen-sail for use in bad weather. I suspect that we eventually ended up being the only fishing boat left in the North Sea still carrying a mizzen-sail. Old habits die hard!

Incidentally on that night in question, such was the strength of the wind that the peak halyard, which runs through a block shackled to an eyebolt in the mast, and held up the yard of the mizzen sail, drew the eyebolt right through the wood — nut, washers and all — and down came the sail. Panic stations! If it had been shackled to a band around the mast in the first instance this would never have happened. I remember climbing up the mast in that gale, and managing to re-shackle the halyard to the band which held the throat halyard, and we were able to get the sail reset and the boat head to wind again. There was certainly an additional band fitted to the mast after that!

On with the story. Before we sailed on that second trip, I had met a retired

Cellardyke line Skipper named David Watson, who at one time had been Skipper of the *Wilson Line*, the last and biggest of all the steam drifters ever to be built. "Dauvit" told me that if I brought up a chart he would show me some of the areas where he used to find fish, and one particular area where they would sometimes catch some big grey skate at this time of the year. I duly went up to visit him at his home.

The next day after the big gale the wind had eased off a bit. I had this newly acquired piece of information firmly in my mind, and was just bursting to try it out. We were just about able to make progress towards this area. Before the gale, on a previous night, we had managed to catch some herring bait surplus to our requirements, and we had them iced below, so we had plenty of bait on board. I remember that when we arrived there in the late afternoon, the weather still hadn't settled down properly, and I suggested to the crew that maybe we should shoot a few lines to see if there was anything to be caught. This was unheard of, and did not go down at all well with the crew. It was considered that shooting lines in the afternoon was a complete waste of bait and time. However, shoot a few lines we did, and surprise, surprise, we got a nearly a hundredweight of skate off each line. Very promising indeed, and I was learning very fast that if I was to be a successful Skipper, I should always carry out my own mind, no matter what.

The next morning the weather was fine, and because we had got this indication that there was fish to be caught, we went to work in earnest. We shot our whole fleet of 35 lines, a stretch of about 12 to 14 miles, in the correct place, in the correct depth of water, and at the right time, and we got one of the biggest day's fishing that I was ever to see while long-lining in the North Sea. About seven tons of fish and halibut, of which about five tons were large grey skate. *Eureka!* I have found it! Not bad work, and I was very pleased with myself for locating the correct spot first time, considering that we had no navigational instruments on board. That trip was to see us landing with the top trip of all the Cellardyke boats, mainly due of course to that one good day's work. The value of the catch on that trip was somewhere about £1,100. It seems so little now, but at that time it was a very considerable amount of money.

Unfortunately we were to learn on our arrival in Aberdeen that the Peterhead herring drifter *Quiet Waters*, a boat of similar size to our own and owned by the Stephen family, had been presumed lost with all hands in an area not all that far from where we had been fishing, very probably on that fateful night of the heavy gale.

We continued to work in the eastern North Sea right through the whole of my first summer as a Skipper until the end of the late Autumn. The rest of the Cellardyke fleet, which were all bigger steam drifters, had by early springtime followed their usual pattern and moved north-west through the Pentland Firth to fish around the Faroe Islands. *Argonaut* at that time, at 72 feet in length, was considered far too small to fish in these western waters, and there would probably have been a revolt if I had even dared to suggest it. It didn't matter though, because that left us with nearly all the southern North Sea long-line grounds to ourselves. With our lower economy, and by doing much shorter trips, we were commanding a much better price for our fish. We were able to carry on successfully fishing those eastern waters as far out as the Skagerrack almost until the end of that first season.

I think by this time the more experienced men in the crew, who had sailed in steam drifters all their careers, were now beginning to get an eye-opener on just how good these modern diesel-engined wooden boats really were. We finished off the season by doing two successful trips around the Faroe Islands themselves.

I mentioned that there were no Decca navigators installed in fishing boats at this time, and it was not always easy to return to exact areas, but using our echo-sounders, with their excellent hard and soft ground discrimination qualities, I was learning all the time. Some of this knowledge that I acquired whilst line-fishing was to serve me in good stead in future years when I later pioneered seine-net fishing on some of these grounds around the long-line fishing areas.

After landing our fish in Aberdeen for the last trip of that year, the long lines were taken ashore as usual and dipped in hot bark to preserve them, and then we sailed home to our home port of Anstruther where all the gear would be stored ashore for the winter.

I remember a story from old Alec Cunningham, who was my fish salesman when I started out with my first new boat. He had been attending a meeting of the Scottish White Fish Producers in Aberdeen one day, and the question arose as to what were a fish salesman's obligations to his fishermen customers. "From the cradle to the grave," one fellow had said, because in the past he had arranged births, marriages and funerals.

We now put on board a full fleet of herring drift-nets, and prepared to set off for the herring fishery at Whitby. I was totally inexperienced as a herring Skipper, except for catching our own bait each night while line fishing, coupled with my few seasons as a cook on a drifter as a young boy. That was when I was encountered what I considered to be a real stroke of luck. A retired Cellardyke Skipper, Rob Gardner, a member of a well-known local fishing family, and always known by his nickname of "The Lion", and certainly one of the more successful Skippers of the past, approached me and asked if I would give him a passage down to Whitby. He wanted to be beside his sons who were fishing there with the family boat. This I immediately agreed to, and we set sail soon after.

The time-honoured method for fishing for herring with drift-nets during the summer fishing from the Buchan ports would be for the boats to steam out to sea, to areas where past experience told the Skippers that they would be likely to find herring. Perhaps even where there had been good reports of herring catches on the previous night. They would leave harbour so that they would arrive at the chosen spot in good time for them to look around for what were considered to be good signs — sea birds such as gannets or herring gulls sitting on the water just waiting, or perhaps an occasional whale breaking the surface, or even the way the colour of the water looked.

Some experienced Skippers could sense the presence of herring or were reputed even to be able to smell them. Whatever way it was, some men could always catch more herring than others, year after year. After deciding that this was where they would try, the boat would steam up wind for a short distance, then slowly turn down before the wind and pay out as much as a hundred drift-nets, stretching for a distance of about three miles. All of this would have to be done just before the sun sank below the horizon, so that the gill nets would be hanging perfectly awaiting the herring rising to the surface at dark.

With the advent of the echo-sounder, however, a lot of this guesswork was now taken out of catching herring. Echo-sounders were originally developed as a method of measuring the depth of water under the ship, a huge advance in itself, but fishermen soon discovered that they had other uses. Skipper Ronnie Balls of Great Yarmouth is credited as the being the first person in the world to discover that it could be used as a fish-finder as well. An echo-sounder in its simplest form is just a machine that transmits an electrical pulse from a transducer set into the ship's hull down to the bottom of the sea and then measures the time that it takes for this signal to return, and displays this information on a scale. Ronnie Balls had noticed that this signal was occasionally being interrupted by something between the surface and the bottom echo, and he correctly deduced that it must be pelagic fish of some kind. The reason that I have said all that was that by 1954 the art of fish-finding was very well developed. The machines were now much more sophisticated, and were presenting the information on a special wet paper instead of an electric impulse on a cathode-ray screen, and giving far more definition and information.

On our passage from Anstruther down to Whitby in the north-east of England, Rob Gardner would have had a fair idea that I had absolutely no experience of fishing for herring in the manner in which it was being done on the grounds that we were now heading for. In addition to telling me how it all worked, and pointing out to me on the chart where the herring were usually found, he said to me that if I wished he would only be too pleased to go to sea with us on that first night and show me how it was done.

I had been Skipper of the *Argonaut* for almost nine months by now, and had been working drift-nets for herring bait all summer, so I wasn't entirely green, but this fishing was completely different. It took place in the dark, and there would be dozens of boats milling around in all directions with searchlights flashing, looking for the presence of other boats' nets. It seemed that everyone was trying to be in the same place at the same time, and that was usually the place where the most herring would be found! There were pairs of ring-net boats with their big nets trying to locate a shoal so that they could encircle it, and then there would be drift-net boats trying to find a clear space to shoot their own drift-nets. Talk about pandemonium!

When we arrived on that first night on the Whitby herring grounds, Rob Gardner showed me the technique that he had used when he was a Skipper. We would steam about, watching the echo-sounder carefully until we came upon indications of herring. They would always be referred to as "marks". We would then steam directly across the wind following the marks, and measuring the time exactly until we came out of the shoal on the opposite side. We would then turn round again, and steam back half that distance time-wise on a reciprocal course. This would ensure that we were now exactly in the centre of the shoal. We would turn again, and steam straight up-wind until we lost the herring marks on the sounder.

When we did, we would carry on for one more minute before turning exactly down-wind on the opposite course, and start to pay out the nets. This minute in time represented about the length of seven nets. When we came back amongst the herring marks again, we would carry on shooting the nets until we lost the marks completely. When we did, we would immediately stop and try to avoid shooting one more net. Experience had shown Rob Gardner that after leaving the shoal, putting out any more nets would be a waste of time. After a quick cup of tea, the hauling process started immediately.

My time spent at that Whitby herring fishing proved to be invaluable, and all the time I was gaining more and more experience. Although I didn't know it at the time, this was to serve me in good stead soon afterwards. As I said before, it was quite frenetic out on the grounds and no one was taking any prisoners. It was definitely the survival of the fittest, and any decisions had to made instantly, or the opportunity would be lost. I found out that I had a flair for this kind of excitement, and we were doing fairly well, and managing to catch more herring than many of the rest of the fleet. The Whitby fishing was always a short season, and after a successful four weeks, we left for home to prepare the nets for the voyage south to the Great Yarmouth fishing.

After a short spell at home, we sailed in early October. It was a long passage to Great Yarmouth, about three hundred miles. This fishing really was "a different kettle of fish", and the experience that I knew that I lacked was definitely needed here. As a result, for most of the early part of the season we were doing pretty poorly. Talk about stress: this was real stress, and it ended up with me having to visit the doctor to try and get something to relieve the pains in my stomach. After examining me he said that he couldn't find anything organically wrong with me. I told him that I knew what was wrong with me — I was suffering from "herring fever". He just gave me a look as if I was from another planet. This was a well-known disease in the fishing industry that Skippers got from time to time when they weren't catching any herring, and more especially when everyone else was.

This fishing wasn't the same as Whitby, and it wasn't the same as the summer fishing. There were many more boats on the grounds, and securing a berth where the best fishing was to be got wasn't always easy. In addition, the herring would rise to the surface several times in a night, and an experienced Skipper needed to be able to estimate the correct time to haul in the nets.

All the boats would normally start to haul at midnight, and if there weren't enough herring showing in the nets to warrant carrying on, we would stop and lie for a while. Sometimes when we did start again there would be a good catch, but this usually meant that by the time we did get hauled and got into harbour, we would be included in the last "pool", which meant a poorer price for the fish. Worse than that, the three o'clock flag would be probably be hoisted by the time we got the herring discharged, and this meant that no boats could go to sea after that, and we would lose that night's fishing.

All of these things I had to learn the hard way. If I had been more experienced even as a deckhand and able to estimate things better, maybe on a few occasions it would have been better to have kept on hauling, and gone in to land with whatever we caught and obtained the best price on offer. Then we would have got to sea that night again. On reflection, perhaps I was being wrongly advised or even manipulated! One thing I realise now is that we should never ever have "bent on" as it was called, on a Thursday night, because it would invariably mean that you would miss Friday night's fishing. Always an important night's fishing. It's all water under the bridge now I'm afraid, but I never got the chance in the following year to benefit from the lessons that I had learned!

Mid-December came, and the herring were getting very scarce on the local Yarmouth grounds. Quite a few boats, particularly those that had done well, had declared their fishing finished. They had taken on board all their spare nets and were now heading for Scotland, and home for Christmas. We were unfortunately not in a position to do this: we desperately needed more fishing time in order to improve our earning. Along with some of the Cellardyke steam drifters, we headed south to the English Channel, to Dover and Calais and the Sandettie Bank mid-channel grounds.

What I will always remember about the harbour at Dover was the tremendous rise and fall of the tide. At low water during a spring tide, sometimes the boat was so far below the level of the piers that it required a good head for heights to descend the ladders. Also when landing herring at low water, the derrick would hardly reach up to the height of the lorry. That apart, the fishing technique required was now more to my liking. It was more along the lines of the Whitby fishing where we had done so well before — short fleets of nets, and steaming around during the dark hours looking for herring marks on the echo-sounder. I had proved myself at that. I also remember that I had even learned to distinguish the difference between herring marks and pilchard marks and this was very important, because we certainly didn't want any of the latter in our drift-nets.

That very first week down in the Channel, while all the boats were milling around searching for herring, I was lucky enough to come across a huge mark of herring just two or three miles off the port of Calais in France. I have no idea if they are still there, but at that time, there was a long line of buoys running parallel to the coast, and the tide was running in the wrong direction. If we had shot on the herring marks, then we would have been sure to have ended amongst the buoys before we got the nets hauled again, with a disastrous result. We had to have patience and wait until the tide turned. The problem was not to show any of the other boats that we had found these marks. We steamed away a bit, doused all the lights and waited. All's fair in love and war!

When I judged that the tide had turned, we steamed back to where we had seen the herring. I could hardly believe my luck! Nobody around! We quickly picked up the marks again, measured the breath of the shoal, and steamed upwind to find the end of the marks. By this time I had developed my own technique. Instead of steaming up the seven net-lengths as I had been taught, I had started to notice that the last nets that we hauled were usually the best, so now I was steaming up two minutes, or the length of fourteen nets, before turning. Everything went well and the nets were placed exactly where I wanted them. Several boats had noticed us shooting our nets, and had rushed to get down alongside us. They were too late: all the boats steaming up and down had scared the herring and they got nothing.

When we started to haul the nets they were full of herring, and it wasn't long before we were underway for Great Yarmouth with some eighty crans of herring (320 baskets). The weather forecast was very bad and as we had a long way to go, and I had decided to take the passage inside the Goodwin sands. When daylight broke in the morning, we were just passing the South Goodwin lightship, and some of the crew were keen to go alongside and pass over some herring for the crew. I had to point out that we needed all our time to get to Great Yarmouth, so we kept on going.

The Great Yarmouth herring buyers had been notified that we were on our way and that our estimated time of arrival would be about 2030 hours. The weather kept on freshening all day till it had developed into very bad gale. Fortunately the wind was from a southerly direction and we were able to make good time. We were running nearly dead before the weather with the mizzen sail squared right across the boat to help to keep the speed up. With hindsight, perhaps we shouldn't have kept the sail up as long as we did.

Great Yarmouth river entrance is a notoriously bad place to be with the wind on and the tide running from the river, and crossing over the bar can be a very dangerous operation. When we arrived, some of the crew thought that we should not attempt to enter. It certainly didn't look good, but the buyers were all waiting, and I decided we should go in. Something about the greed of gold being greater than the fear of death readily springs to mind. With the Mate standing by to help me with the wheel if needed, and another man watching the throttle, we managed to enter the harbour safely. I have to report from that night that I always remember that my legs turned more than a little bit rubbery during the process.

We got the big price that we were looking for and the herring were sold for more than £8 per cran, earning us over £800 for our catch. This was fabulous money in 1954, and literally turned our voyage to Yarmouth from what was beginning to look like a disastrous one into a success overnight, and it merited a small mention in *Fishing News*.

The sad news that we were to learn on our arrival was that the South Goodwin Lightship had been lost with all hands during the night. It shows just how bad the weather had been, and perhaps we should never have attempted to make that voyage north to Great Yarmouth to land our herring.

After the weather had moderated, we set sail for the English Channel once again, hoping for a repeat of our good fortune. I can't remember all the details, but when we arrived on the fishing grounds we were lucky enough to find another big shoal of herring. After measuring the breadth of the shoal, we steamed upwind to find their extent. This time I decided to experiment a little bit more, and instead of steaming up one minute and seven nets as I had been shown, I decided to carry on up three minutes and the length of twenty-one nets before turning and starting to shoot.

My experiment was successful, and once again we were to net a big catch. This time it was a hundred crans. We again landed the herring in Great Yarmouth, and once again because nearly all the boats had left for home, we got a good price for our catch. These two last landings had virtually turned what was looking like a poor voyage, into a very successful one. Sadly there was to be no repeat. I wanted to return to the English Channel once more, but I was out-voted. All the Fife boats had left for home by this time, and the crew thought that they had been away for long enough, and they wanted to go home as well.

Looking back, it had all been new to me and although I seemed to have learned the trade very quickly, sadly it was to be the very last herring fishing that I would ever attend. Seine-netting for haddock, cod, whiting and flat-fish in the North Sea would be our normal winter fishing from now on, and my newly-found skills and my experiences as a Skipper of a herring drifter would never ever be put to the test again. Even more sad was the fact that within three or four years the herring themselves would completely disappear, and the whole East Anglian fishing voyage along with all its infrastructure would disappear along with them. The Scottish fleet had being going south to fish from Yarmouth for nearly a hundred years, and now it was to come to a complete end.

Early in the New Year, on 15th January 1955, my wife and I were married. It seemed that just after the fleet returned from the Yarmouth fishing it was always the traditional time for herring fishermen to be married, and I was to be no different. We honeymooned in London, and would then have a short break until the start of the long-line fishing in the North Sea at the beginning of March. In addition, I had now moved from my parents' home in St Monans to set up home with my wife in West Anstruther, where we rented one half of my new in-laws' house for the princely sum of one pound per week!

That year was to see the start of a new era as far as catching our own herring bait was concerned. Stocks were declining, and herring had become very scarce in the North Sea, and some nights we were not even catching enough to bait our full stretch of lines. The rest of the boats were having much the same experience. One night we shot our drift-nets as usual after the previous day's lines were safely on board again, and got absolutely no herring at all. This was serious now, and we were just wondering what we should do, when I suddenly had the bright idea that I would contact one of the Norwegian coastal radio stations and ask if they could help. I contacted Stavanger radio and the operator asked me to hang on and he would make some enquiries for me. It wasn't long before he came back and told me that they had plenty of frozen herring at the cold store in Egersund.

As far as I know, up to that time no Scottish fishing boat had ever been into Egersund, and we certainly had no large scale chart on board to guide us in. The entrance is notoriously very tricky with lots of rocks around, and we had to wait until daylight was just breaking so that we could see the rocks and still see the sectored lights. We eventually managed to feel our way into the harbour.

The herring that we purchased were just beautiful. They were big herrings, frozen properly, and they made ideal bait. They were maybe even better than the fresh herring that we were accustomed to using. There had always been a reluctance with North Sea line-men to use what they referred to as "overday's bait" instead of newly-caught herring, but in this situation that we were in, beggars couldn't be choosers. It was certainly far better than no bait at all, and this was beginning to happen far too often.

After we saw how well the frozen herring were fishing, that was the end of the drift-nets, and if we were to be totally honest, I'm sure that no one was sorry. It now became our normal routine to steam straight to Egersund and buy our bait instead of trying to catch them each night. Although I certainly didn't tell any of the other boats my little secret for a while, they were not too long in latching on to this, and some of them were even making the long journey to Norway to buy their bait before they started their trips to Faroe Bank.

As I said before, the *Argonaut* and my job as a fishing Skipper owner were all-consuming, and sometimes I very much allowed my heart to rule my head. One story I remember on that subject was that one morning as I was preparing to leave home in Anstruther to catch the bus for Leuchars railway station, and then after that the train to Aberdeen for the start of another line-fishing trip, the phone rang. It was my father! Did I know that it was a heavy SE gale, and that he had been on the phone to Aberdeen earlier on, and the harbour was closed to all shipping. In his opinion it would be a waste of time travelling to Aberdeen that day, because we wouldn't manage to get out in any case. We argued for some time, and he finally persuaded me to go down to the bus stop, and tell the crew to come off the bus. This I did, and when I returned home I didn't even sit down, I walked backwards and forwards in front of the fire like some animal in a cage, not even bothering to take off my coat!

After tea that night, my wife opened the front door and looked out, and returned to inform me that the weather had changed, and there was not even a breath of wind. That was all I needed: who could I take my anger out on? Who could I blame for not getting away to sea that day? My father of course! I lifted the phone and dialled his number. When he replied, I told him that he had cost me a day's work and that he was never to interfere with me again. After he had apologised, I banged down the phone and immediately felt guilty, because I remembered my early days when I had started with him as a boy and how strong he had been in his heyday as a Skipper of a steam trawler. I did think though that it was a bit strange that he taken all that from me without some reply.

It wasn't to be the end of the matter though, for a few minutes later my phone rang. It was my father again. "David, I have just been sitting here thinking, why didn't you go away today?" I was flabbergasted. "Why didn't I go away today?" I said. "I didn't go away because you stopped me." "Oh well," he said, "in that case I don't think you were very hard to stop. When I was the Skipper of a steam trawler, nobody would ever have stopped me when I wanted to go to sea!" *Touché!* I suppose the truth of the matter was that deep down I had known all along that it was a complete waste of time travelling to Aberdeen if we weren't going to be able to leave the harbour, but I just wouldn't allow myself to admit it.

We certainly did well in our time as line fishermen, there was no doubt about that, but it meant long spells away from home, especially in the summertime. For long periods each year, we would try and get into a routine where we would sail from Aberdeen on a Monday, and land back on a Tuesday, sixteen days later. We would then sail on Thursday again after a day-and-a-half at home, and we would land on a Thursday fifteen days later and be at home for a long weekend. That meant only one weekend at home every five weeks. Perhaps I didn't realise it at the time because my work had started to take over my life, along with the fact that we didn't know anything else, but it was a very hard life, and I don't know how crew members put up with such a punishing routine. Unlike some modern Skippers, there was no shift system in operation, and I was there myself on every single trip, and so were the men who sailed with me for many years.

The most successful trip that I ever saw while long lining, was caught almost by chance. I had been walking down by the harbour in Anstruther between trips, and I had met Jimmy Brunton, a retired former long-line Skipper. He had owned and skippered the steam drifter *Noontide* for many years. He lowered his voice and asked me confidentially if I had ever worked lines on the fifty-odd fathoms depth on the very top of the Faroe Bank. I had better explain that a fathom measures six feet, about two metres. These banks were originally volcanic eruptions, I presume, and they rose almost vertically from the depths, and then started to level out around 100 fathoms in depth. They would then very gradually shoal towards the centre of the bank, before starting gradually to deepen again towards the other side.

After I told Jimmy that I hadn't fished there, he then told me his story. Years ago whilst he had still been a fishing Skipper, they had been shooting their lines one morning in bad weather and they had been forced to maintain a course almost dead before the wind. By accident they had come right up on to this shoal water, and had stopped shooting out any more lines. Two hours later when they started to haul, they found that the ground was so hard and the tide was so strong, that they could hardly get the lines back on board again. Jimmy also told me that they got very good fishing of beautiful fish from the few lines that were on this shoal water. They had apparently never ever been brave enough to try it again.

I was pretty ruthless in those early days, and losing a few lines wasn't going to bother me very much. Although this information that Jimmy Brunton had given me was several years old, and despite the fact that he had warned me to be wary, I was just bursting to get there and try my luck. I decided that on this very next trip

I would make for that shoal water, and shoot the whole fleet of lines there. This we duly did, and sure enough when we saw that some of the dhan-buoys that marked the end of our lines were dipping beneath the water with the strength of the tide, we knew immediately that trouble was brewing. We were going to have a very long, hard struggle to get those lines back on board again.

Struggle we certainly did, and after a long, hard day and night till early next morning, we finally finished hauling. When we tallied up, we found that we had caught the biggest day's catch that most of us had ever seen, mainly consisting of big halibut, thick roker skate, cod and big haddock. All prime fish. To cut the tale short, we fished in that same area on that very hard ground for the whole trip, and got equally good fishing nearly every day. It was very hard work, and needed all my young man's energy to keep persevering. We had many line breakages, which meant that we would often have to run to the opposite end of the lines and haul in reverse. We would get other breaks, and then we would have to grapple the long-lines up from the bottom, perhaps several times, which was not easy on that very hard ground. We eventually got back to Aberdeen with the boat fully loaded with prime fish, which included ten tons or two hundred hundredweight of big halibut, and many tons of cod and large haddock and thick roker skate. All the signs of what had been a virgin fishing ground.

The £3,200 that we earned for that catch doesn't sound like very much fifty-odd years down the line, but in 1958, before inflation had got fully into its stride, I can assure you it represented a great deal of money. It was a catch record that was to stand for many years, and was only surpassed long after I personally had finished with line-fishing.

I mentioned "grappling" or "grading" or "creeping" for broken lines: all terms used in the various fishing ports for recovering lines that had broken away after becoming entangled with various obstructions, and which were now lying on the bottom. It sometimes wasn't easy to recover lost lines in that deep water when the bottom was very hard and where the creepers themselves kept coming fast and wouldn't travel over the ground. Perhaps if the tide was too strong and the boat and creepers would travel too fast over the ground and miss the lost lines completely, they would have to be brought up and the whole process repeated. Perhaps the weather was too bad and it wasn't easy for men to sit on the rails of these open-decked boats and hang on to the heavily weighted creepers. It was an art form and some Skippers became very good at it, but only with the help of the crew member who was holding the line attached to the creepers. Some of those experienced men could tell exactly what was happening down there simply by feel, and would supply the Skipper with all the information he needed to keep the boat and creepers travelling properly across the lines at the correct speed.

This was all before the days of Decca navigators and a long time before the days of GPS navigators, and recovering lost lines was a laborious progress. You would always have a dhan buoy with an electric light and a string of buoys rigged ready and attached to a basket filled with thick line much longer then the depth of the water you were working on, and attached to a heavy anchor. If the line came fast, and you eventually broke the line, you would drop the marker buoy as quickly as possible to mark the position. You would then have to steam to the other end of your whole fleet of lines to find the original buoy that you had dropped when starting to shoot in the morning. This was so that you could haul back in the opposite direction. This could maybe mean steaming for five or six miles. If you broke first thing in the morning when starting to haul, it maybe meant a journey of ten miles to the other end.

After recovering the starting end of the lines, sometimes you would maybe come fast to the bottom again, and you would stop on the point of breaking the line and attach another buoy to the line. Then the creepers would have to go over and try to get hold of the lines. Sometimes when you did get hold of them you would break the line trying to lift them off the bottom. If you did get them up first time, you would have to attach another dhan buoy and anchor to the long stretch of line and then haul back the short distance to the buoy that was attached to the second fast line. When they were recovered, the dhan-buoy attached to the main lines would have then to be recovered and hauling restarted. It was a long, laborious process and patience and perseverance were a virtue. It was absolutely no use getting angry. No matter how tired you were, bearing in mind it could well be the twelfth consecutive day's work of the trip, and you could be pretty exhausted, there was only one way to recover those lost lines, and you just had to get on with it!

As the halibut got fished out for the season, and the other fish became fewer as well, all the boats would fall into a routine whereby they would start their trip at Faroe Bank, looking for a few high-value fish. If they judged that they weren't catching enough, they would maybe make a shift further west to the Bill Bailey bank or even Lousy Bank. What we would usually do if that didn't work out was to steam another two hundred miles further west to Rosemary bank to the north of Rockall. After perhaps a day's work there, we would move to Rockall bank itself, and then we would work all the way down the west side of the bank until we had filled up the fish room with mainly ling and skate. These were all low-value fish, and we needed a full load plus the halibut caught on the Faroe Banks to make a profitable trip.

Later on in the summer when the halibut had completely taken off we would sail from Aberdeen and head direct to Rockall bank with the sole intention of filling up the boat with these low-value fish as quickly as possible. Our favourite spot was a bank known to us as the forty-five miles bank which was to the south west of the rock itself. There was always plenty of big ling and skate there at that time. We would also fish further out towards the seventy-five miles bank and the ninety-five miles bank where on occasions in the early days I have seen very good halibut fishing. Maybe after only three days' fishing, we would be heading for Fleetwood with thirty-five to forty tons of fish on board. After landing our fish there, we would take on ice, fuel, fresh bait and stores, and sail immediately for Rockall bank again. We had no refrigeration in those days, and the fish holds weren't even insulated, and carrying enough ice for those big loads of fish was

Argonaut I entering Fleetwood harbour to land a catch of fish from Rockall.

always a problem. I remember on one of these occasions when we had landed in Fleetwood, we had loaded so much ice on board that the boat was considerably down by the head. Someone suggested to me that it would be better if we left the harbour as quickly as possible, before someone from the Board of Trade noticed and made us take some of the ice out.

I remember another trip after we had landed in Fleetwood and we were unable to get bait there. I had phoned and ordered bait to be delivered from Aberdeen to Portpatrick harbour. I always remember that because we had some time to kill we dropped into Ramsey Harbour on the Isle of Man because I knew that the famous TT motorcycle races would be passing through there the next day. When the boat refloated in the morning we sailed for Portpatrick, and oh boy did I get a shock when we arrived! I had never ever been in there before, and when we entered in the dark in the middle of the night, there was hardly enough room to turn the boat. We managed of course, and loaded the bait and headed out into the Atlantic for Rockall bank again.

When I think back to that period in the early 1950s, and the boats that we had then, they really weren't fit enough for what we were all trying to do with them. They were excellent sea boats of course and had reliable Gardner engines, but after all they were only open-decked boats and just seventy-odd feet long. They really were far too small to be loaded so heavily, and in truth they weren't really man enough for what was being asked of them.

During my first four seasons as a line-boat Skipper on *Argonaut*, I mentioned before that we even had a wooden wheelhouse before we eventually replaced it with one made of steel. We also persevered with the big herring hatch on the foredeck for many years after we had long finished catching herring. We just spread a tarpaulin over the hatches and fastened it down with wedges. None of the boats at that time had steel bulkheads or proper insulation and when we were fully loaded with fish, why the bulkheads didn't collapse, I will never know. It gives me the shivers sometimes when I think about it. Why some of those boats didn't get into serious trouble in all the years that we were working those deep western waters I will never know, but fortunately it didn't ever happen!

The very fact that the whole fleet of Anstruther, Peterhead and Fraserburgh boats, which were long-line fishing in those western waters around that time, were all considerably under-powered with only 152-hp main engines maybe had something to do with it. They really didn't have enough power to do much damage to themselves. Inflatable rubber dinghies and other life-saving apparatus were not compulsory at that time, so needless to say we had none of these items on board, and there were certainly no helicopters at our disposal to bail us out if we needed help. The problem with long-line fishing was that once you put the twelve-mile stretch of lines on to the sea bed, it could perhaps take sixteen hours or more to get them back. During that time, the weather could change dramatically and very often did.

Another story that I must tell is about my very first line-fishing trip to Iceland. After sailing from Aberdeen, along with two Cellardyke boats, *William Wilson* and *Silver Chord*, we had arrived at Faroe bank at much the same time and were all waiting to shoot our lines in the same place in the morning. I knew it was going to be one of those days right from the start. No one would give an inch and the three boats ended up shooting their lines almost down on top of each other. To make matters worse, the weather soon deteriorated into a south-easterly gale.

Hauling back that day was not easy, and meant that we were continually having to dip our lines under other boats. By the time we got hauled, I can always remember it was well into the next morning and it was a Sunday. All this happened nearly fifty years ago, but I can remember as if it was yesterday. We didn't catch a lot of fish that day: the weather was bad, and our spirits were at a very low ebb indeed.

When we eventually finished hauling back our lines, I happened to say in an unguarded moment, "I think we will go across to Iceland." One of the crew, who really ought to have known better, immediately challenged me by saying that I was frightened to go to Iceland! "Do you think so?" I replied. "Square the mizzen-sail across the boat, and then we will see." This was the same boat that a few years earlier was considered too small to fish at Faroe bank, and now we were on our way to Iceland. We set off at full speed before the wind, away into the north-west. It was definitely the line of least resistance after the long, difficult day that we had just put in, and it was fine to get the watch set and crawl into our warm beds without worrying to much about the consequences.

After a few hours' sleep, I awoke and got up feeling refreshed and then immediately an awful feeling hit me: what had I done? I had never been to Iceland before, and for that matter, neither had any of the crew. I didn't even know if we

Winning isn't everything

were carrying enough fuel on board to get us back to Aberdeen. We only carried 950 gallons at best, which would hardly last one of the new modern trawlers for a day, and coupled with that, any fisherman reading this story will find this fact hard to believe, but I didn't even have a fishing chart for Icelandic waters on board. All I had was a Consol chart for that whole western area which didn't have any depth of water or bottom information on it and didn't even show the Icelandic coastline. By good fortune it had a dotted outline, which I presumed was meant to indicate the 100-fathom line around Iceland.

We carried on steaming all that day, and then I had a stroke of luck. I could now hear the Skippers of two Aberdeen-owned line boats starting to chat on the radio. We had a direction finder on board, so I was able to take a bearing of them and head in their general direction. I decided not to contact them at this point, and kept my own counsel for several reasons. One of them being that I certainly didn't want to reveal the extent of my ignorance.

Just before the next morning dawned the weather had eased up somewhat, and the echo-sounder showed that the water was starting to shoal. Soon it had come from being very deep water to what I presumed was the 100-fathom edge. Perfect timing! At that time however, long before digital readouts, the Kelvin Hughes echo-sounders were notorious for showing a false echo which was the true depth plus a further 350 fathoms, and you had to be very careful not to get caught out. Several boats had made this mistake in the past, and had ended up shooting their lines into very deep water with dire results.

It was in the days some time before the first of the three Cod Wars between Iceland and the UK, so there was not a problem with that, and we could work wherever we wanted with out infringing any laws. Whilst the crew were cutting up the bait and getting things ready, I manoeuvred around to satisfy myself we were on the right depth, and we started in the usual manner when newly arriving at a different fishing ground. We shot a few lines in 130 fathoms, then some in 125 fathoms, then some in 120 and so on and so forth, gradually shoaling the water, till we finished shooting the last of our lines up on the "flat" in 60 fathoms.

When we started to haul two hours later, I couldn't believe my luck. *Eureka*. I have found it. There was a fish on almost every hook, and all prime fish at that, including quite a few halibut. Alas, when we hauled out into the deeper water later in the day, the amount of fish we were catching grew much less, and the quality grew poorer. I wasn't unduly worried though, because now I knew exactly the depth of water that the best fishing was to be had, and tomorrow would be another day.

That was how the fishing generally worked on Faroe Bank. If the best fishing was to be found, for example, on 102 fathoms on one side of the bank then it would be near enough on 102 fathoms on the other side. When we were hauling back the lines, we would always note the exact depth of water that the best fishing was coming from, especially the depth of water where almost every halibut was being caught. We were very fastidious about that because it was very important, and for the rest of the trip, we would then concentrate on that depth of water right around the bank. It was all to do with the water temperature and the feeding. On with the Iceland story. The next morning I knew that I had to be very careful because we were now going to shoot our lines on the "flat"' and this could be Grimsby and Hull trawler territory. All went well however; no other boats were to be seen, and for the next three days we got very good fishing indeed. The fourth day was different however, because half-way through the day a trawler appeared on the scene.

As I said, this was some time before the start of the three so-called Cod Wars, and he must have found this good fishing same as ourselves, because he was soon to be joined by many of his friends. We lost a few lines to these trawlers before we finally got finished hauling, and I knew it was now time for us to clear out. Right had to give way to might, and we certainly could not compete with those big trawlers!

Now it was time to contact my fellow countrymen from Aberdeen, the Skippers that I had been listening to for the last three days. They were Skippers who had spent all their lives long-line fishing mainly at Iceland, but they were more than a little inclined to patronise a young fishermen from Cellardyke like myself, who only fished with lines in the summer for about eight months of the year. Little did they know that we had only been on the grounds for a few days, and already we had the boat half full of fish. "Come away up beside us, ma loon," they told me, "and take a berth down alongside us in the morning." I needed no second invitation.

Next day there they both were, lying far too long in the morning for my liking, and there we were, with the bait all cut up ready, and me jumping from one foot to the other, anxious to make a start. We just had to wait until they were ready. We shot our lines down along with them, and although we got very good fishing, surprise, surprise, for whatever reason, they both cleared out that night and left us to fish there for several more days until it was time to go home. They will probably have all passed on now, long ago, but I bless them for their concerns.

The engineer was already starting to warn me that we might not have enough fuel to get home, but I wasn't all that worried, because we would be passing the Faroe Islands, and I thought that we might go in there and top up the tanks. When we eventually did get to the Faroes, after weighing up the situation I thought we might manage to get as far as Scrabster in the North of Scotland. Then I thought we might get through the Pentland Firth, and go into Wick. To cut the story short we finally managed to get as far as Fraserburgh and got our fuel there. We were horrified to find out how little fuel we had left. The tanks were almost empty! These eight-cylinder 152-hp Gardner engines were certainly very economical, and their fuel consumption rate was amazing, but the 950 gallons that we carried still wasn't much to last us for a fifteen-day trip to Iceland.

It was about this time that our daughter had been born, and my wife and I had moved into our first real house. Like so many others at the time we moved into to an excellent three-bedroomed council house at 8 Mayview Road in Cellardyke, and for my sins I had now become an adopted "Dyker". It was a fine big two-storey house, one of a set which had been originally built as fishermen's houses with space for fishing gear. We had very good neighbours in that street who were nearly all great-line fishermen, so much so, that the street was to earn the nickname of "Halibut Avenue". We were to spend the next ten years in that house.

We didn't return again to fish at Iceland for a long time after that first exploratory voyage, simply because we were doing so well elsewhere that we didn't really need to go, plus the fact that the seventy-two hours that we needed to steam to Iceland was a long boring journey.

A few years further on we had an Aberdeen fisherman named Alex Bruce crewing on board *Argonaut* with us for the summer season. Alex had been a former great-line Skipper, and during this one particular trip, he asked me if I had ever been to Iceland. I told him that we had, and I also told him that although we had got a very good trip on that occasion, I wasn't just exactly sure where we had been working. He told me that he knew the grounds at the south end of Iceland very well, and that when he had been a Skipper, he had always got good fishing there about this time of the year. I think he must have been planning all this, because he said that by the time that we had landed in Aberdeen and returned to sea again it would be a neap tide, or a "dull" tide as we called it, and would be ideal for what he had in mind. "Right," I told him, "that's good, we will go to Iceland next trip, and if we don't get any fish, then it will be you to blame." He told me that he wasn't at all worried about that and that he was quite confident that we would do well.

After we had made our landing, and had our few days at home, we sailed from Aberdeen bound for Iceland. This time we were well prepared, we had four forty-five gallon drums of diesel fuel oil lashed to the front of the wheelhouse and hose connections to run it down into the fuel tanks. Big deal! Talk about going to sea "schooner rigged". This extra fuel was supposed to be our safety-net to get us home again.

Half way between Faroe and Iceland we met the Peterhead-owned Aberdeen line boat *Caledonia* going in the opposite direction. The Skipper called me on the radio, and asked me where I thought I was going. He told me that they had tried everywhere, and that there was no fish on the south Icelandic line grounds, and he urged me to turn back. He said that he was on his way back to Faroe Bank area to finish his trip. I called my friend Mr Bruce and asked him what he thought of this situation. "Never mind him," he said, "just keep on going." So that was just what we did!

The first fishing ground that we arrived at was usually protected by very strong tides, and could only be worked during neap tides, and that was why we were there at that time. My pilot showed me where we should shoot, and on what depth of water, and advised me that we should only shoot fourteen lines instead of our usual fleet. I told him that I couldn't do this as this felt to me as only being a half day's work, and that we would shoot our normal thirty or thirty-five lines. He told me that I could please myself, but he had learned from long experience that if we did, we would get no fish from the first fifteen lines that we would haul. The fish would all be eaten by the sea lice on the bottom. As usual we shot the full fleet of lines and it was amazing, he was absolutely right, it was a waste of time and all we got back were the heads and carcases of the fish. On the second half of the lines that we hauled, again just as he had forecast, we got excellent fishing. I suspect more than a few Aberdeen long-liners had experienced all that in the past, because it was amazing that he could be so accurate.

Next day we moved west to a new spot on a similar corner of the next "flat" and now he said I could shoot all the lines that I wanted to, because there would be no sea lice. We got another good day's fishing. That night we moved again further west to another new spot, and more good fishing. Every day we shifted grounds, and every day we got good fishing. We were back in Aberdeen in less than a fortnight, and made the second biggest trip that I ever earned up to that time as a great-line Skipper. It was amazing. If we had listened to this other boat that we had met on our way to Iceland, we might have turned around and gone back to the Faroe Islands. It made me wonder why Alex Bruce was no longer the Skipper of his own boat!

Next trip we set sail again for Iceland and once again it was a neap tide or a "dull" tide as we say here in the East Neuk. I was quite a quick learner, and now I was the expert! There were no other line-boats in the area, and we simply started at the same place as on the previous trip, and made the same moves each night that we had made before. We got good fishing on each day. Once again we were back to land our fish in Aberdeen within the fortnight, and made another fine trip.

After a couple of days at home, we once more set sail for another trip to Iceland, but it was now getting near to the end of September, and a little late to be so far North in such a relatively small boat, where the weather could suddenly turn nasty. It certainly did just that! One morning we arose to haul the lines, and it was now a strong gale of wind. When I went into the wheelhouse and looked at the compass, I could not believe my eyes. Instead of the wind being southerly as I had half expected it to be, it was now blowing hard from the west. I knew that instead of hauling the lines up through the wind in a comfortable fashion, we would now have to haul them broadside on to the wind, and from the lee side. The very worst way!

The wind freshened and freshened all day long, and by the time we had got half the lines hauled it was now getting very near to being a storm and I knew it was time to stop hauling before someone got washed overboard. We quickly bent on an anchor and a dhan-buoy with an electric light on to the end of the remaining lines, and started to prepare the boat for a long night of very bad weather.

The mizzen-sail was set properly, and because we had no automatic pilot in those days, it would only be that big sail that would keep the boat's head up through the wind and enable us to survive the gale. All the baskets containing the lines were lashed down securely, along with the wooden lifeboat that we carried,

Winning isn't everything 119

You must remember that the *Argonaut* of that era was only 72 feet long, and a completely open-decked boat with no whale back.

All that night, I kept in close contact with a few of the big, modern Aberdeen diesel trawlers that were in the immediate area, and they couldn't understand how we were managing to keep out of trouble. The wind was so strong at times, and the swell so big, that they themselves were just lying over the broadside, and doing the best they could to survive. I was well aware that the wind couldn't possibly keep blowing at that strength for ever, but I can tell you that for a long while that night it was just about all that we could handle!

By the next afternoon it began to moderate very quickly, and now we were starting to think about finding the dhan-buoys on our lines again. We did have a Decca navigator on board by this time, but its accuracy was almost useless being so far north from the transmitting stations. I knew the exact depth of water that the lines were lying on, and by following the edge, we started looking for the dhan that we had dropped when we had stopped hauling. It wasn't to be seen, and we had to carry on to where we had started to shoot originally on the previous morning.

We were lucky enough to find the dhan, and managed to recover the rest of the lines which took us nearly all night to haul. Because they had been in the water for so long, and some of the hooks still had bait on them, we were lucky because we almost got two days' fishing in one. It was amazing how quickly we could change from just trying to survive, to wondering how many fish were on the lines!

Incidentally, that was when we all saw something that any fisherman will find almost unbelievable. Whilst we were hauling the last line we could not see the buoy attached to the ends, although it should have been floating just alongside the boat. The dhan-buoys of the day were just wooden poles with cork floats on them, and the height of the swell on the previous night must have been so big, that somehow or other it must have pulled the dhan down, and "drowned" it. It had sunk all the way to the bottom and we had to haul it up! I had heard people speak of this phenomenon before, but this was certainly the first time I had ever witnessed it for myself. Considering the strength of weather that it took to make it happen, I don't think I ever wanted to see it again!.

In 1962, after I had spent about eight years as a line-fisherman, my father was now pressurising me to give up long-line fishing, and to prosecute seine-set fishing in the North Sea all year round. I was finding it very hard to agree, because I really loved long-line fishing and the excitement of fishing for halibut. What I would usually do towards the end of each February in order to save any argument, was after we had landed our last seine-net trip for the season in Aberdeen, we would come straight home to Anstruther without phoning him and put all the seine-net gear ashore. He would get to hear about it eventually.

This year he came along from his home in St Monans and his first question was to ask what we had earned on our last trip at seine-netting. After I told him, he put on his most sarcastic voice and said to me, "Do you know what I think about you, David? I don't think that you can count! It seems to me that you are one of the few people that I know who can make any money seine-net fishing in the winter, and yet when the spring and the better weather comes, and the summer fishing is about to start, you rush off to the Faroe Bank and the great-lines. All I am going to say to you is that no matter how much you earn for your first trip long-lining, it won't be as much as you had on your last trip at the seine-net."

Sadly, he never was to find out if he was right or wrong. We were fortunate on that first trip of the season to get very good fishing, and caught a very quick trip of fish including a fine catch of halibut. We curtailed the length of our trip and sailed for home to get a good price. There were no mobile phones in those days for people to contact home and get all the news. Unless you put in a 'link call' through one of the coastal radio stations you just arrived when you arrived. Many a time I said goodbye to my wife and family, and sixteen days later practically turned up on the doorstep unannounced.

Fishing boats are always berthed in these main coastal fishmarkets strictly in order of arrival, and it was very important for the great-line boats that they got into Aberdeen early to secure a good berth. The main reason for this was that it enabled them to get their halibut properly weighed, and laid out in an orderly manner on the market floor. It all took time, and also, because the catches were auctioned in strict rotation, it was important that they got their fish sold as early in the morning as possible to enable the merchants to catch the railway transport to their customers in the south. It was very important for the line-boats to maximise the value of their catches.

When we arrived in Aberdeen that morning from that first trip of the season, my brother Robert and I decided to go home for the day and travel back up in the early morning by car to unload our catch. No one else was interested in coming with us, so immediately we got moored up we rushed to the station to catch the train. We had left instructions for a taxi to be waiting for us at Leuchars railway junction, but instead of a taxi, we found my wife and my brother Robert's wife waiting to tell us the sad news that our father had died only that very morning.

It was 2nd May 1962 and he had died during the night from a heart attack aged only 59 years. He had spent nearly eleven years of being virtually an invalid, after he had retired from going to sea. It was such a shock for me that I wondered if I would ever be able to fish the same again. My father had always been my hero, and although I very seldom ever took it, it would be hard to contemplate the future without his advice and counselling. The funny thing was that that very summer would indeed be the final year of great-line fishing for us, and the end of the first part of my career as a Skipper. After eight seasons, I finally took heed of the message that my father had been trying to get over to me for a long time, and I was never to see another hook ever baited in anger again.

It seemed strange that the very next year, in April 1963, for first time in my eight years as a Skipper we were not to be off to the Faroe Islands for the arrival of the halibut on to the shallow waters of the Faroe Bank. I think maybe the main reason that I decided to move away from line-fishing, was more for practical reasons rather than because of my father's advice. The boat was now nearly ten years old, and she had been very hard driven and fully loaded most of the time, and by now her keel was partly hogged and we were having a hard time keeping her watertight. I don't think she was ever designed to do the work that she had done, and maybe the White Fish Authority specifications to which she had been constructed possibly weren't heavy enough in the first place. Whatever it was, I felt that she was getting past her best and that she wasn't going to see me through the rest of my career.

Reluctantly we were now also beginning to realise that we would need a new boat in the near future. It was obvious that this one wasn't going to last for ever, and I knew that something would have to be done about it sooner rather than later. I was looking for some reassurance from someone to help me to make up my mind. I made an appointment to meet Dr Bennet Rae, the head of the Marine Laboratory in Aberdeen, to ask his opinion about the prospects for the future. As I might have expected from a marine scientist, I got no real encouragement, and I left our meeting probably no wiser than I was before I had gone in.

On the way out of the building though, by sheer coincidence I happened to meet one of the men that I knew, who worked for the Marine Laboratory as a sampler in the fish market. A lot of stock assesment is done by monitoring the fish actually being landed, and this was one of his main jobs each morning. They would measure the size of a sample of the fish, and then they would remove the otolith or earbone, from which they could determine the age of the fish by counting the rings on the bone as on the rings on a tree.

This man asked me what had brought me down to the Marine Laboratory on that morning, and I told him that I was considering building a new boat, and that I had been down to see Dr Rae. "What did he tell you?" he asked, and I told him that I hadn't been told too much. "David," he said, "go and build your new boat. I have just been to sea on the Fisheries Research Vessel doing their annual spring research cruise, and the scientists are all very excited. In fact they are all saying that they have never seen so many young immature haddock in all their careers." It was a lucky chance meeting for me, and this was all the encouragement that I needed. I took his advice, and immediately went ahead with the new boat. His advice turned out to be absolutely correct, and as a result, it put us in the right place at the right time with a brand new boat.

You have to remember that this was another era, and I was a very careful young man. Although we were doing quite well, I didn't want to lose all the progress that I had made in my life by making a wrong decision. In spite of all that I had been told about the new, huge year class of haddock, I still had some reservations about building this new boat. The first plan that we submitted to the White Fish Authority was so ridiculous that I can't believe that we were even contemplating it. It was an application for a grant to build a new hull only, and to remove everything from the old boat and reinstall it on the new hull and then taking the old hull to the beach and letting it break up. I can still remember the surveyor of the day telling me that it was probably the daftest idea that he had ever heard in his life, and that we would very likely end up renewing everything anyway. He was probably correct, and his advice was for us to forget our original plan and to sell the old boat and build a completely new boat from scratch, which we did. I don't know if I was ever really completely serious about the first project but it would surely have been a big mistake if we had gone ahead with the idea. All I remember was, that we didn't want anyone to buy the old boat after us, and be disappointed with their purchase.

Although we originally sold the boat to Ireland for conversion to a yacht, that didn't happen, and it wasn't too long before she found her way back into the industry again. The very thing we hadn't wanted to happen. I was contacted by Skipper Owner John Warnock of Kilkeel in Northern Ireland who was interested in her, and I had shared her history and put him fully in the picture regarding her condition. He was determined to buy her. He renamed her *Fisher Lad*, and when I spoke to him several years later, he assured me she was "as tight as a drum." I must confess that I was amazed. Fishing for prawns and herring in the sheltered waters of the Clyde and the Irish Sea must have prolonged her life, and she was to last almost another thirty years under her new owners before finally being decommissioned.

People reading this will be surprised at my cautionary approach about building a new boat, but you have to bear in mind that this was still 1963, and the heady days of the late 1960s, 70s and the 80s were still in the future. It was a euphoric period in the industry, when, with the help of various government grants, some Skippers like myself were replacing their boats every few years. This was still the era in which, when somebody built a new boat, they assumed that it would be the family boat for almost the rest of their working lives.

Fortunately for us, this huge 1962–63 haddock year class that the scientists had recorded was to be the start of the historic "gadoid explosion". We were to witness the birth of the biggest year class of haddock in human memory ever to be born in the North Sea, and here I was at 33 years of age, just about the right age to take full advantage of it. I had ten years' experience at working the offshore grounds mainly as a line-fisherman, and now I was soon to have a new boat which was to be bigger, more powerful, and faster than the normal, and I certainly had all the energy and the ambition to take advantage of that! The new boat was to be designed by my uncle, Bruce Smith, and she was to be built by his brother, my Uncle Philip, at the yard of Smith and Hutton's in Anstruther just as our first boat had been exactly ten years earlier.

It was a lucky decision for me perhaps to give up line-fishing when we did, and my father had been correct all along, because 1963 was now to see us fully committed to seine-netting the whole year round. As I said, this was the start of the so called "gadoid explosion" in the North Sea, and every boat was soon landing record catches of haddock with the inevitable result that the market price collapsed. Whole catches were sometimes left unsold, and were taken away for reduction to meal and oil. The Scottish fisherman's traditional answer to cheap fish has always been to land more, and this year was to be no different!

I decided that I had had enough of this, and thought that we would try something different by sailing round to the hake grounds off the west coast of Scotland and base ourselves at Oban. When we set off, we didn't even have a chart for the south end of the Minches, but it was the summertime, and we managed in some way or other to feel our way down to the Skerryvore lighthouse grounds where most of the boats were fishing.

I had acquired a bit of a reputation as a successful fisherman in the North Sea by this time and it had followed me around. We hadn't even had our first haul completed, when someone was kind enough to inform me that this was a different type of fishing from the North Sea, and that we wouldn't be able to catch hake in competition with the boats with the slightly bigger horsepower and also the boats with the variable pitch propellers. I didn't say much, and although I hadn't fished this area before, and had absolutely no information about the grounds, I had enough confidence in myself to believe that this wouldn't be the case, and that I would quickly find my feet.

I was to be proved correct, because before that first summer had finished, we eventually caught the largest individual haul of hake that anyone had seen that whole year, and before the end of the season we were also to land the all-time record catch of hake in Oban. I have absolutely no idea if this record still stands, but I am confident that it does.

This record catch was made mainly by good fortune, and of course a good deal of perseverance. At that time the Scottish inshore fleet fishing on the west coast didn't work at the weekends, although we sometimes did in the North Sea. I had been informed quite forcibly when we had arrived in the area that these inshore grounds had to be rested and that they wouldn't stand up to boats fishing at weekends. I acknowledged that fact, and played by the local unwritten rules and had fished faithfully along with the rest of the fleet all that summer, and had gone home at the end of each week like everyone else. We were doing very well.

Now it was September, and the new boat was almost ready, and was scheduled to be launched in Anstruther in the middle of the following week. I decided that we would keep playing the game and that we would go out to St Kilda and fish for haddock and megrims over the weekend. When we got through Pabbay Sound in the Outer Hebrides it was a strong north-west gale, and the weather was so bad that I knew we were just wasting our time trying to go any further. I knew that when we eventually got to St Kilda we wouldn't be able to work anyway. Reluctantly we were forced to turn back.

Where would we go to fish for the next three days? I had tried my best to stick to the understanding of no fishing on the local grounds during the weekends, but the weather was against us, and we had to be home for Wednesday and the launch of the new boat. I decided that I would try and get down to the Dhube Artach grounds before daylight and try there. Those were the days some time before power blocks had been developed for hauling the nets, and the weather was almost too bad for us to work even there. We were just able to manage. The hake fishing got better as the days went on, which was usually the case with a westerly gale, and we were able to gather a record catch during the next three days.

The dilemma facing us in the building of our new boat was choosing the type of engine to be installed. Up until that time, the engines that were most favoured by Scottish fishermen were either a Kelvin diesel or a Gardner diesel, the same as we already had in our present boat. They had been proven over the years to be by far the most reliable, particularly the Gardner. Many fishermen had already found out to their cost that if they chose some other make of engine apart from these two that I have mentioned, it was almost a recipe for disaster. In fact, so reluctant were Scottish fishermen to bypass these two types of engines with their proven track records, that many fishermen who would have maybe liked to build bigger boats, deliberately limited the size to suit the power ranges available from these two manufacturers.

By 1963 things were beginning to change, and so-called inshore fishermen were now starting to venture further afield. It was obvious that there was now a need for larger boats. The Bergius Company from Dobbie's Loan in Glasgow had realised this, and were now offering more powerful ranges of their Kelvin engines. The Gardner Company which was without doubt nearly always most people's first choice, were standing in the way of progress for the Scottish fleet at that time. Either they did not have the technical knowledge to increase the horsepower of their engines, or else they could not or did not seem to want to do the development work on turbo-charging. All they had to offer was the adding of more cylinders and slightly increasing the revolutions. This was definitely not an option, as the Gardner engines were already too long in size and taking up far too much of the engine room as it was. They did eventually offer a twin package of two engines standing side by side driving through a single gearbox, but this didn't really find favour with Scottish fishermen.

The new boat that we were now building was to be 80 feet in length, and as such was slightly bigger than the normal at that time. As I said, Kelvin had just introduced a new range of more powerful engines at that time, so we had initially ordered a Kelvin diesel. One cold autumn night after the construction of the new boat had already started, I received a visit from a young engine salesman from the Caledonian Tractor Company near Glasgow called Raymond Munroe. I was determined that I wasn't going to invite him in to my house, for we had already decided on the type of engine that we were installing, and I kept him standing on the doorstep for so long, that he was embarrassed and I was embarrassed. I finally relented, and invited him in.

He was a good salesman with full confidence in his product. Before he finally left my house that night around midnight, he had practically convinced me that the ideal engine for the new boat should be an American-made Caterpillar marine engine. I told him that I was very impressed with all that he was telling me, but, because I had to confess that I had never heard of a Caterpillar marine engine until that time, and I would have to make an awful lot of enquiries for myself before I finally made up my mind. I was very well aware of all the pitfalls of installing a completely new type of engine, which in the end could prove to be unreliable and end up costing us a lot of money.

In those days, there was a large fleet of Swedish herring trawlers landing into Aberdeen almost daily, and as far as the North Sea was concerned they were far and away the most progressive fishermen of the day. I remember that one of my favourite sayings at that time was that what the Swedes did one year, the Danes did the next, and we did the following year. I don't think I was too far away from the truth.

The Whyte family were running a well-known fish-selling company in Aberdeen at that time, and they employed a man named Asser as an interpreter and to look after these Swedish trawlers who mostly were their customers. I knew that he was the man that I should speak to, and I asked him if he knew of any Swedish fisherman who had a Caterpillar engine installed in his boat. He told me that he did, and that furthermore this particular fisherman that he had in mind was now having it taken out to replace it with a much more powerful version from the same makers. I knew that this was the Skipper that I had to contact. I wrote him a letter, and he replied telling me that he had had his first Caterpillar engine for four years, and that he was now installing a bigger one and that he could think of no better engine. That was all I needed to convince me. I immediately cancelled the Kelvin engine, and ordered a Caterpillar of 320-hp, more than double the capacity of the Gardner engine that we had at present.

I am not quite sure whether that particular engine was the first Caterpillar to be ordered for a fishing boat in the UK, or the first one to be installed. Either way I believe it was a very fortuitous meeting for me with that young salesman that night, because we would always have a Caterpillar engine on all the boats that we owned after that, and they would all give excellent service.

The new Caterpillar turbo-charged engine took a bit of getting used to at first, because it was now running at twice the revolutions of its predecessors, and it was also more than a good bit noisier! In a way though, it was to open up the flood gates for the introduction of reliable, modern high-speed diesel engines into the Scottish fleet. Fishermen could now more or less build any size of boat they required, along with any size of engine that they required, and not be constrained by the power range of the engines that they had always been used to.

Argonaut II was a forerunner in the Scottish seine-net fleet at the time with quite a few innovations. In addition to being, at eighty feet, bigger and faster than the normal type of seine-net fishing boat, and fitted with the new, more powerful Caterpillar engine, she was also fitted with a Norwegian Liaaen-type controllable pitch propeller. She was also fitted with hydraulic steering gear, and that in itself was an innovation.

You have to remember that this was still 1964, and it was still some four or five years before the very first hydraulic seine-winch was introduced by the Northern Gear and Tool Company from Arbroath. It was still the era of geared belt-driven winches The idea of having a variable pitch propeller was to give us more flexibility in our towing speeds in all weather conditions, whilst maintaining a constant engine and winch speed. I must say that it all worked very well.

Argonaut II was also fitted with hydraulic load cells on the fairleads leading on to the winch. They were to measure the loads on the seine ropes on both sides individually. This pressure could then be read from gauges in the wheelhouse, and enabled us to set our towing speeds to suit all kinds of situations. We would now also be able to tell almost immediately if we had encountered a snag with the gear.

These load cells had just been newly developed by the Industrial Development Unit of the White Fish Authority at Hull, and they worked perfectly. However they were very soon to be superseded when hydraulic seine winches were eventually developed, and fishermen very quickly realised that the pressure gauges on the new winches were providing them with exactly the same information.

There was another story that I recall from the building of the second *Argonaut* which was something similar to that of the new engine. We had originally ordered a Kelvin Hughes MS 29 echo-sounder to be installed because that was the best and most reliable instrument of the day. The Kelvin Hughes Company had served the Scottish fishing industry well, and some years earlier they had been the very first company to introduce a depth-recorder where the soundings were recorded on wet paper instead of on to a cathode-ray screen.

Going back a few years to 1947, I remember all this very well because I had just started as a seventeen-year-old deckhand learner with my father on the steam trawler *Cairnburn* from Granton. The Marconi company had just purchased fifty of these new machines from Kelvin Hughes and had then installed them on a rental basis on to various trawlers. My father's boat was one of them. When anything went wrong with the machine, I was usually the first person that my dad turned to, in order to try and get it working again.

Anyway the story was that whilst our new boat was being built, I had met my friend David Wood who was now working as an agent for British Ropes, and who had been in his day a very successful herring ring-net Skipper. David always had his ear close to the ground regarding new developments, and he asked me what kind of fish-finder I was installing in the new boat. "Fish-finder?" I replied, "I don't really know all that much about them." Like all seine-net fishermen at that time, all we were mainly concerned about was the ability of the machine to accurately distinguish hard ground from soft ground, and of course, the ability to record pelagic fish echoes

He told then me that he had heard on the grapevine that a newly developed cathode-ray fish-finder, better known as a *Fischlupe*, was an absolute must for displaying fish echoes close to the bottom. He thought that I should be installing one. They were produced by the German firm Electroacustic, and the firm of Woodson's in Aberdeen were their agents. That was enough for me, and I called Woodson's immediately and ordered the new machine.

After thanking me for the order, they then dropped the bombshell. They told me that the Kelvin Hughes sounder and Electroacustic's *Fischlupe* both operated on the same frequency, and that they would not be compatible, and that their signals would interfere with each other. When I asked how I could resolve this, they told me I could also install an Electroacustic echo-sounder as well as the fishfinder. Now I had a problem: the German company was very much an unknown quantity as far as Scotland was concerned at that time, and the performance track record of their echo-sounders was something that no one was familiar with.

You have to remember that these were the days long before dual-frequency sounders became commonplace, with their high frequency signals for fishfinding, and low frequency for ground discrimination, and the 28 kh that they all operated on initially was very much a compromise. It was also an age when the Kelvin Hughes company very much ruled the roost regarding echo-sounders, and bypassing them after all this time was a very difficult decision to have to make.

It was also an time before we realised the full impact that the so called "gadoid explosion" of haddock and other fish in the North Sea was going to have on the fishery, and how successful we would all become in a very short time. Counting the pennies was still very much on my mind, but it was a false economy really, and we could easily have installed the Kelvin Hughes echo-sounder as a back-up to be used independently. Such was my thinking then, so I reluctantly decided we couldn't afford both, and cancelled the order. The Kelvin Hughes transducer, which had just been newly installed, would have to come out again.

I remember it all well. When my Uncle Philip, who was the builder, told the local Kelvin Hughes agent what I was planning to do, he came up to my house on Sunday morning like a foaming lion, and demanded to know what on earth I was thinking about. I told him! He then asked if he could phone his boss in Glasgow, and a very long conversation took place. When he came back into the room, he told me that they had decided that if I cancelled the order, I would have to pay for the carriage of the machine up to Anstruther, his time for installing the transducer, and his time for removing it again and then the cost of the carriage back.

I let him continue for a while and then I said "Please stop. Before you came up here today I had a very guilty conscience about all of this. Now that I've heard what you have to say, just go ahead and take the transducer out, send everything back, submit your bill, and it will be paid immediately. And I have further news for you. I will never install another piece of Kelvin Hughes equipment as long as I am a boat owner."

Sometimes it doesn't do to burn your boats, because it was only a few months later that we were nearly in collision in thick fog with a very large Polish trawler whilst making our way to North Shields to land our fish. Without hesitation I got on a link call to Glasgow, and because they were the best available at that time, I ordered a Kelvin Hughes type 17 radar to be fitted as quickly as possible. To give credit where it is due, George Leiper, who was the manager there and had always been the fisherman's friend, bore no grudges. He personally travelled down to North Shields during the weekend and with the help of the local agent, we had our new radar installed ready for sea by Sunday night. There were no hard feelings!

I understood their fears very well, because this was the first time that they had any real opposition in the market place for a long time, and now it was to be from a German company. The microchip, the Japanese domination of world electronics and the invention of the first marine colour echo-sounder by the Koden Company in 1975, were still ten years or more in the future. When it did happen, I'm afraid that Kelvin Hughes along with their German counterparts had no real answer. A lot of their long-standing loyal customers were forced to seek their up-to-date electronic equipment elsewhere.

Going back to the installation of the radar, it was amazing that we had recently built a new boat without it, although other boats were starting to install it at that time, and as I said, within a few months we would be doing the same. Up to now as a Skipper, radars seemed to be well down our list of priorities. The danger aspect of steaming around in poor visibility just didn't seem to bother us too much because we were used to it. I suppose if we had realised at that time that radar would in some ways ultimately increase the catch it would have been different, but up to that point it was just regarded as an added expense!

I can remember looking back ten years to my first year as a Skipper, and thinking nothing of leaving Aberdeen in thick fog, steaming down to the Island of Stroma and from there on through the Pentland Firth, and then sailing right through across to the Faroe Islands without ever seeing a single thing. We just got on with it like everyone else, and did it simply by taking bearings on the various radio beacons with our direction finder. I often wonder how many near misses we might have had in that time with all those big trawlers from the Humber and Aberdeen passing close by on opposite courses.

This was now the start of a completely new era indeed. For the first time ever, new, bigger fishing boats were being built complete with powerful engines which were not Kelvins or Gardners. They were also starting to install depth-recorders, fish-finders, and radars which were not Kelvin Hughes, and also all kinds of other navigational aids.

This second new boat was to cost over £40,000, and was named *Argonaut II* by my wife at the launching ceremony at the shipyard of Smith & Hutton's on 7th September 1963. This was followed by a reception and a dinner dance in the former Star Hotel in St Andrews. We must have moved up in the world from the lemonade and buns of the launching ceremony of the first *Argonaut*. We left Anstruther harbour in the new boat on 1st January 1964, which was almost ten years to the day since I had started out as a very young Skipper owner with her predecessor.

I remember at the time being very concerned about getting the towing speeds exactly right, which was very important in Scottish seine-netting. So much so, that I remember on that New Year's Day morning we took both boats out into the Firth of Forth and sailed them alongside each other in an effort to match up the speeds. You have to bear in mind that this was all new to everyone, and the new engine was now turning at twice the revolutions of the old one. Coupled with the fact that we also had a Liaaen controllable pitch propeller from Norway, I really

The author and his wife about to perform the launching ceremony of *Argonaut II* at Anstruther harbour.

had no idea what the towing speed would be. Simple proportion helped a lot to solve the problem, and we sailed that very same night. We started fishing the next day, and the new boat fished very strongly right from the start. In a very short time I began to wonder what I had been worrying about.

You have to remember that hydraulic seine-net winches hadn't been developed at this juncture, so we also had to cope with the new gearing on the Smith's of Anstruther down-drive. It was designed and manufactured here in Anstruther, and was a very important piece of machinery in a fishing boat's inventory at that time. In addition to transferring the power from the crankshaft of the main engine down to the shaft which ran forward underneath the fish room for driving the belt-driven Lossiemouth seine-winch, it also incorporated a built-in clutch. This Ferodo clutch had replaced what had formerly always been a "kick in" clutch, which couldn't have been all that good for the crankshaft of the engine. It was quite an innovative piece of machinery in its time, and eventually most boats in Scotland were to have them fitted.

As we had the first of the new high-speed engines, I realised very early on that the gearing in this "down-drive" would now no longer be correct, and that the resulting winch shaft speed would not be suitable for the new boat. I went to Mr Smith, and explained all this to him. At first he absolutely refused to change the ratio of the gears inside his equipment. He was an engineer of course and not a fisherman, and he just didn't like the idea of someone telling him that his successful product was soon to be outdated.

After I explained to him that I could visualise this as being the start of a new generation of seine-net boats all fitted with higher speed engines and that his equipment wouldn't be right, he finally relented. He asked me to tell him what I needed and he agreed to make it. I told him it was just simply a case of changing the ratio. I remember that I suggested that he should change the ratio from 2:1 to 4:1. It did the trick and they were able to keep their product up-to-date and retain their market.

As I said, the new boat was a great success, and when we went back to the west coast hake grounds in the following summer we now had the biggest boat with the largest horse-power engine, and, coupled with a variable pitch propeller, we certainly had a big advantage over most of our neighbours. It appears that we were very lucky to have fished there at that particular time. I have been told since by fishermen that had fished these grounds all their lives, that our presence at the west coast for those two consecutive years coincided with the best hake fishing that had been seen there for many years.

I was reading recently that Cecil Fynn of Campbeltown recorded that in 1960 he thought that he was seeing the biggest brood of juvenile hake that he could ever remember, and he had fished the west coast all his life. The adult fish that we were catching four years later during our time there must have been the result of that very good year class of maturing hake.

Towards the end of that summer, the hake fishing on the Oban grounds started to get poorer and poorer as the weeks went by. Eventually when we all came out on a particular Monday morning which was usually the best fishing day of the week, there were very little to be caught, and that night it was decision time. The boats were all lying around trying to make up their minds in which direction they would head in search of fish. A rumour had started that there was news of good hake fishing in the Clyde itself, and some of the boats decided to shift down there. I knew absolutely nothing about the Clyde grounds so I wasn't sure what we would do. I decided to toss a coin, and it would be either be follow the leader down to the Clyde, or back to the North Sea where we belonged. Luckily for me, the penny came down in favour of going to the Clyde, and I got in line with the rest of the fleet.

Our very first haul was a complete disaster. Because we knew nothing about the grounds, we were positioned much too far to the west, and I had shot the gear where the ground was far too hard. We finally ended up being separated from all our gear, and had to grapple it up from the bottom. When we eventually recovered all our gear and shifted more to the east beside the rest of the boats, we found very good fishing.

Amazingly we were all up landing in Ayr with very good catches of hake that very same night. I was delighted, for hake were fetching a very good price indeed, and it was better by far than landing big catches of haddock into Aberdeen where a big portion of the catch was sure to remain unsold and go for processing to meal and oil for very little reward. It was to be a very good few weeks' fishing after that, and we eventually ended up by landing what was the then record catch of hake for the Clyde waters up to that time. Whether that record still stands or not, I do not know. We will give much of the credit for our success to the powerful new boat.

My crew and I had found it very strange at first to be fishing in these sheltered waters completely surrounded by land on all sides. It was a far cry from what we had been used to up until then. A funny thing about that very first week's fishing, was that Ivan Boardley, the Ayr fish salesman who handled the selling of our catches, presented me with a bottle of whisky and told me that it was for landing the biggest week's catch that he had ever sold. I was amazed and asked him about the rumours of the boats' earnings that had originally brought us all down to the Clyde. "Oh that," he said, "that was for two weeks' fishing, not one!" It was a good job for all of us that we didn't get the fishing news just right, or we might never have been there at all.

As the season was now drawing to a close and the summer run of hake were gradually being fished up, we ended up having to supplement our week's earnings by steaming out from the Clyde to Tory Island to the north of Ireland, and even out as far as Eagle Island to the west of Ireland to catch other bottom fish. All that happened in 1964, and by the time that we finally left the west coast, we certainly had enjoyed being inshore fishermen for those couple of summers. Sadly after that year, I was never to fish in the Clyde waters again.

All these new fishing opportunities were to coincide with a rampant rise in inflation in the country, and the whole fleet was to see a rapid rise in their earnings. I remember in the first or second year of the new boat we grossed over £50,000 for the year's catches. It must have been an impressive feat at that time because I remember receiving a letter from George Murray, an Aberdeen trawler owner, congratulating me on our achievement and equating it with the running of the four-minute mile.

Argonaut II was a very successful boat and such was the euphoria sweeping the industry at that time that Joe Croan of Caley Fisheries decided to donate a splendid "Golden Haddock" trophy for the inshore vessel grossing the most money for one year's catches. In an unguarded moment he also said that any Skipper winning his trophy for three years in a row could keep it.

Argonaut II and myself and crew, were to win this trophy in 1966, 1967 and 1968. We were also again the highest-grossing crew in the following year in 1969, but Joe decided that I couldn't have his trophy again, because we had moved over to the new *Argonaut III* in mid-year. I thought that it was a bit cruel after all our hard work, but I think there might have been some politics involved somewhere along the line! He said that I couldn't have the original trophy as he had promised, but that he would have an exact replica made at the same jewellers in Edinburgh. To be fair to Joe, he was as good as his word.

A story from the presentation dinner. We were finding the fish very scarce that week and it was now Wednesday and we didn't have nearly enough fish on board. We shot away after dark just to try a haul and immediately got good fishing. We

The author with the crew of *Argonaut II* and donor Joe Croan at the Golden Haddock Award presentation in 1967. Four brothers and a brother-in-law are also in the picture.

worked all through the night and the daylight haul on Thursday morning we got a huge haul. We got underway for Aberdeen market and were still gutting on Friday morning when the porters came down to start landing. We landed the catch and got home on Friday afternoon as usual. It was time to bathe and change into our dinner jackets and travel to Edinburgh to Bruntsfield Links Golf Club where the dinner was being held. By the end of the evening, I calculate that the crew and myself had been on our feet for sixty hours without a rest. Some difference from the present time, when I find now that if I don't get my eight hours' sleep every night, I am like a dead dog. Oh to be young again!

During my long career there are three things that I am most proud of. On *Argonaut II* in 1965 I indisputably introduced the very first hydraulic power block to the British fishing industry, and later, on board *Argonaut III*, I also introduced the first shelter-deck to the Scottish fleet, and proved that seine-netting could easily be prosecuted with the complete middle of the boat covered in for the protection of the crew. This eventually became standard on every unit in the fleet, and was to make such a difference to men's working conditions and safety, that eventually it was to lead to the introduction of full shelter-decks.

I certainly didn't invent the power block, because this had been done much earlier by a man named Marco Puretic in California in the USA. In its infancy it was simply a vee-shaped wheel with rubber cladding on it to provide more friction, and it was used to haul in those giant ring-nets which were used for tuna fishing and the catching of other pelagic fish. It was driven I believe by some kind of continuous rope arrangement, which must have made it a very Heath Robinson affair indeed. It wasn't until the Norwegians took up the idea and introduced hydraulic power to the blocks that it was to become the success that it is now.

I had been watching all of this in the international fishing publications for some time, and I wondered if in some way it could be adapted for hauling a seine trawl. I contacted the Industrial Development Unit of the White Fish Authority in Hull and told them that I had an idea that I would like them to look at. We were landing our fish mostly into North Shields at that particular time, so I arranged to meet with development engineer Dr Norman Kerr on the quay side there at about 0300 hours in the morning, so that I could explain what I had in mind. No trips off from the sea to travel to Hull for discussions at that time. Oh no! That would have been unthinkable!

I explained to them that my idea was for a fairly tall steel pedestal type construction rising up from the deck and situated on the starboard quarter, with one of those vee-shaped power blocks in some way mounted on top. To this very day, I still don't know if anybody elsewhere in the world had ever tried to haul a bottom trawl with one of these powered blocks before we did, and I must confess that although I was very keen to try out the idea, I had my misgivings. I very much wondered if the wings of the net would separate themselves out during the hauling operation, or would become entangled and the experiment would be more bother than it was worth. There was only one way to find out, and that was to get one set up on board the boat and try it. Dr Kerr and his team took the idea away back to Hull to have a look at it. They contacted me next trip to say that they had discovered this power block which was manufactured by the same David Johanson's firm of Hydema of Norway. It was of a double-sheaved construction, and it might just be the answer for keeping one wing of the trawl net clear of the other. I readily agreed. They also told me that they had drawn up plans for a crane-type arrangement which would make the mounting of the block much more flexible. It would have a hydraulic ram to enable it to be lifted and lowered so that the net could easily be lifted in and out. Their original idea to me was to then have blocks and tackle leading from each side of the deckhouse to control its port to starboard movement. I very quickly scorched that idea, and told them that I thought that it surely would be just as easy to build in another hydraulic ram for swivelling it from side to side. This was done, and the whole idea immediately became a complete success, and every new installation for the next few years was very much a copy of our original idea.

I remember to this day my pleasure at seeing the culmination of all my efforts when we sailed out to Aberdeen Bay for a test run, and put the net over the side and then hauled it back with the new power block. Some people had needless reservations about stability whilst the planning was going on, but it was obvious right from the start that this wasn't going to be a problem. My own fears of the net becoming entangled as it was coming in vanished in minutes, and it also became immediately apparent that a single vee-block would do the job equally as well as a double one. It was almost impossible to keep each wing of the net in its own separate vee in any case, but it really didn't matter.

Very soon the whole British fishing fleet would have them fitted, and without a doubt the power block proved to be the single most labour-saving piece of equipment ever introduced to the fishing industry. Even my original idea of mounting the block on a simple pedestal later proved a success, because nearly every small boat in the country would eventually adopt that particular idea. Later on when they eventually progressed to become mounted on very sophisticated multi-purpose cranes, their new added flexibility allowed them to be used for every purpose imaginable in the handling of all kinds of fishing gear.

There is an interesting story about the development of the power block for hauling a trawl. After it was proven to work, the two Norwegian companies of Rapp in the north and Hydema in the south could very quickly see the huge manufacturing possibilities for their companies, and engaged on an expensive court battle to secure a monopoly. I believe it nearly lead to both their bankruptcies, and the verdict was eventually given in favour of neither of them. The judge had ruled that they were trying to patent gravity! The blocks only worked because of the weight of the net on the inboard side of the block creating the friction. The eventual twist to the end of the story was that Joe Croan managed to persuade both companies to amalgamate and to form the well-known company of Fishing Hydraulics of Ellon.

The huge hauls of fish that were being caught in later years after that, in all kinds of weather, and the much bigger and heavier nets that were now being gradually introduced, would have been impossible to handle without power blocks. For the next forty years or so, going to sea without one would have been almost unthinkable. On the safety aspect, I'm sure that more than a few of the accidents that might well have happened over the years without the use of the power block, had been avoided.

Mind you, I seem to recall that in spite of the fact that it was glaringly obvious to all and sundry what the advantages in using the power block were, especially as we personally were doing so well at the time, not every one was convinced, or perhaps maybe didn't want to be convinced. I remember standing on the pier at Oban harbour chatting to this very successful Moray Firth Skipper and looking down on our respective vessels and telling him about the power block, and telling him that he should be having one fitted. His answer to me was that they were too fussy with their gear to haul their seine-net with a block. I don't know where that left me, but he must have blushed a few times to himself later when he was eventually forced to fit one like every one else. It was inevitable that innovators like myself would always have their critics.

By 1969, Joe Croan had sold out his Granton trawling interests to the Humber firm of Associated Fisheries but was still in overall charge of their Scottish operations. They subsequently bought over the important Peterhead fish-selling and boat-owning firm of Caledonian Fisheries from its owner Provost Robert Foreman. This now made Joe the boss of the newly renamed Caley Fisheries.

I asked Joe why he had sold out his own business to someone else, and his reply to me was that he thought it was "twelve o'clock". What he meant by that, I presume, was that he thought that we had now seen the best of the fishing industry. He might have been correct as far as his core business of running a large trawling fleet and a transport group was concerned, but more than a few single boat owners who went on to do very well for themselves long after that time, might well have disagreed.

Although the second *Argonaut* was only just over three years old by this time, Joe phoned me to say that they had ordered three new boats, two to be built at Irvine's yard in Peterhead, and one at Jones's yard in Buckie. They were now looking for Skippers to become part owners. Robert Gardner and his cousin Alex Gardner from Cellardyke had signed up for the first two from Irvine's yard, to be known as *Forthright* and *Steadfast* respectively, and he was very keen for me to take on the third boat. In time both of these boats would become very successful.

I told Joe that I wasn't interested in the other boat if it was to be in partnership with Caley Fisheries or anyone else for that matter. I told him that I would only take it on if we got the sole ownership of the whole boat. In return, we would give an undertaking to Joe that we would guarantee to give Associated Fisheries all the fish sales. Joe agreed to all of this and the new boat was started. She was designed by G. L. Watson, the famous Glasgow firm of marine architects, and built by Jones of Buckie, long renowned for the quality of their workmanship.

I can still remember my feelings on the day that she was scheduled to be launched as if it was just yesterday. It was a most beautiful, sunny autumn day and she was everything that anyone could have wished for. The aluminium gold alloy masts, a relatively new introduction, were glistening in the sun. The wooden hull was shining as if it had been polished with Simonize, and my brother Robert and I were there with our families and friends. She was all that anyone could have wished for in a new fishing boat and certainly justified our faith in the builders. New buildings from the Jones yard in Buckie had to be launched into the open sea, and it was a pity that there was a very heavy swell running on that day. *Argonaut III* couldn't be launched immediately after my wife had performed the christening ceremony, and she was put into the water on another day when the weather improved.

Looking back on her final cost of £70,000, it seemed like a huge sum of money at the time, and I have to confess that during the building I had more than a few attacks of cold feet. There was no doubt that we were doing very well at the time, but that still didn't stop me worrying whether we were making the right decision. I must have mentioned that fact to someone, because I was soon approached by a representative of another firm who informed me that they would like to take over the new boat. I could only guess at who would want the new boat, but now it was crunch time. I shared my reservations with Skipper Alec Elder who had been a very successful Aberdeen trawler Skipper in his prime and who was now working for Joe Croan as a consultant.

I don't know what advice I was expecting Alec to give me, but I was certainly more than a little surprised when he advised me to go home and ask my wife. He told me that very often in the past, when he had been trying to make a decision about something, he had done this and he had usually got the right answer. When I went home and told my wife the whole story, she immediately replied without hesitation, "Keep the new boat! Who wants it anyway, and what are they going to do with it that you can't?" I think I most definitely got the correct answer!

Looking back, I don't think I was ever really completely serious about not taking the boat on her completion, and after seeing her it was a good job that I didn't. It would have been the biggest mistake of my life up to that time. Although the previous *Argonaut II* was only just over three years old, people were already starting to build bigger boats, and if I wanted to keep my place in the industry then I had to do the same. Inflation was now rampant, fish prices were rising all the time and so were our earnings. *Argonaut III* was the most beautiful wooden boat that I had seen up to that time, and a credit to her builders, and it wasn't long in that new boat before we would become the first inshore boat to earn more than £100,000 in one year. It's a funny thing, but when a boat looks good, then she generally is a good boat, and our latest was no exception!

We had supposedly made our last landing for that year in North Shields, but I felt that we still hadn't achieved the magic figure that I was looking for. We sailed immediately for one more day's fishing at the Coral Bank and we arrived back in Anstruther on Christmas Eve. With the fish still iced on board, we just managed to get back to our homes before Santa Claus arrived. We consigned the 200 boxes

Argonaut III on fishing trials at Buckie harbour

of fish to North Shields by road a few days later and we were well rewarded for our perseverance. Ironically, when the final totting up was done, it was revealed that we had reached our goal for the year without the addition of that extra day's work. I had been determined that I wasn't going to miss my target by falling at that very last hurdle. Very soon after that, even that total year's earnings were surpassed, and as far as I am aware in a very short time I would later set the £200,000, £300,000, £400,000 and £500,000 marks for a year's earnings in our class of boat.

Later, on board *Argonaut III*, along with David Johanson of the Hydema Company of Frederickstad in Norway, I also introduced into Scotland the first hydraulic rope reels for the automatic stowing of seine-net ropes. These had been developed in Denmark on a Danish anchor seiner shortly before that, but needed to be greatly adapted and redesigned before they would be accepted by the majority of the Scottish "fly dragging" seiners.

After discussions at their factory in Fredrikstad, we decided along with the Hydema Engineers that we would need an individual reel on each side of the ship so that we would be free to start shooting the ropes immediately the fish from the previous haul had been lifted on board. Under the original Danish system it would have meant that we would have been at a disadvantage if we had had to lie and run ropes across from one reel to another. Working in the midst of a big fleet of predatory seine-net boats such as our own, when there were fish to be caught, would have meant that we could easily have lost our next "berth", and that would have been totally unacceptable.

For the very same reason, we also needed to develop a system whereby a frayed splice in a rope could be laid out for repair whilst the ropes were still coming in. It could then be respliced whilst the net itself was being hauled, and we would be ready to shoot again immediately on cue. Time is precious! All this took a great deal of working out, and the boats that inherited the new system after we had developed it took it all for granted.

Hydema had previously incorporated a patented "slot" into the side flanges of their large trawl winches which they were manufacturing for Canada at that time. These slots were meant to transfer the sweep lines of the trawl on to a side drum so that they could develop more torque for hauling in the sweeps of the net. When they showed me a film of the winches in operation, I immediately saw the possibilities for building similar slots into the flanges of the new rope reels. I could see that they would serve the same purpose for laying out a rope to be spliced. Before they started to build the new reels, I had suggested that they first made up a half model, and I sent over a long length of the type of ropes that we were using at that time, so that they could test out the idea.

They first tried to simulate the operation by pulling the ropes from the prototype reel by a lorry doing about ten miles per hour, but it wasn't too long before I got a phone call telling me that they didn't think it was going to work. I travelled over to Norway again, and when I arrived they immediately arranged a demonstration. I wasn't long in the yard when I spotted that their mistake was that they were trying to pull the ropes off the bottom of the reel as in a trawl winch. I realised straight away that when we were hauling the ropes would go onto the bottom of the reels, and when we were shooting, they would have to come off the top. I knew right away that the problem was now solved, and I asked them to go ahead with the construction.

Their introduction of these new rope reels would now mean that the crews would no longer have to stand on the foredecks in all weathers, and drag away the ropes as they came from the rope coilers. It would also mean that they would no longer have to lift and stow them in preparation for the next haul. All back-breaking work! The ropes would now go directly from the winch barrels and be automatically spooled straight on to the new reels. It would now free some of the crew for other duties. In addition, if they weren't employed in gutting fish, they could now have some time off awaiting the completion of the next operation.

I remember when the Peterhead firm of Smith's Engineering completed the installation and the reels were first put on board. It was on a Sunday night, and we had quite an audience at the harbour when we were running the ropes from the pier on to the drums. Interested Skippers had come from all over to see if they thought the idea would work. It had coincided with the completion of some repairs which were being made to the main engine, and the Caterpillar engineers were anxious to go out into the bay to give the engine a test run.

It was wintertime and it was now dark, and there was quite a fresh wind blowing from the south-east. After the engineers were satisfied with the main engine, I decided that we would leave the harbour and go down to Aberdeen Bay and have a full-blooded haul. I was just desperate to see those reels in action. I always remember when we came astern to shoot the net revving up the engine blew off one of the newly-fitted pipes in the engine room and we lost all the hydraulic oil.

The boat was now rolling all over the place because we had no ice or boxes on board, and I can just remember one of the plumbers hanging his head down into the bilges trying to repair a pipe and being sea-sick at the same time. We refilled the system with fresh oil, and carried on shooting the gear and because we had taken so long, by the time we got back to the buoy we couldn't see the light. Just typical! Eventually we found it and started to complete the haul. Right away I could see the possibilities and I was just delighted.

We went back to Peterhead and because there was still some work to be done we decided to travel home to Anstruther again. The crew weren't saying too much, and I could sense that they all had their private reservations about what was taking place. I was the first to be dropped off at my house from the mini bus, and I just knew they would be revealing their true feelings to each other immediately I got out. I also remember that I beat then all to it, because I put my head back into the bus and looked them all between the eyes and I said, "Some of you men don't think this is going to work, do you?" There was a silence. I had hit the nail right on the head. I then told them all that I had news for them, because I was going to make these reels work, no matter how long it took, or how much it cost me.

That first trip was a complete success as far as the idea was concerned, and it wasn't long before the crew started to appreciate just what it was now going to mean to their workloads. The only snag was that the pipe connection where it came up through the deck, kept blowing out, and we kept losing all the oil from the system. We had to borrow hydraulic oil from various boats in order to keep going, and eventually we ended up having to make up our own hydraulic oil by mixing one part of lubricating oil with two parts of diesel oil. Not too good for the new motors and pumps, but I was determined that I wasn't going back to the harbour until all the boxes were filled with fish. I knew that many people would be watching the result of that first trip with great interest, and eventually we

Trawler owner David Craig presents the author to HRH Queen Elizabeth before she boards the boat.

landed in Peterhead with a good catch. I had proved my point.

It wasn't too long before the whole Scottish seine-net fleet would be having rope reels installed. Some boats around that time were looking for a cheaper alternative, and had decided to cut large holes in their decks immediately below the rope coilers and let the ropes fall down into a type of bin arrangement. It wasn't really a success, and it wasn't too long before they all eventually abandoned that idea in favour of the hydraulic reels.

In 1975 we had the blockade of Aberdeen. The whole inshore fleet descended on the port and moored their boats right across the harbour to prevent the passage of any boats out or in. This was a protest against the conditions in the industry at that time. I was part of the team from the Scottish Fishermen's Federation who were overseeing the running of the operation. We would be contacted by the Skippers on the ground for instructions to who should be let in. It only lasted about four days which was long enough to keep the media's attention. The same operation was being carried out on the Clyde and also at Leith. I don't know what we achieved by all of this. Maybe not a lot.

It was at this time that after seven years of very successful fishing with *Argonaut III*, we decided to build yet another new boat. This time it would be a steel boat to be built at the Campbeltown Shipyard in Argyle on the Clyde. She would be 80 feet long, and would be named *Argonaut IV*. Her yard number was 32, and in 1976 she cost £290,000. She was an excellent boat like all her class, with a bigger fishroom.

Winning isn't everything

In 1977 I had the unusual honour of the Queen and Princess Anne visiting this new boat. They were on their way to Balmoral and had been invited to open the new Aberdeen fish market in July. The Queen had expressed a wish to visit a fishing boat, and the harbourmaster at that time had asked me if I would make my boat available. We had to be in on the night previously so that the police security team and frogmen could inspect the boat, and after landing our catch we moored up at the floating jetty so that the Queen could easily get on board. She was very well briefed and asked a lot of intelligent questions regarding the boxing of fish at sea, and appreciated that it was a lot of work to do this.

At a dinner in the early part of 1979 I was awarded an engraved silver salver from our own firm of Aberdeen Inshore Fish-selling Co. Ltd., which recorded that *Argonaut IV* had grossed £527,000 for her year's earnings in 1978. This is nearly thirty years ago now, and would be a respectable year's earnings even now. Unbelievably, that was the same year in which *Argonaut IV* was the second-highest grossing white-fish boat in the whole of Britain. We were only outstripped by the 185-foot Humber distant water stern-trawler *C. S. Forester*.

On 13th December 1978 I was awarded the MBE for services to the industry. It was an euphoric trip down to London and the Palace with my family to be given my award by the Queen. This would be the third time I had been introduced to her.

Those were heady days now for the whole of the Scottish inshore fishing industry, with Icelandic waters now being off limits for the British deep water trawling fleets. Along with inflation and the resultant increase in fish prices coupled with an unbelievable increase in fish stocks, we in the inshore section section were filling the vacuum and boats were now seeing their earnings increase by more and more each year. These were to be the euphoric years of the so-called Scottish inshore fleet, resulting in the huge build-up of the white fish catching industry. Fish selling firms were offering ambitious young Skippers their first real chance in life by financing boats for them, and it seemed that new boats and launching ceremonies such as I described earlier, were being reviewed in *Fishing News* almost every week. In almost every case they proved to be success stories.

It seems to me on looking back, that all these years passed almost like a dream, and I can hardly remember even the half of it. I just know that my crew and I, in the series of boats, all named *Argonaut*, were to top the annual grossings table in Scotland each and every year all through the late sixties and seventies. For almost twenty years or more I believe. There were little or no restrictions to speak of, and every fisherman at that time thought that he had a God-given right to go out and catch everything in sight. I know that I certainly did anyway!

These were exhilarating times in the mid seventies and big hauls of cod were quite commonplace. In addition to all the hauls that we successfully caught and got on board, we lost four huge hauls of cod in as many years. Two we got along side but couldn't hang on to them because of the great weight and ended up bursting the bag and losing all the fish, and another where we couldn't even get a start to haul the net because there were so many fish and we had to cut the ropes and let the net go as well.

The fourth was the daddy of all big hauls. We had spent two days head on to the wind with a strong south-easterly gale on the Bressay shoal east of Lerwick and on the third day when daylight broke it was a fine morning with not a boat to be seen. Shooting round on the gear I could hardly believe the amount of fish marks I was seeing on the fish finder and I remarked to my brother that there would be so much fish in the net that we maybe wouldn't be able to haul it. He said that we had always managed before, but I knew that this time it was different. Well, at the end of the haul when the net broke the surface, I could hear the cries of the crew, and when I looked back I was confronted with a sight I had never seen before. The whole net was just a mass of cod, absolutely full of fish. It jumped out of the water and split the net from just behind the footrope right down to the extension on the cod end. We thought at first that we had lost them all but when we hauled the net alongside we managed to salvage about 200 boxes of cod. What had been in that net when it came up goodness only knows. I am certain that it was the biggest haul ever seen by a boat of our class, and I am sure that there might have easily been a thousand boxes of fish in that net.

Many people have asked me at various times over the years if I have ever had any strange catches during my career, and the answer is that I have. We used to fish quite a lot around the Eckofisk oilfield, and I believe I've seen everything in the net from bicycles to bagpipes. The mind can only boggle over how they came to end up on the sea bed! I also can remember toilet pans, shoes and many other articles of clothing.

I also remember another trip because of something that happened that had some significance. We were fishing in the North Sea at the Fisher bank, which had been a favourite spot of mine at one stage. There must be many Scottish fishermen who have gone all their lives to sea, and have never ever seen a porbeagle shark, let alone caught one. I know that up until that day, I don't believe that I myself had ever seen one. I had seen many big sharks caught in the past whilst I had been a line fisherman, but they were all the wrong kind and were of no value.

We had just hauled the seine-net on this particular morning with a big catch of cod and haddock, when one of the crew spotted a big fish tail sticking up from amongst the fish and we immediately recognised it as being a shark of some kind. We attached a rope becket around it, and heaved it forward with the winch until it was clear of the rest of the fish. It now dawned on us then that it could be a porbeagle shark, and that it might be valuable. The crew kept on scooping up the rest of the fish into boxes in preparation for their being gutted, when another large tail appeared. A becket was put around it, and it was also heaved forward clear of the fish. Before the crew eventually got all the fish filled up from the pounds, nine large porbeagle sharks were uncovered amongst the fish from that one single haul.

Because we were getting good fishing, we remained in that area all the rest of that day, and by night time we discovered that we had caught sixteen of those

Winning isn't everything 143

large fish. We stowed them down into the fish hold and covered them with ice, and when we landed into the fish market at Aberdeen, there was great interest amongst many of the fish merchants. I think they were sold as a lot for about £1,100, a not inconsiderable sum of money at that time, and I think that they were bought to supply Italian restaurants in London.

Argonaut IV berthed at the ice factory in Pittenweem.

Decision to Retire

I CAN ALWAYS REMEMBER the exact day that I decided to retire. It was in mid-February 1992 and the weather was definitely unseasonable for the northern North Sea at that time of year. It was flat calm and the sun was shining. We were working around the Cormorant oilfields far to the north-east of the Shetland Islands, and we were getting very good fishing. On top of all that, there was not another boat in sight all around the horizon. The kind of situation that most Skippers dream about.

I was standing at my post in the wheelhouse watching the gear coming in and thinking to myself, just how much longer am I going to do this? I was 62 years old and was just about the oldest full-time Skipper still working. I had already been at sea for forty-seven years, of which nearly forty years had been as Skipper of my own boat, and my brother, who had been my partner for so long, had already retired. I could see myself now having to spend far too much time at sea at my age. Maybe I would jeopardise my health and all that I had ever worked for, if I carried on for much longer. My brother Robert and I had always been an ideal partnership. He generally let me make most of the decisions, and he successfully skippered the boat when I wasn't there. I made up my mind in a flash. This would be my last trip at sea, and when I went home, I wasn't coming back.

This was quite dramatic after all those years, and I called my son David to the wheelhouse and told him that he was to be the first to know what I had decided. He asked me what had suddenly brought this on, and I told him that it didn't matter. After this trip was finished he would now be the Skipper. He was only twenty years old at that time, and I could see the alarm bells starting to ring, and he told me that he didn't think he was ready for this. "You have one week to learn," I said, "because I am serious about my intentions."

I could appreciate his dilemma. It hadn't always been easy for David politically on board his father's boat, just as it wasn't easy for many other Skippers' sons. Sometimes they could cause many problems! David wasn't like that, he was popular with the crew as a fellow deckhand whilst he quietly got on with his work and waited his time. His uncle had always been there, and so had his brother-in-law, my daughter's husband. He was fifteen years older than David. On top of that I had men who had sailed with me for twenty-four years and who knew what I was going to do almost before I knew myself. It wasn't going to be easy for him to leapfrog over everybody and start giving orders to men with all that experience.

I was different from a lot of other Skippers, I had always kept my own counsel, and I hadn't at any time encouraged anyone to come into the wheelhouse and share my problems, including my own son. On top of that, David was always very conscious of where he was in the pecking order on board the boat among those long-serving crew members, and didn't come into the wheelhouse to see me very often. I have to say that when I was a young seventeen-year-old sailing with my own father these things really didn't bother me too much, but David was different from me.

We landed our fish in Aberdeen, and as true as my word I packed up all my gear and I retired from fishing. David went off with the boat on that very next trip and made an impact right away by getting a very good trip for his first time in charge, which I was almost certain he would do! He didn't contact me once during that first trip to ask for my advice and the very same on the next trip. The next trip after that was different, it was the month of March now and the haddock had left the bottom to spawn and he was struggling. They were close to the Shetland Islands and within phone range. Now he contacted me, and his voice said "Any ideas?" Between the two of us we got things sorted out.

That very same summer David asked me to take the boat to sea again so that he could have a break, and I told him that I would, but I was only willing to do one trip. It was a successful trip, and one trip led to two, and I was back, and I was liking it again and I could have gone on, but I realised that it was the end this time. I told David that in future if he wanted someone to take the boat to sea, it would have to be his brother-in-law.

In August 2003, after being in charge of the boat for nearly thirteen successful years, David phoned to tell me that he had just landed in Aberdeen and that he had no more haddock quota left to catch for the rest of the year. He had tried everywhere unsuccessfully to rent enough fish to last the rest of the year. This was before the system of renting quota was really established.

We sold the boat to Irish owners on 20th September 2003, and it was the end of an era for us.

I have often been asked if I have had any frightening experiences during my long career, and the answer to that is that twice I have nearly lost the boat. The first experience was when *Argonaut III* was nearly new and we had a big day's fishing in the eastern North Sea. We had lain over the broadside gutting until about two in the morning and the weather started to get bad and we still had 70 boxes to gut so I suggested we stop and get underway for Peterhead. We set the watch and when we got up at breakfast time I could hardly believe my eyes, the weather was so bad. We were running before a SE by east gale, the very worst direction in the North Sea in my opinion. I called out the crew to gut the rest of the fish from the day before and I would watch the weather for a while, then I would come out and give them a hand. I saw this huge wave come roaring down as high as a tenement building and I shouted to the crew to hang on to the rail around the wheelhouse. It hit the boat and knocked her right over on her side, filling the wheelhouse with water through the open window.

When the boat righted herself we could see a man in the water, way down to leeward, and all the seine net ropes were dangling over the side. I knew we were only going to get one chance to get down to him, and keep the ropes out of the

Decision to retire

propeller. I went astern first and then ahead and we sailed right down to him and luckily got him on board. The next thing were the cries from the fishroom. My brother had been thrown across the floor and had broken another man's leg. The fish had all been spilled from the top tier of boxes and were piled up against the ship's side. Hard to believe! We got the ropes on board and the boat head to wind, and the man up from the fishroom and aft to the cabin, and his bed.

To let you know how far the boat had been over, one man who slept in the for'ard top bed found his bag with his shaving gear at the back of the back bed on the opposite side of the cabin. The boat had been over past the horizontal. A near thing!

The other near thing was in *Argonaut IV*, just a few months before I finally retired. We had been fishing close to Norway when we got this bad forecast, and I did a thing that I normally never did — I decided to go into Egersund. We were running slowly downwind before the sea with the watch set and I was standing leaning on the wheel when the other man on watch let out a cry that a huge wave was about to overtake us. It broke over the stern and filled the cabin through the galley door. The boat buried her whaleback in the water and took off at a great speed, and the stern lifted totally from the water. The boat finally slowed down and the engine stopped. I switched off the automatic pilot and steered the boat by hand, keeping her straight downwind. My watchmate let out a cry that there was another sea bearing down on us, as big as the first one. We kept running straight downwind and I managed to keep the boat on course. It's a good job, because I believe if she had broached on one side or the other she would maybe have rolled over and capsized. When she finally slowed down and laid over the broadside we went down to the engine room to investigate and we dicovered that the propeller overspeed had cut in and shut the engine down. After that we lay head to wind with no further trouble. My brother was the first to say to me, "Fancy you getting caught like that — you who had preached to everyone in the past that if you are going to go in for shelter go in before the weather comes, and not when it is there." A very narrow escape nonetheless.

The Political Era

THERE HAD ALWAYS BEEN many fishermen long before my time who had involved themselves in fishing politics and the forming of Fishermen's Associations and Federations of Associations in their desire to improve conditions for their fellow fishermen.

There were also many fishermen during my long career who were natural born leaders on the political scene. Willie Hay who came to power after the 1975 blockade and went on to become president of the Scottish Fishermen's Federation comes readily to mind. Although I was always more than willing to give up my precious leisure time to represent the fishing industry and my fellow fishermen, I never held any executive position in my long association with the Scottish White Fish Producers Association and the Scottish Fishermen's Federation, and I most certainly didn't seek one.

I always considered myself first and foremost to be a fisherman rather than a politician, and it wasn't always easy to be both. Those who did so are to be commended. I always made it my bottom line that I was more than willing to give up as much of my precious leisure time as was required of me, but I was not going to give up any of my business time. That would have been counter-productive!

That attitude maybe sounds selfish, but not when you consider that there were so many of my fellow fishermen around, who were not even willing to give up one minute of their leisure time except when there was a perceived crisis which they thought might affect them. Having said that, I was the Chairman of our local Anstruther branch of the Scottish White Fish Producers' Association from the early 1970s until I retired from the chair in December 2004 and I also represented the Association at Federation level. During all those years, I was a conscientious attendee at most Association meetings.

The way things are set up in the UK, fishermen's representatives are on many occasions only a lobby group at best, and it was often a very thankless task. On so many evenings after returning home from these tiring journeys and long meetings, when I would have been perhaps been better off resting my body after a hard week at sea, my wife would ask of me, "And what did you achieve today?" I think on more occasions than not, I would truthfully have had to reply, "Not a lot!"

Looking back over that early period just after 1972, when the UK first joined the EEC as it was known then, it was extremely important that that the Scottish Fishermen's Federation and the other UK Federations were present at all the negotiations leading up to the signing of the Common Fisheries Policy. Mind you, in the early days of the EU, it was UK Government officials that we were mostly lobbying at that time, and maybe, just maybe, in the beginning, we did have slightly more influence than we seem to have at present.

It has always very difficult to try and formulate any long-term strategy, just as it remains to this day. Most of the time when dealing with Government departments and politicians, it always seemed as if we were only responding to the latest crises, and we never at any time seemed to be charge of our own destinies. It was always a damage limitation exercise at best and it was like trying to hold back the tide. The goalposts were continually being moved, and very often it seemed like the whole pitch as well. The situation is far worse now, and looks like getting worse still. There are now so many people calling the tune that we have never even heard of. The rules are being amended so often, that it is very difficult for anyone who is not involved in the day-to-day running of the industry to keep topical. We need real support from our own government at this very critical time for the industry, particularly in securing economic quotas for the boats, but I don't think we are ever going to get it.

During the very early part of my time in fishing politics, we were mostly dealing with our own government officials who were then dictating the policy and drawing up the rules. Now it is all being presided over by a veritable army of officials and countless various committees composed of representatives of all the various European countries who are all very much concerned with looking after their own corners. At a time when the industry seems to be rapidly decreasing in size, it seems that it needs ever more and more people to run it.

Each November and December when catch quotas for the following year are being allocated, it is a stressful time for everyone concerned. It's when the annual horse-trading and all the posturing between the various countries takes place. The pattern was always the same, nothing on white fish was ever decided until the mackerel and herring figures were established. This was what the Norwegians were mostly interested in. The hurried decisions that were usually made on the rest of the stocks, in the middle of the night when everyone was very tired, weren't good for the industry either.

Fishermen can't help but feel that there is always an axe hanging over their heads and therefore find it very difficult to plan for the future. I'm still an optimist though, and I am still of the opinion that there will always be a catching industry, albeit greatly reduced, and that the people who remain in the industry and work hard will continue to prosper.

I am not saying that our membership of the EU has been a bed of roses up to now, and I count myself as one of its very severest critics, whether in fishing matters or otherwise. As far as my own career and the careers of people of my generation are concerned, there is one thing that we absolutely mustn't forget. When criticising the EU now, as we are all prone to do with good reason perhaps, it is very easy to forget that previous to 1972 and our membership of the EEC, the North Sea was simply swarming with Russian and other Eastern Block owned trawlers. Large fleets, complete with mother ships and the rest of their

The Political Era

infrastructure, were everywhere, and I'm certain that conservation and the long-term prospects for the future wouldn't have been very high on their agendas. When the North Sea was fished out, as surely it must have been, they would have just moved on to another of the world's oceans.

This period would have been about 1970, and just immediately before 1972 and our own entry into the EEC. At that time another exceptional year class of haddock had been born into the North Sea, and these Russian trawlers were fishing mainly for haddock. Some of the Aberdeen trawler Skippers who were of Polish origin and had come to the UK during the war, had become fishermen, and could understand the Russian language. They had said that these Russian Skippers at that time were sometimes reporting catch rates of 40 tons per hour of mostly immature haddock.

It was obvious that that situation couldn't continue for ever, and who knows just what size of mesh they were using at that time if the Rockall example of more recent times is anything to go by. More to the point, who cared? As I seem to recall, perhaps our own social consciences weren't just quite so developed in those days either. Long before that, those of us who are old enough will surely remember those huge fleets of Polish fishing boats fishing in the North Sea mainly for herring.

In 1972 when we became members of the EEC and the fishing parameters were set, what never ceases to amaze to me even to this day, was that these large fleets of Eastern Block fleets just seemed to quietly leave the scene. No cod wars! No haddock or herring or mackerel wars! No banner headlines in the *Fishing News* and the rest of the press. They just simply disappeared seemingly overnight. I have always wondered what persuaded them to move on. What promises were they given? Were they quietly compensated behind the scene, or perhaps given other assurances, or concessions of something else? We shall probably never ever get to know, but the most important thing was that they all left!

One thing I am absolutely certain of is that if all these boats hadn't gone when they did, and had carried on doing what they were doing, my successful career in the North Sea and the successful careers of many of my peers might have been a vastly different story. Who knows? The huge build-up and the success story that was the Scottish Fishing Fleet between 1963 and the 1990s might never have happened. I am firmly convinced in my own mind that our own UK government or even the Norwegian government, would have never have got round to tackling the problem. The unrestricted pressure on the fish stocks would have been far too great for them to have survived for so long.

The huge new year class of haddock of about 1970, in my opinion almost ranked along with the previous huge year classes of the early 1960s and also the large 1999 year class of haddock which is mostly sustaining the fleet now. What happened to that 1970 year class? Where did it go? I always suspected that it didn't make nearly the impact on the landing figures for that time that it should have done. My suspicions were, that along with the Russians, we now had the huge build-up in the Danish industrial fishing industry and it was now a completely different story.

Denmark had joined the EEC at the same time as we did, and as such were members of the same club as we were, and they could fish when and where they wanted just as we were doing ourselves. They had many hundreds of large industrial trawlers who at that time were almost completely out of control regarding mesh sizes and any other form of control, and who were landing almost whatever they wanted. Of course there are figures available for all that period, there are always figures, but what do they tell us? Absolutely nothing as far as I am concerned. I would put no degree of trust in their statistics whatsoever. Their landings were so vast, that I am sure it would have almost impossible to monitor them even if their authorities had had the will and the resources to do it, which I am sure they didn't.

Some of these boats could land individually almost more in one single trip, than some of the bigger Scottish seine-netters could land in a whole year, with the biggest percentage of their catch being immature fish, and only suitable for reduction to meal and oil. I honestly believe that if the true amount of the total landings of these so called industrial fish over the years was ever to be known, and I am sure that with the best will in the world it can't, the figures would be so astronomical that no one would ever actually be able to comprehend it.

Everyone remembers the heyday of this immoral trade, with queues of boats lying in ports such as Esbjerg with their decks awash, waiting to be discharged. The fishmeal plants simply couldn't cope with the volume of the landings, and in fact whole new ports such as Hirtshals further north, and others, were built to help handle this trade. What we also have to bear in mind, was that all this just didn't go on for a few years. It started to build up nearly forty years ago and is still going on to this day, albeit not nearly to the same degree. Even in this day and age of increased regulation, I am certain that we will never ever get to know the whole truth of the composition of what these boats are landing. They have recently become self-regulatory and the monitoring of their landings is to be carried out at the factories. The very idea is farcical. If their past performances are anything to go by, we all have a good idea what that will mean.

One of my contentions is that if EU inspectors had not been able to gain access to Denmark to monitor these landings when they did, and obtain some sort of control over them — enough to convince hundreds of these owners that the game was up, and that they should decommission their boats — I have a suspicion that the whole North Sea would probably have been barren long before now anyway, and that there would have been nothing much left to fight over. I think that if all these environmental groups such as Greenpeace and their like were to take a much closer look at industrial fishing in the North Sea, then they would be doing some real good, instead of engaging in publicity-seeking stunts like harassing small fishing boats engaged in catching fish for human consumption.

I have figures from Denmark which recorded a huge dip in their industrial landings in 1989 to 1991. These figures exactly coincide with the dip in landings

The Political Era

of the Scottish fleet for human consumption at that same time. It proves beyond doubt to me that instead of the so called "pout" that they were supposed to be catching, they were catching the same fish as we were.

Plenty of hope left yet. We are continually being told by the scientists that the successful 1999 year class of haddock is a single year class, and at the time of writing, there is no other important year class to follow. It will happen, of that I am sure. I have always maintained that one very good year class every few years is all that is needed in any case, and if it is properly managed, it should sustain the fleet that is left for a long time to come. If we take the example of Georges bank on the eastern seaboard of America, another miracle has happened there. Fishermen there are now seeing the largest new year class of haddock for many many years. These things just happen not because of what is being done, but in spite of what is done!

Being part of the Scottish Fishermen's Federation lobby groups at the annual quota talks in Brussels, Bergen or Luxemburg over the years, was always going to be a doubtful honour at the best of times. There weren't too many victories to be got, or away draws either for that matter.

I remember one particular trip from Aberdeen to Bergen in mid-winter to attend some of these negotiations. A small eight-seater plane had been chartered to cut down the costs. The trip across went well, but immediately we got there, heavy snow started to fall. The pilot announced that he was away to the mountains to ski, and we could contact him at any time. By the middle of the day we were told that the talks had collapsed, as so often happened, and we all decided that we should just go home again. We recalled the pilot.

I'll never forget when he turned up at the airport and told us to wait in the lounge as the de-icing machine wasn't working. I have to confess that my thoughts immediately turned to Matt Busby and Manchester United and the Munich air disaster. We eventually boarded the plane, and I remember it skidding all over the place on the runway as we tried to take off. We had no sooner left the ground when the first snow shower hit the windscreen, and then another and another. Halfway across the North Sea we had to reduce height because the wings were freezing up and the pilot had to use the pneumatic expanders to crack the ice. I was never so glad to see Buchan Ness lighthouse again on our way to Aberdeen airport, not even on a fishing boat in a strong south-east gale. That was definitely the last time for me in a small plane over the North Sea in winter!

The EU might still manage to completely destroy the Scottish Fishing industry yet, who knows, but I am sure that it will be caused by political decisions rather than with commercial failures. I defy anyone who was involved in those weary all-night lobby groups in Brussels pre-1982, not to have thought that when the twenty years derogation to the CFP was signed, that we had gained an important victory by being allocated the lion's share of all the major fish stocks in the North Sea. How on earth did we get from that point, to the predicament that we are seeing now?

If I was ever asked to pinpoint the very start of the Scottish Fishing Industry's long period of prosperity, and indeed I think coincidentally, the long period of prosperity of nearly all sections of the British working community, I would have to say it was in 1964. We had the biggest year class of haddock for forty years, just maturing, and the North Sea had filled up with haddock and later cod, in a very short space of time. This was the so-called "gadoid explosion" that I mentioned before. There was no obvious reason for this to happen except that nature had provided once more. Some set of favourable conditions had come together in the North Sea and the waters around the British Isles, and caused this to happen. There is no other explanation. Following that, unions were strong and wages were rising and there was still full employment throughout the country. Inflation had started to go through the roof, and so had fish prices. The Humber fleet had all but disappeared because of lack of fishing opportunities in more northern waters, and we in the inshore sector were ideally placed to fill the vacuum.

I got plenty of recognition during my long career. During the glory years I had a very high profile in the industry, and without doubt for a long time I was the best-known fisherman in the British Isles, but it all seems a long time ago now.

I have many good memories from my lengthy career: maybe more than most. One of the highlights would have to be when my wife and I were invited to attend the Queen's jubilee celebrations in the great hall in Edinburgh Castle in the presence of the Queen herself, and all her close relations. Security was exceedingly tight and we had to park our cars on the castle esplanade and be chauffeur-driven up to the Castle itself. Along with the Queen's own relatives, there were also eighty commoners present. Forty personalities from stage and screen, and forty from other walks of life, my wife and I amongst them. I was informed that I had been invited as a successful seagoing fisherman, and not as a representative of any of the various fishing organisations. I felt very proud of that fact!

My wife and I were introduced individually to all the Royal family in turn, the Queen and Prince Philip, Princess Anne and Prince Charles, and also the Queen Mother. After a magnificent dinner, the lights were dimmed, and in the company of many people that we had only read about previously, we were royally entertained by various famous Scottish artists. It was a very moving occasion for my wife and me, and one that I will never forget.

I have been introduced to the Queen three times in all during my fishing career: at the above Jubilee celebrations, and then once again in 1977 when the Queen came on board *Argonaut IV* at Aberdeen, after she had opened the new fish market. Also at the palace when I received my MBE.

Another important occasion for me was when Edward Heath had breakfast on board *Argonaut IV*. He had been invited to perform the opening ceremony at the fishing exhibition and started off his day by visiting the fish market. We had been forewarned that he would be coming on board and had the white tablecloth all laid out for him. He tucked in to fried lemon sole and even had a second helping. I'm sure that when as a fifteen-year-old boy I was coiling that big tar-covered rope down in the *Procyon*'s fo'castle in the spring of 1946, even in my very wildest dreams I couldn't have imagined that all this would ever happen to me.

Golf

I SUPPOSE I COULDN'T REALLY finish my tale without some mention of my retirement and my passion for the game of golf. Like so many of the St Monans boys of my era, it had all started with carrying clubs at Elie Golf Club during the school summer holidays, and went on from there. Caddying at Elie had always been a long-standing tradition with the fisher boys from St Monans, and my own father and all his brothers had done it long before that, when they were schoolboys. In fact my father, who to my knowledge had never ever played a round of golf in his entire life, knew every hole at Elie links like the back of his hand. You only had to tell him what you had scored at a certain hole, and he knew immediately where you meant. I have heard it said that on more one occasion during the many poor spells at the fishing between the two great wars, it was only the income from the boys carrying clubs, small as it may have been, that enabled many of the homes to keep going.

My uncle Alec, who later became a trawler Skipper, used to tell me that unbelievable as it seems, he had managed to get engaged to caddie for four rounds in one day. Admittedly they did play much faster in those days, and they did carry fewer clubs, but it still takes some doing for a small boy of perhaps twelve or thirteen years of age. On top of that they had to walk every day from St Monans to Elie and back along the railway line, carrying their sandwiches with them. He must have been very tired!

There is a copy of an official caddy list for 1920, which hangs in the entrance hall of Elie Golf Clubhouse. All the names of the caddies on that list are identical to the names of all the boys that I grew up with in St Monans, although the names on the list must have been of their fathers, uncles and grandfathers from an earlier era. Quite uncanny. I also have a copy of an official caddy list from the Old Course in St Andrews where the name of one of my mother's ancestors is included: a George Corstorphine. This was perhaps her great-uncle who, along with his brother and families, had moved from Cellardyke to St Andrews to fish from there and had ended up being sometime caddies at the Old Course.

When I started to play golf after I had finished my National Service and got back to fishing again, it was natural that I would join the Earlsferry Thistle Club and play over the Elie links. I played there for about six years before joining Anstruther Golf Club, and also Crail Golfing Society, where I have been a member ever since.

Like so many others who have led a busy life during their working years, I had very little opportunity to play regularly, and then only social golf and never in formal competitions. Having said that, I still managed to attend the annual

Herring and Fish Trade Golf Alliance at Duffhouse Royal Golf Club at Banff for thirty-two unbroken years. Somehow or other, no matter how busy I was, I always managed to make time for that.

When I retired from my seagoing career in 1992 I was aged 62, and I had made a conscious decision: that this was the rest of my life, and that everything that had happened before that was to finance what I wanted to do from then on. I should make the very most of it to compensate for all the hard work and time separated from my wife and family, and that I should endeavour to enjoy the fruits of all my labour. I also decided that from then on the game of golf was going to play a major part in it. I immediately embarked on some kind of a mission, and by Friday 19th June 2004 when I had reached the age of 73, I had finally completed playing my 500th different golf course.

I was invited by some very good friends to come down for the big occasion and play at their home course at Alresford Golf Club in Hampshire, and I flew down to Southampton to do so. I received the courtesy of their course, and also a special dispensation to play from their medal tees, which are usually reserved for competitions only. The Captain and some of the members came out to accompany me, and it gave me great pride to go around in 79 shots from the proper medal tees, which from my playing handicap of ten equalled the standard scratch score of the course. I just couldn't have been more pleased with myself. To finalise it, they arranged a dinner for me that night, and presented me with a framed picture of their clubhouse to commemorate the special occasion.

I have played over fifty different courses in the United States, and I have also played in Australia, Japan, Canada, Hawaii, Nova Scotia, Denmark, the United Emirates, Turkey and most of the well-known golfing holiday destinations in Spain and Portugal and around the Mediterranean. For many years we have spent holidays on the Canary Islands, and I have played all the courses there including the new course on the small island of Gomera which lies to the south of Tenerife. I have done some bizarre things to track down a new course that I have wanted to play, including ferry journeys and plane flights. I have attended the annual Masters championship at Augusta in Georgia on three occasions, but up to the time of writing, I haven't managed to secure an invitation to play the course yet. I live in hope! Up-to-date I have now played on 545 different courses.

Since I retired from the sea I have been playing on the self-styled Scottish "seniors circuit" for the past fourteen years, and it would be very difficult indeed to name a golf course in central Scotland that I haven't played on. I was quite proud to be still playing off nine handicap at age 74. My wife accompanied me to a lot of those competitions during those years, and showed remarkable loyalty in doing so. We made many good friends during the process. I have also been a keen member of the Midlands Golfing Alliance for about twenty years, and they try and hold one meeting each week during the winter. I have been a faithful and regular attender, and have played over the many famous old courses between Forfar and Dunfermline.

They say that having a hole in one is every golfer's dream, but I had to wait until I was sixty-two years old before I realised mine. It was whilst I was playing the fourth hole at Vilamoura Old Course in the Portuguese Algarve. Soon after that I added another five, making six in total. They include holes-in-one at Crail, at Anstruther, another one in Portugal, also one in Tenerife, and one in a Pro-Am at Hilton Head in America. Judging by these results, I suspect that holes-in-one are probably directly proportional to the amount of golf that one plays. I hope that I am still counting, but you just can't make them happen, and they seem to have become very conspicuous by their absence at the moment!

I have played golf around the Pinehurst area in America, and also in a few Pro-Ams at Hilton Head in the Carolinas, including the famous Harbour Town course where the Heritage Classic is played each year. I have also represented Crail Golfing Society against the Brookfield Country Club in Atlanta. I have taken part in competitions in Ireland, and I attended the very first Ryder Cup match held on the new Kiawah Island course in America. Definitely not as a competitor though, I might add!

There is one funny story I remember from that occasion on the flight home from Savannah to Atlanta. I was wearing my recently-purchased black shirt with the Ryder cup logo on it, along with my new red trousers. In conversation, the lady sitting in the neighbouring seat asked if I was English and why was I in America? I explained to her that I had been over for the Ryder Cup which was a competition between European and American golfers, and was held every four years. I could see that she had never even heard of the Ryder Cup but she seemed suitably impressed with my explanation. When the plane landed in Atlanta and we both stood up to collect our luggage from the overhead lockers, she said goodbye, and wished me good luck in my next competition! I wish!

To finish my tale

IT WAS A HEART-RENDING DECISION for all my family to sell *Argonaut IV* to Irish owners on 20th September 2003, and some tears were shed. It was especially hard for my youngest son David who had successfully skippered the boat for the thirteen years since I had retired. Although still a relatively young man, he was a very good fisherman indeed, and the boat was still operating very profitably compared to some of the very expensive newer boats that were servicing big borrowings. It was a very big decision for us to sell, and wasn't easy for him to accept, but it was brought on by several other factors. The most important of which was that the boat, although in excellent condition, was nearing thirty years of age, and wouldn't last for ever. Replacing her wouldn't be easy.

The climate in the industry at that exact time was looking fairly bleak indeed, with so many people reluctantly giving up and accepting a decommissioning package to leave the industry. It was very difficult at to see how we would ever be able to successfully and viably finance a new build. Recently introduced legislation was restricting the fleet to only fifteen days' fishing per month, and people weren't geared up to the fact that they would be able to rent the use of other people's days from them. It was beginning to look like a hopeless situation. The *Argonaut*'s personal quota of haddock for the year was almost finished, and it was then only August, and we were simply unable to rent extra quota.

Since then of course, the situation has changed somewhat. Other people's days are available for rent to enable boats to spend longer at sea and have more fishing time, and it also seems to be quite easy to rent other people's fish quotas. All this comes at a very heavy price of course, and as they say, "It all has to come out of the cod-end." At the moment I am hearing that some boats have finished their own quota as early as February and will be renting fish for the rest of the year. Coupled with the dramatic rise in the cost of fuel, which on some occasions can swallow up to 50% of their gross earnings, the situation is still not rosy by any manner of means. Young fishermen are flocking to work in the oil industry, where they can have more time off between trips. It's no wonder that crew members are becoming very hard to find. Very few new entrants are coming in to the industry.

Coincidentally, another reason for selling *Argonaut IV* was, at that exact time my eldest son who was successfully running two retail fish operations in St Monans, decided that he was going to make an offer for the famous Anstruther Fish Bar which was on the market for sale. When his bid was successful, we had to decide fairly quickly if we would sell the boat, and that my youngest son David Smith and my son-in-law David Wilson would purchase these two retail outlets from him whilst they were available. At the moment they all seem to be quite happy with the changes that they have made to their lives, but only time will tell if our decision was correct.

Like so many other long-established fishing families, the Smiths of St Monans are now finally out of the catching side of fishing after so many generations. What a shame! At the time of writing, we have still retained our fishing licence and our fish quotas, but whether we will ever use them again is very debatable. It will certainly not be my decision!

I am immensely proud to have been a fisherman, and I am very glad that my father gave me all the encouragement and support that he did when so many others at the time were doing the very opposite. I have had a very exciting and rewarding life, and I have enjoyed absolutely every moment of it, doing all that I ever wanted to do. I realise how lucky I have been because not everyone gets the opportunity to do that. If it were possible, I would like to do it all over again!

Also, looking back over my life, I have taken great pride in seeing my family becoming well-established. Like so many fishermen who were separated from their families for long periods and did not have the opportunity to watch their own children growing up, I have certainly taken great pride in the progress of my grand-children, and have enjoyed the pleasure of their company. Who knows, with a little bit of luck, I might even live to see my two new great-grand-children grow up as well.

Printed in Great Britain
by Amazon